GENERATIONS
of
FAMILY FAVOURITES

SOUP 2 NUTS

Lisa

Please enjoy !!

GENERATIONS
of
FAMILY FAVOURITES

SOUP 2 NUTS

RJ Woodward

RJ WOODWARD

iUniverse, Inc.
Bloomington

Generations of Family Favourites
Soup 2 Nuts

iUniverse books may be ordered through booksellers or by contacting:

iUniverse
1663 Liberty Drive
Bloomington, IN 47403
www.iuniverse.com
1-800-Authors (1-800-288-4677)

ISBN: 978-1-4620-6004-7 (sc)
ISBN: 978-1-4620-6005-4 (ebk)

Printed in the United States of America

iUniverse rev. date: 10/18/2011

INDEX

<u>Generations of Family Favourites—Soup 2 Nuts</u>

Prologue

Every family has come up with ways and means to do things that have passed down through the generations. I have spent a good part of my life wishing someone in our family would take the time to compile some of their favourites.

As children we were encouraged to express ourselves to do different things to help out. Many of these hints have been tried, tested and loved by all. They have been expressed in a level that even the youngest reader can attempt their first creations without fear of failure.

Take this book and make it part of your way of doing things, mark your favourite, add your own to the extra pages provided and encourage future generations to pass them on. A small wish but a great demand.

Our family is a circle of love and strength. With every birth and every union, the circle grows. Every joy shared adds more love. Every crisis faced together makes the circle stronger. Memories have been cherished as well as our recipes.

"Look to this day . . . . for yesterday is already a dream and tomorrow is only a vision."

"A friend is someone who knows the song in your heart, and can sing it back to you when you have forgotten the words."

Author of:

Eyes Closed, Too Hear

- ISBN/SKU 9781450261975 soft cover
  9781450261982 E-book

Generations of Family Favourites

- ISBN/SKU 9781450290357 soft cover
  9781450290364 E-book

Generations of Family Favourites Book Two

- ISBN/SKU 9781462013036 soft cover
  9781462013043 E-book

Generations of Family Favourites Book Three—Specialty

- ISBN/SKU 9781462044795 soft cover
  9781462044801 E-book

Reaching Beyond

- ISBN/ SKU 000506793 soft cover
  9781462061372 E-book

Chapter 1

General

*"It's better to be a lion for a day
than a sheep all your life."*

—Elizabeth Kenny

~°~°~°~°~°~°~°~°~°~°~°~°~°

**"Why worry about things
you can't control when you can keep
yourself busy controlling
the things that depend on you?"**

—Unknown

~°~°~°~°~°~°~°~°~°~°~°~°~°

ASTROLOGY

Aries—March 21-April 20
Taurus—April 21-May 21
Gemini —May 22-June 21
Cancer—June 22-July 22
Leo—July 23-August 21
Virgo—August 22-September 23
Libra—September 24-October 23
Scorpio—October 24-November 22
Sagittarius—November 23-December 22
Capricorn—December 23-January 20
Aquarius—January 21-February 19
Pisces—February 20-March 20

~°~°~°~°~°~°~°~°~°~°~°

*"Your sons and daughters shall prophesy,
your old men shall dream dreams,
your young men shall see visions."*

—Bible, Joel 2:28

BIRTHSTONES

January	Garnet (Dark Red)	*Constancy*
February	Amethyst (Purple)	*Sincerity*
March	Aquamarine (Pale Blue)	*Energy*
April	Diamond (White)	*Purity*
May	Emerald (Green)	*Hope*
June	Pearl (Cream)	*Health*
July	Ruby (Red)	*Passion*
August	Periodot (Olive Green)	*Joy*
September	Sapphire (Deep Blue)	*Wisdom*
October	Opal (Iridescent)	*Hope*
November	Topaz (Golden Yellow)	*Fidelity*
December	Turquoise (Green Blue)	*Contentment*

~°~°~°~°~°~°~°~°~°~°~°~°~°

"Every experience is a life lesson".

There are five things that you cannot recover in life:

The Stone . . . . after it's thrown,
The Word . . . . after it's said,
The Occasion . . . . after it's missed,
The Time . . . . after it's gone.
A person . . . . after they die

<u>WEDDING ANNIVERSARIES</u>

1 Paper   2 Cotton   3 Leather   4 Linen
5 Wood   6 Iron   7 Wool   8 Bronze
9 Pottery   10 Tin   11 Steel   12 Silk
13 Lace   14 Ivory   15 Crystal   20 China
25 Silver   30 Pearl   35 Coral   40 Ruby
45 Sapphire   50 Golden   55 Emerald
60 Diamond   65 Blue Sapphire
70 Platinum   80 Oak
90 Granite

~°~°~°~°~°~°~°~°~°~°~°~°~°

Location is a critical factor:

A home with everything you need, in the wrong location, is probably not the right home for you.

~°~°~°~°~°~°~°~°~°~°~°~°~°

Overcoming What Stops You:

Find your passion: We all have something we're great at.

Believe: It is hard to be led if it is you that you're following, but you have to believe that you are worth the successful outcome, or you will always end up back in at the starting line.

Take Action: Taking all that pent up fear that holds one back and use positive actions to point one's self in the right direction. If one can imagine what might go wrong if they take a risk, then they can imagine what can go right! *"Remember courage is acting in the face of fear"*

~°~°~°~°~°~°~°~°~°~°~°~°

Life's little lessons and good advice

Philosophy. *"A philosophy professor stood before his class and had some items in front of him. When the class began, wordlessly he picked up a very large and empty mayonnaise jar and proceeded to fill it with rocks, about 2" in diameter.*

He then asked the students if the jar was full? They agreed that it was. So the professor then picked up a box of pebbles and poured them into the jar. He shook the jar lightly. The pebbles, of course, rolled into the open areas between the rocks. He then asked the students again if the jar was full. They agreed it was.

The professor picked up a box of sand and poured it into the jar. Of course, the sand filled up everything else. He then asked once more if the jar was full. The students responded with an unanimous—yes.

The professor then produced a bottle of red wine from under the table and proceeded to pour the entire contents into the jar effectively filling the empty space between the sand.

The students laughed.

"Now," said the professor, as the laughter subsided, "I want you to recognize that this jar represents your life. The rocks are the important things—your family, your partner, your health, your children—things that, if everything else was lost and only they remained, your life would still be full."

"The pebbles are the other things that matter like your job, your house, your car. The sand is everything else—the small stuff."

"If you put the sand into the jar first," he continued "there is no room for the pebbles or the rocks. The same goes for your life. If you spend all your time and energy on the small stuff, you will never have room for the things that are important to you. Pay attention to the things that are critical to your happiness. Play with your children. Take time to get medical check-ups. Take your partner dancing. There will always be time to go to work, clean the house, give a dinner party and fix the disposal."

"Take care of the rocks first—the things that really matter. Set your priorities. The rest is just sand."

One of the students raised her hand and inquired what the wine represented.

The professor smiled, "I'm glad you asked. It just goes to show you that no matter how full your life may seem, there's always room for a good bottle of wine!"—Raymond Watson

~°~°~°~°~°~°~°~°~°~°~°~°~°

1 square foot = 144 square inches

~°~°~°~°~°~°~°~°~°~°~°~°~°

Moving:

Go through all your closets and collect everything you have stashed away. This includes your valuables that are hidden way back on a shelf.

~°~°~°~°~°~°~°~°~°~°~°~°~°

<u>Keeping a healthy home:</u>

Reduce toxins

Less desirable weather may make fall and winter seem like an ideal time to tackle your indoor painting projects. However, you need to be mindful of the volatile organic compounds (VOCs) found in many interior paints and finishes. VOCs are one of the biggest threats to indoor air quality; they include a variety of chemicals, some of which may have both short—and long-term health effects. For indoor jobs, select paint with low or no VOCs to keep your air fresher. Additionally, some houseplants such as ivy and gerbera daisies can help to naturally remove VOCs from your indoor air.

Clean your indoor air

Ragweed and pollen will trigger allergy symptoms for millions of people this fall; however, the worst allergy triggers are often found inside the home. Installing a whole-home air filtration system can help to remove indoor allergens including dust, mildew, pet dander and pollen from the air you breathe. For example, the AccuClean (TM) System by <u>American Standard Heating & Air Conditioning</u> removes up to 99.98 percent of the allergens from your filtered air, so even if its allergy season outdoors, your indoor air is crisp and clean.

Prevent mold

During the cooler fall and winter months, people tend to seal up their homes and spend more time inside, which traps moisture and humidity—both significant contributors to indoor mold growth. Maintain healthy indoor humidity levels by venting bathrooms and clothes dryers and using an exhaust fan while cooking. Install an <u>air humidifier</u> to provide year-round control of your indoor moisture level, and keep your home at 50 percent humidity or lower to reduce the chance for mold growth.

Watch out for CO

Protect your indoor living environment from carbon monoxide or CO by installing CO detectors or alarms throughout your home. This fall, make sure your home's heating system, including items such as a furnace or heat pump, vents and chimney, are inspected and serviced by a professional contractor. And, if there is a fireplace in your home, open the damper before lighting a fire to help prevent the build-up of potentially poisonous gases inside of your home.

Keep a seasonal routine

Most homeowners already know it's important to test their smoke alarms on a monthly basis, but how often do you change the alarm's batteries? One way to keep track of alarm maintenance is to make battery changing a seasonal activity. For example, beginning this fall, replace the batteries in your smoke alarms (and CO detectors), every time you reset your clocks.

~°~°~°~°~°~°~°~°~°~°~°~°~°

"If this is coffee, please bring me some tea; but if this is tea, please bring me some coffee."

~Abraham Lincoln~

~°~°~°~°~°~°~°~°~°~°~°~°~°

Paper Shredding:

Deadbolts, alarms, and guard dogs can't always keep a home safe. Many people are unaware of how much sensitive information they toss in the trash each day from junk mail, old bill statements, or even return addresses. It is possible to obtain credit card numbers, bank account information, and social security numbers from discarded mail and personal paperwork. Using a paper-shredder, however, can drastically reduce the risk of identity theft and increase household security.

~°~°~°~°~°~°~°~°~°~°~°~°~°

Health Benefits From Simple Foods:

Note*** treat as a guide this does not circumvent prescribed medicines and their effects.

Apples

Protects your heart—Prevents constipation—Blocks diarrhoea—Improves lung capacity—Cushions joints

Apricots

Combats cancer—Controls blood pressure—Saves your eyesight—Shields against Alzheimer's—Slows aging process

Artichokes

Aids digestion—Lowers cholesterol—Protects your heart—Stabilizes blood sugar—Guards against liver disease

Avocados

Battles diabetes—Lowers cholesterol—Helps stops strokes—Controls blood pressure—Smoothes skin

Bananas

Protects your heart—Quiets a cough—Strengthens bones—Controls blood pressure—Blocks diarrhoea

Beans

Prevents constipation—Helps haemorrhoids—Lowers cholesterol—Combats cancer—Stabilizes blood sugar

Beets

Controls blood pressure—Combats cancer—Strengthens bones—Protects your heart—Aids weight loss

Blueberries

Combats cancer—Protects your heart—Stabilizes blood sugar—Boosts memory—Prevents constipation

Broccoli

Strengthens bones—Saves eyesight—Combats cancer—Protects your heart—Controls blood pressure

Cabbage

Combats cancer—Prevents constipation—Promotes weight loss—Protects your heart—Helps haemorrhoids

Cantaloupe

Saves eyesight—Controls blood pressure—Lowers cholesterol—Combats cancer—Supports immune system

Carrots

Saves eyesight—Protects your heart—Prevents constipation—Combats cancer—Promotes weight loss

Cauliflower

Protects against Prostate Cancer—Combats Breast Cancer—Strengthens bones—Banishes bruises—Guards against heart disease

Cherries

Protects your heart—Combats Cancer—Ends insomnia—Slows aging process—Shields against Alzheimer's

Chestnuts

Promotes weight loss—Protects your heart—Lowers cholesterol—Combats Cancer—Controls blood pressure

Chili peppers

Aids digestion—Soothes sore throat—Clears sinuses—Combats Cancer—Boosts immune system

Figs

Promotes weight loss—Helps stops strokes—Lowers cholesterol—Combats Cancer—Controls blood pressure

Fish

Protects your heart—Boosts memory—Combats Cancer—Supports immune system

Flax

Aids digestion—Battles diabetes—Protects your heart—Improves mental health—Boosts immune system

Garlic

Lowers cholesterol—Controls blood pressure—Combats cancer—Kills bacteria—Fights fungus

Grapefruit

Protects against heart attacks—Promotes Weight loss—Helps stops strokes—Combats Prostate Cancer—Lowers cholesterol

Grapes

Saves eyesight—Conquers kidney stones—Combats cancer—Enhances blood flow—Protects your heart

Green tea

Combats cancer—Protects your heart—Helps stops strokes—Promotes Weight loss—Kills bacteria

Honey

Heals wounds—Aids digestion—Guards against
ulcers—Increases energy—Fights allergies

Lemons

Combats cancer—Protects your heart—Controls blood
pressure—Smoothes skin—Stops scurvy

Limes

Combats cancer—Protects your heart—Controls blood
pressure—Smoothes skin—Stops scurvy

Mangoes

Combats cancer—Boosts memory—Regulates
thyroid—Aids digestion—Shields against Alzheimer's

Mushrooms

Controls blood pressure—Lowers cholesterol—Kills
bacteria—Combats cancer—Strengthens bones

Oats

Lowers cholesterol—Combats cancer—Battles
diabetes—Prevents constipation—Smoothes skin

Olive oil

Protects your heart—Promotes Weight loss—Combats
cancer—Battles diabetes—Smoothes skin

Onions

Reduce risk of heart attack—Combats cancer—Kills
bacteria—Lowers cholesterol—Fights fungus

Oranges

Supports immune systems—Combats cancer—Protects your heart—Straightens respiration

Peaches

Prevents constipation—Combats cancer—Helps stops strokes—Aids digestion—Helps haemorrhoids

Peanuts

Protects against heart disease—Promotes Weight loss—Combats Prostate Cancer—Lowers cholesterol—Aggravates Diverticulitis

Pineapple

Strengthens bones—Relieves colds—Aids digestion—Dissolves warts—Blocks diarrhoea

Prunes

Slows aging process—Prevents constipation—Boosts memory—Lowers cholesterol—Protects against heart disease

Rice

Protects your heart—Battles diabetes—Conquers kidney stones—Combats cancer—Helps stops strokes

Strawberries

Combats cancer—Protects your heart—Boosts memory—Calms stress

Sweet potatoes

Saves your eyesight—Lifts mood—Combats cancer—Strengthens bones

Tomatoes

Protects prostate—Combats cancer—Lowers cholesterol—Protects your heart

Walnuts

Lowers cholesterol—Combats cancer—Boosts memory—Lifts mood—Protects against heart disease

Water

Promotes Weight loss—Combats cancer—Conquers kidney stones—Smoothes skin

Watermelon

Protects prostate—Promotes Weight loss—Lowers cholesterol—Helps stops strokes—Controls blood pressure

Wheat germ

Combats Colon Cancer—Prevents constipation—Lowers cholesterol—Helps stops strokes—Improves digestion

Wheat bran

Combats Colon Cancer—Prevents constipation—Lowers cholesterol—Helps stops strokes—Improves digestion

Yogurt

Guards against ulcers—Strengthens bones—Lowers cholesterol—Supports immune systems—Aids digestion

~°~°~°~°~°~°~°~°~°~°~°~°~°

What you can do to fight over-packaging:

*You are the consumer. You're the end user.
Ultimately, what you say goes.*

~°~°~°~°~°~°~°~°~°~°~°~°~°

"A gentle heart is tied with an easy thread."

—George Herbert

~°~°~°~°~°~°~°~°~°~°~°~°~°

Honey:

Honey is the only food on the planet that will not spoil or rot. It will do what some call turning to sugar. In reality honey is always honey. However, when left in a cool dark place for a long time it will do what I rather call "crystallizing". When this happens I loosen the lid, boil some water, and sit the honey container in the hot water, turn off the heat and let it liquefy. It is then as good as it ever was. Never boil honey or put it in a microwave. To do so will kill the enzymes in the honey.

Cinnamon and Honey

Facts on Honey and Cinnamon: It is found that a mixture of honey and Cinnamon cures most diseases. Honey is produced in most of the countries of the world. Scientists of today also accept honey as a 'Ram Ban' (very effective) medicine for all kinds of diseases. Honey can be used without any side effects for any kind of diseases.

Today's science says that even though honey is sweet, if taken in the right dosage as a medicine, it does not harm diabetic patients. Weekly World News, a magazine in Canada, in its issue dated 17 January,1995 has given the following list of diseases that can be cured by honey and cinnamon as researched by western scientists:

HEART DISEASES:

Make a paste of honey and cinnamon powder, apply on bread, instead of jelly and jam, and eat it regularly for breakfast. It reduces the cholesterol in the arteries and saves the patient from heart attack. Also, those who have already had an attack, if they do this process daily, they are kept miles away from the next attack. Regular use of the above process relieves loss of breath and strengthens the heart beat. In America and Canada, various nursing homes have treated patients successfully and have found that as you age, the arteries and veins lose their flexibility and get clogged; honey and cinnamon revitalize the arteries and veins.

ARTHRITIS:

Arthritis patients may take daily, morning and night, one cup of hot water with two spoons of honey and one small teaspoon of cinnamon powder. If taken regularly even chronic arthritis can be cured. In a recent research conducted at the Copenhagen University, it was found that when the doctors treated their patients with a mixture of one tablespoon Honey and half teaspoon Cinnamon powder before breakfast, they found that within a week, out of the 200 people so treated, practically 73 patients were totally relieved of pain, and within a month, mostly all the patients who could not walk or move around because of arthritis started walking without pain.

BLADDER INFECTIONS:

Take two tablespoons of cinnamon powder and one teaspoon of honey in a glass of lukewarm water and drink it. It destroys the germs in the bladder.

CHOLESTEROL:

Two tablespoons of honey and three teaspoons of Cinnamon Powder mixed in 16 ounces of tea water, given to a cholesterol patient, was found to reduce the level of cholesterol in the blood by 10 percent within two hours. As mentioned for arthritic patients, if taken three times a day, any chronic cholesterol is cured. According to information received in the said Journal, pure honey taken with food daily relieves complaints of cholesterol.

COLDS:

Those suffering from common or severe colds should take one tablespoon lukewarm honey with 1/4 spoon cinnamon powder daily for three days. This process will cure most chronic cough, cold, and clear the sinuses.

UPSET STOMACH:

Honey taken with cinnamon powder cures stomach ache and also clears stomach ulcers from the root.

GAS:

According to the studies done in India and Japan, it is revealed that if Honey is taken with cinnamon powder the stomach is relieved of gas.

IMMUNE SYSTEM:

Daily use of honey and cinnamon powder strengthens the immune system and protects the body from bacteria and viral attacks. Scientists have found that honey has various vitamins and iron in large amounts. Constant use of Honey strengthens the white blood corpuscles to fight bacterial and viral diseases.

INDIGESTION:

Cinnamon powder sprinkled on two tablespoons of honey taken before food relieves acidity and digests the heaviest of meals.

INFLUENZA:

A scientist in Spain has proved that honey contains a natural 'Ingredient' which kills the influenza germs and saves the patient from flu.

LONGEVITY:

Tea made with honey and cinnamon powder, when taken regularly, arrests the ravages of old age. Take four spoons of honey, one spoon of cinnamon powder, and three cups of water and boil to make like tea. Drink 1/4 cup, three to four times a day. It keeps the skin fresh and soft and arrests old age. Life spans also increase and even a 100 year old, starts performing the chores of a 20-year-old.

PIMPLES:

Three tablespoons of honey and one teaspoon of cinnamon powder paste. Apply this paste on the pimples before sleeping and wash it next morning with warm water. If done daily for two weeks, it removes pimples from the root.

SKIN INFECTIONS:

Applying honey and cinnamon powder in equal parts on the affected parts cures eczema, ringworm and all types of skin infections.

WEIGHT LOSS:

Daily in the morning one half hour before breakfast on an empty stomach, and at night before sleeping, drink honey and cinnamon powder boiled in one cup of water. If taken regularly, it reduces the weight of even the most obese person. Also, drinking this mixture regularly does not allow the fat to accumulate in the body even though the person may eat a high calorie diet.

CANCER:

Recent research in Japan and Australia has revealed that advanced cancer of the stomach and bones have been cured successfully. Patients suffering from these kinds of cancer should daily take one tablespoon of honey with one teaspoon of cinnamon powder for one month three times a day.

FATIGUE:

Recent studies have shown that the sugar content of honey is more helpful rather than being detrimental to the strength of the body. Senior citizens, who take honey and cinnamon powder in equal parts, are more alert and flexible. Dr. Milton, who has done research, says that a half tablespoon of honey taken in a glass of water and sprinkled with cinnamon powder, taken daily after brushing and in the afternoon at about 3:00 P.M. when the vitality of the body starts to decrease, increases the vitality of the body within a week.

BAD BREATH:

People of South America, first thing in the morning, gargle with one teaspoon of honey and cinnamon powder mixed in hot water, so their breath stays fresh throughout the day.

HEARING LOSS:

Daily morning and night honey and cinnamon powder, taken in equal parts restores hearing. Remember when we were kids? We had toast with real butter and cinnamon sprinkled on it!

~°~°~°~°~°~°~°~°~°~°~°~°~°

Put it in a box:

If you cannot decide to toss or keep an item, put it in a box for 6 months. If you don't open the box before then, you can let it go without regret.

~°~°~°~°~°~°~°~°~°~°~°~°~°

"Cream and milk, when they turn sour in the night, often indicate that thunderstorms are about."

~°~°~°~°~°~°~°~°~°~°~°~°~°

Uses for Tea

Cleaning:

1. **Clean carpets:** Clean up musty, dirty carpets by sprinkling dry, used green tea leaves on the carpet. Let them work their magic for about 10 minutes and vacuum them up.
2. **Clean antique rugs:** Delicate Persian and Oriental rugs can benefit from a sprinkling of tea leaves. Sprinkle nearly dry, whole tea leaves on the rugs and gently sweep them away.
3. **Shine wood floors:** The tannins in black tea can help shine and colour hardwood flooring. Carefully rub some brewed tea into the floor following your normal cleaning routine without using too much water, let it air dry.
4. **Polish furniture:** Brewed tea also can help clean and shine wood furniture. Dip a soft cloth in a

small amount of tea, and use it to wipe down the tables, chairs and more.

5. **Clean mirrors and windows:** Tea can remove stubborn, greasy fingerprints from glass and make it sparkle. Simply rub a damp teabag on the glass or fill a spray bottle with brewed tea.

6. **Clean toilet stains:** Rumour has it that used tea bags can magically remove stubborn stains in the bottom of the toilet bowl. Just leave them in the toilet for several hours, then flush and brush the bowl.

7. **Get rid of fishy smells:** Rinse your hands with tea after eating or preparing fish (or other stinky foods) to eliminate odours.

8. **De-stink fridges:** instead of baking soda try using tea bags in the fridge to absorb odours.

9. **De-stink cat litter:** Likewise, used tea leaves can help deodorize litter boxes when mixed into the litter. Dry, green tea leaves are recommended.

10. **Prevent fleas:** Tea is rumoured to help prevent fleas, so sprinkle some dry used leaves around pet bedding.

11. **Kill dust mites:** Carefully spray diluted black tea on the carpet to kill dust mites. Colour test the carpet first in an inconspicuous spot.

12. **Clean the fireplace:** Sprinkling wet tea leaves on fireplace ashes while scooping them out may help reduce blowing dust.

13. **Make potpourri:** The herbs and flowers in herbal tea bags may have run out of flavour, but they often still have a good scent. Dry out herbal tea bags and add to potpourri or scented sachets.

14. **Make a car air freshener:** Likewise, you can freshen up the car without a chemical-laden commercial air

freshener. Put lavender tea or other soothing herbal tea in a bag under the seat to fight odours.

Personal:

1. **Soothe a sunburn:** Wet tea bags can soothe sunburns and other minor burns. For a full body sunburn soak in a tea bath.

2. **Soothe tired eyes:** Warm, wet tea bags can reduce puffiness and soothe pain around tired eyes . . . and tea bags on your eyes look a little less ridiculous than cucumber slices.

3. **Soothe pinkeye:** You can also use warm, wet tea bags as a compress to soothe the pain of pinkeye.

4. **Soothe razor burn:** A wet tea bag can also reduce and soothe razor burn.

5. **Drain boils:** Cover a boil with a wet tea bag overnight, and it should drain painlessly.

6. **Soothe blisters:** Hot tea bags are also rumoured to draw out infections when left on fever blisters and canker sores.

7. **Preventing skin inflammation:** Soaked Chamomile tea bags can be used to prevent skin inflammation caused by the radiation therapy.

8. **Dry poison ivy rash:** Dry a weepy poison ivy rash with strongly brewed tea. Simply dip a cotton ball into the tea, dab it on the affected area and let it air dry. Repeat as needed.

9. **Save a broken fingernail:** To salvage a partially broken fingernail, use a piece of mesh tea bag to create a splint of sorts between the nail and the broken piece. Coat in nail polish.

10. **Make soap:** Tea is a useful addition when making glycerine soap. The texture and scent can help make the soap smell and cleanse better.

11. **Help recover from injections:** A wet tea bag on an injection site can be soothing, for babies or adults.

12. **Soothe bleeding gums:** For an older child who loses a tooth, try putting a cold, wet tea bag in the mouth where the tooth was lost. It can reduce bleeding and soothe pain.

13. **Make mouthwash:** Similarly, toothaches and other mouth pain can be soothed with a rinse of antiseptic peppermint tea mixed with a little salt.

14. **Shine dry hair:** Brewed tea makes a good conditioner for dry hair. Rinse with (unsweetened) tea and leave to dry for a while, then rinse again with water.

15. **Dye hair:** Brewed tea also is a good natural hair dye. Mix rosemary and sage into dark black tea and let the mixture stand overnight. Strain the mix and thoroughly work it into your hair. Repeat as needed for the desired colour.

16. **Improve skin:** To protect and beautify skin, try bathing in green tea. Another widely recommended skin booster is chamomile tea in a facial steamer.

17. **Cure acne:** Some acne suffers swear by washing their faces with green tea to cure or reduce their acne.

18. **De-stink feet:** Soaking your feet in strong tea for 20 minutes per day may be a relaxing and effective way to reduce foot odour.

19. **Heal warts:** To help plantar warts on the feet heal faster, press a warm, tea bag onto the wart for 20 minutes per day.

20. **Improve breath:** Gargling with strong tea can help reduce halitosis

21. **Get smarter:** Caffeinated teas have proven effects on mental alertness, but some traditional Chinese practitioners swear that tea leaves in pillows can also help mental alertness. They say after sleeping on tea leaf pillows, people can wake up more clear headed and quick thinking.

22. **Cure the common cold:** The same Chinese traditionalists also swear by tea as a time tested remedy for many cold symptoms. Of course, others maintain that a cold will seven days with tea treatment or one week without.

23. **Prevent dizziness:** People drink tea for a variety of health reasons, but many older adults do not realize that black tea could reduce their dizziness when standing up. The tea boosts blood pressure, reducing the threat of dizziness. There are many other articles claiming the benefits of black tea, including reduced risk of heart attacks, kidney stones, Parkinson's disease and ovarian cancer.

Kitchen:

1. **Tenderize meat:** Marinate tough meat in black tea to make it more tender.

2. **Smoke it:** Add tea to a smoker to make tea infused cheese and meats.

3. **Boil eggs:** The Chinese also like to add tea leaves to the water after boiled eggs are cooked. This adds some flavour and colour to the boiled eggs.

Garden:

1. **Add to compost:** Pouring strong tea into a compost bin will help speed up the process and encourage more friendly bacteria to grow, improving the compost.
2. **Fertilize roses:** Spread used tea leaves around rosebushes, then add mulch and water. The tannic acid and other nutrients will benefit the plants.
3. **Help houseplants:** Occasionally use brewed tea instead of water to feed ferns and other houseplants that like rich, acidic soil.
4. **Add to potted plants:** A few tea bags in the bottom of a planter can help soil retain water, and adds valuable nutrients.

Others:

1. **Dye fabrics:** Green and black teas have long been used in dyes for fabric and paper, particularly for generating a beige faux-antique look.
2. **Paint with tea:** Some artists use strong black tea to paint backgrounds or accents on black and white sketches.
3. **Strengthen puppy pads:** A footbath with strong black tea is rumoured to help strengthen the pads of dog feet.
4. **Repel mosquitoes:** Burning tea leaves is said to repel mosquitoes with none of the side effects of chemical bug sprays.

5. **Tell the future:** "Reading the tea leaves" is more than a political expression. Telling fortunes in the pattern of tea leaves in an empty teacup is an ancient art that is still occasionally practiced.

Making Great Tea:

Start with fresh cold water and bring it to a full boil. For black tea, begin steeping immediately for 3-5 minutes, depending on how strong you want it. With green and white tea, let the water cool down for a few minutes before pouring it over the tea and only let it steep 2-3 minutes. Buy the best tea you can afford—the very cheaper varieties seldom taste as good.

Also, make sure your kettle doesn't have a build-up of lime. If necessary, put in a cup of vinegar and enough water to fill the kettle; bring it to a boil and let it sit for five minutes. Empty, rinse well, and continue. Boiling water in the microwave is not recommended; it's fine in a pinch at the cost of the perfect flavour

~°~°~°~°~°~°~°~°~°~°~°~°

Try to buy a home that meets most of your needs for the next 5 to 10 years, or find a home that can grow and change with your needs.

~°~°~°~°~°~°~°~°~°~°~°~°

More is not necessarily better:

"There's really no need for most of us to have, say, two microwave ovens, or three bicycles."

~°~°~°~°~°~°~°~°~°~°~°~°

"We gather to ask for your blessing,
We gather to thank you in prayer.
Please bless all this food we are sharing
And keep us in your tender care"

~°~°~°~°~°~°~°~°~°~°~°~°~°

Uses for Lemon Peels

1. Clean greasy messes

Greasy pans? Splattered stove tops? Messy counters? If your kitchen has been the victim of some sloppy sautéing, try using lemon halves before bringing out possibly toxic chemical cleaners. Sprinkle some salt (for abrasion) on a juiced lemon half and rub on the greasy areas, wipe up with a towel. *(Be careful using lemon on marble counter tops, or any other surface sensitive to acid).*

2. Clean your tea kettle or coffee pot

For mineral deposit build up in your tea kettle, fill the kettle with water, add a handful of thin slices of lemon peel and bring to a boil. Turn off heat and let sit for an hour, drain, and rinse well. For coffee pots, add ice, salt and lemon rinds to the empty pot; swish and swirl for a minute or two, dump, and rinse. Hello, sparkly.

3. Clean your microwave

All it takes is one exploding bowl of food to render the interior of your microwave officially gunked, sometimes gunked with cement-like properties. Rather than using strong chemical cleaners, try this: Add lemon rinds to a microwave-safe bowl filled halfway with water. Cook on high for 5 minutes, allowing the water to boil and the steam to condense on the walls and tops of the oven. Carefully remove the hot bowl and wipe away the mess with a towel.

4. Deodorize the garbage disposal

Use lemon peels to deodorize the garbage disposal (and make your kitchen smell awesome at the same time). It is a great way to finally dispose of spent lemon peels after you have used them for any of these applications.

5. Polish chrome

Mineral deposits on chrome faucets and other tarnished chrome make haste in the presence of lemon—rub with a squeezed lemon half, rinse, and lightly buff with a soft cloth.

6. Polish copper

A halved lemon dipped in salt or baking powder can also be used to brighten copper cookware, as well as brass, chrome, or stainless steel. Dip a juiced lemon half in salt (you also use baking soda or cream of tartar for the salt) and rub on the affected area. Let it stay on for 5 minutes. Then rinse in warm water and polish dry.

7. Clean a stainless sink

Use the same method described to polish chrome, applied to any stainless sink.

8. Keep insects out

Many pests abhor the acid in lemon. You can chop of the peels and place them along thresholds, windowsills, and near any cracks or holes where ants or pests may be entering. For other ways to combat pests naturally, see 7 Steps to Chemical-Free Pest Control.

9. Make a scented humidifier

If your home suffers from dry heat in the winter, you can put lemon peels in a pot of water and simmer on the lowest stove-top setting to humidify and scent the air.

10. Refresh cutting boards

Because of lemon's low pH, it has antibacterial properties that make is a good choice for refreshing cutting boards. After proper disinfecting (see: How to Clean Your Cutting Board) give the surface a rub with a halved lemon, let sit for a few minutes, and rinse.

11. Keep brown sugar soft

If your brown sugar most often turns into brick sugar, try adding some lemon peel (with traces of pulp and pith removed) to help keep it moist and easy to use

12. Make zest

Zest is the best! Zest is simply grated peel, and is the epitome of lemon essence—it can be used fresh, dried, or frozen. If you don't have an official zester, which looks like a very fine cheese grater, you can use the smallest size of a box grater. To dry zest, spread it on a towel and leave out until dried, then store in a jar. To freeze, use a freezer-safe container. Use zest in salads, marinades, baked goods, grain dishes, etc.

13. Make Vegan Lemon Biscotti

Once you've made some zest, make these Vegan Lemon Biscotti cookies.

14. Make twists

Strips of peel, aka twists, are good in cocktails, sparkling water, and tap water. Use a vegetable peeler to make long strips, or use a knife and cut the peel into long strips, cutting away the white pith which is bitter. These can be frozen in a freezer-safe container or bag.

15. Make lemon extract powder

Make zest or twists and dry the strips skin-side down on a plate until they are shrivelled and dried up, about 3-4 days. Put in a blender and pulverize into a powder. Use the powdered peel in place of extract or zest in recipes.

16. Make Lemon Sugar

To make lemon extract powder and add it to sugar, or take fresh twists, put them in a jar with sugar and let the peel's oil infuse the sugar.

17. Make Lemon Pepper

Mix lemon extract powder with freshly cracked pepper.

18. Make candied lemon peel

Orange or grapefruit peel can be candied too. Yum. Candied peels are pretty easy to make, and can be eaten plain, or dipped in melted chocolate, used in cake, cookie, candy, or bread recipes. These recipes for candied citrus and ginger use Sucanate, the most wholesome sugar you can buy.

19. Lighten age spots

Many folk remedies suggest using lemon peel to help lighten age spots—apply a small piece to the affected area and leave on for an hour. You can also try one of these 5 natural ways to lighten age spots.

20. Soften dry elbows

Use a half lemon sprinkled with baking soda on elbows, just place your elbow in the lemon and twist the lemon (like you are juicing it) for several minutes. Rinse and dry.

21. Use on your skin

Lemon peels can be very lightly rubbed on your face for a nice skin tonic, then rinse. (And be careful around your eyes.)

22. Make a sugar scrub

Mix 1/2 a cup of sugar with finely chopped lemon peel and enough olive oil to make a paste. Wet your body in the shower, turn off the water and massage sugar mix all over your skin, rinse, be soft!

*"Problems are not stop signs,
they are guidelines."*

—*Robert H. Schuller*

Lemon Juice:

- For a sore throat or bad breath, gargle with some lemon juice.
- Clean discoloured utensils with a cloth dipped in lemon juice. Rinse with warm water.
- Toss used lemons into your garbage disposal to help keep it clean and smelling fresh.
- Use one part lemon juice and two parts salt to scour chinaware to its original lustre.
- A few drops of lemon juice in outdoor house-paint will keep insects away while you are painting and until the paint dries.
- Remove scratches on furniture by mixing equal parts of lemon juice and salad oil and rubbing it on the scratches with a soft cloth.
- To make furniture polish, mix one part lemon juice and two parts olive oil.
- To clean the surface of white marble or ivory (such as piano keys), rub with a half a lemon, or make a lemon juice and salt paste. Wipe with a clean, wet cloth.
- To renew hardened paintbrushes, dip into boiling lemon juice. Lower the heat and leave the brush for 15 minutes, then wash it in soapy water.

- To remove dried paint from glass, apply hot lemon juice with a soft cloth. Leave until nearly dry, and then wipe off.
- Rub kitchen and bathroom faucets with lemon peel. Wash and dry with a soft cloth to shine and remove spots.
- Fresh lemon juice in rinse water removes soap film from interiors of ovens and refrigerators.
- Create your own air freshener: Slice some lemons, cover with water, and let simmer in a pot for about an hour. (This will also clean your aluminum pots!)
- Fish or onion odour on your hands can be removed by rubbing them with fresh lemons.
- To get odours out of wooden rolling pins, bowls, or cutting boards, rub with a piece of lemon. Don't rinse: The wood will absorb the lemon juice.
- Save lemon and orange rinds to deter squirrels and cats from digging in the garden. Store rinds in the freezer during the winter, and then bury them just under the surface of the garden periodically throughout the spring and summer.
- After a shampoo, rinse your hair with lemon juice to make it shine. Mix the strained juice of a lemon in an eight-ounce glass of warm water.
- Mix one tablespoon of lemon juice with two tablespoons of salt to make a rust-removing scrub.
- Before you start to vacuum, put a few drops of lemon juice in the dust bag. It will make the house smell fresh.
- Get grimy white cotton socks white again by boiling them in water with a slice of lemon.
- Clean copper pots by cutting a lemon in half and rubbing the cut side with salt until the salt sticks.

Rub the lemon onto the metal, rinse with hot water, and polish dry.

- Suck on a lemon to settle an upset stomach.

~°~°~°~°~°~°~°~°~°~°~°~°~°

If your goal is to go to court to punish someone for what they have done to you, remember there is a good chance he or she will fight back and try to punish you. As the old saying goes, "If you seek revenge, first dig two graves."

~°~°~°~°~°~°~°~°~°~°~°~°~°

Barbecue Safety

- Place your barbecue on a stable base. A wobbly grill is a serious hazard.
- Before using your gas grill, check all the connections for leaks. This is important whether you use portable propane tanks or have a direct natural gas line. The best way to check for leaks is to get some soapy water (mix some liquid dish soap and water in a dish) and put it on all the joints and connections. Watch for tiny bubbles to form. If they do, you have a leak that needs to be fixed BEFORE you light the grill.
- Check for grease build-up and clean if necessary. Excessive grease can flare in unexpected places at unexpected times.
- Check for badly rusted and corroded burners. This is the part of your gas barbecue that is likely to need replacing the most frequently. These parts

wear out quickly . . . but the good news is, they are easy to replace. Many hardware and department stores carry universal replacement burners, or they can be ordered from your unit's manufacturer. This is an extremely hazardous situation. The heat from the excessive gas from this hole could cause external fires, skin burns, and even an explosion of the propane tank. If your burners are beginning to corrode, **change them!** It's an easy process and very inexpensive. **It could save a life!**

- Never leave young children unattended in the vicinity of a hot barbecue . . . and don't let them play close by.

- If using charcoal briquettes, use the minimum amount of lighter fluid necessary to start the coals.

- Always light your gas barbecue with the lid open. If it doesn't start after a couple of tries, turn off the gas and wait five minutes for the gas to dissipate before trying again.

- Loose fitting, flowing clothing is a hazard as it can be blown over the flame and ignite.

- Because you're dealing with fire, have a fire extinguisher or the garden hose handy or close by in the event of a serious flare-up. But if it's a grease fire DO NOT use water as it will spread the grease and flare up.

- When you've finished cooking on a gas barbecue, be sure to turn off the gas valve on the tank or on the gas pipe.

- Never bring a barbecue grill indoors (which can be tempting in bad or cold weather), or into any unventilated space such as a garage. This is both a fire and carbon monoxide poisoning hazard.

Winter Survival Kit for Your Home:

Keep several days' supply of these items:
Food that needs no cooking or refrigeration,
such as bread, crackers, cereal, canned foods,
and dried fruits. Remember baby food and
formula if you have young children.
Water stored in clean containers, or purchased
bottled water (5 gallons per person) in case
your water pipes freeze and rupture.
Medicines that any family member may need.
If your area is prone to long periods of cold
temperatures, or if your home is isolated, stock
additional amounts of food, water, and medicine.

~°~°~°~°~°~°~°~°~°~°~°~°~°

Copies of Emergency Documents Should Include:

Specifications for adaptive equipment (in case it needs to be replaced)

- Proof of ownership or lease of your residence. (This is important when applying for disaster assistance after the quake.)*¨ Social security numbers of family members.*
- Vehicle, boats, etc. make, identification and license numbers.*
- Charge and bank account numbers.*
- Insurance policy numbers.*
- Securities, deeds and loan numbers including company name, address and telephone numbers.*
- Will/living trust and letter of instructions.*

- Photos or video of all valuables for documentation of insurance claim. (This inventory should be backed up on disk if it is on computer. Consider documenting your inventory by going through your areas with a video or camera and capture all your possessions on film.)*
- Important business documents.'
- Family records (birth, marriage, death certificates).*
- List style and serial numbers of medical devices such as pacemakers.

~°~°~°~°~°~°~°~°~°~°~°~°~°

Cleaning techniques and dust protection measures can extend the life of your PC dramatically.

~°~°~°~°~°~°~°~°~°~°~°~°~°

General Cleaning Tips—Computer:

- Never place your computer on the ground, always use a computer table or shelf for this purpose.
- To clean the computer case first unplugs your system power from the electrical outlet. Remove all cables and connectors from the back side of your computer.
- Now blow the air around all the hardware components and keeping away your blower nozzle 4 to 5 inches away from main board components. You can use a vacuum cleaner also for this purpose but compressed air is the better solution to clean a system.

- At the end, using lightly dampened cloth or spray any cleaning fluids on the computer case and use a paper towel to dry it.
- Never clean inside computer components or other circuit board with a damp or wet cloth.
- Always be careful not to eat or drink around the computer.

Going Bananas

After reading this, you'll never look at a banana in the same way again.

Bananas contain three natural sugars—sucrose, fructose and glucose combined with fibre. A banana gives an instant, sustained and substantial boost of energy.

Research has proven that just two bananas provide enough energy for a strenuous 90-minute workout. No wonder the banana is the number one fruit with the world's leading athletes.

But energy isn't the only way a banana can help us keep fit. It can also help overcome or prevent a substantial number of illnesses and conditions, making it a must to add to our daily diet.

Depression: According to a recent survey undertaken by MIND amongst people suffering from depression, many felt much better after eating a banana. This is because bananas contain tryptophan, a type of protein that the body converts into serotonin, known to make you relax, improve your mood and generally make you feel happier.

PMS: Forget the pills—eat a banana. The vitamin B6 it contains regulates blood glucose levels, which can affect your mood.

Anaemia : High in iron, bananas can stimulate the production of haemoglobin in the blood and so helps in cases of anaemia.

Blood Pressure: This unique tropical fruit is extremely high in potassium yet low in salt, making it perfect to beat blood pressure. So much so, the US Food and Drug Administration has just allowed the banana industry to make official claims for the fruit's ability to reduce the risk of blood pressure and stroke.

Brain Power: 200 students at a Twickenham (Middlesex) school (England) were helped through their exams this year by eating bananas at breakfast, break, and lunch in a bid to boost their brain power. Research has shown that the potassium-packed fruit can assist learning by making pupils more alert.

Constipation: High in fibre, including bananas in the diet can help restore normal bowel action, helping to overcome the problem without resorting to laxatives.

Hangovers: One of the quickest ways of curing a hangover is to make a banana milkshake, sweetened with honey. The banana calms the stomach and, with the help of the honey, builds up depleted blood sugar levels, while the milk soothes and re-hydrates your system.

Heartburn: Bananas have a natural antacid effect in the body, so if you suffer from heartburn, try eating a banana for soothing relief.

Morning Sickness: Snacking on bananas between meals helps to keep blood sugar levels up and avoid morning sickness

Mosquito bites: Before reaching for the insect bite cream, try rubbing the affected area with the inside of a banana skin. Many people find it amazingly successful at reducing swelling and irritation.

Nerves: Bananas are high in B vitamins that help calm the nervous system.

Overweight and at work? Studies at the Institute of Psychology in Austria found pressure at work leads to gorging on comfort food like chocolate and chips. Looking at 5,000 hospital patients, researchers found the most obese were more likely to be in high-pressure jobs. The report concluded that, to avoid panic-induced food cravings, we need to control our blood sugar levels by snacking on high carbohydrate foods every two hours to keep levels steady.

Ulcers: The banana is used as the dietary food against intestinal disorders because of its soft texture and smoothness. It is the only raw fruit that can be eaten without distress in over-chronicler cases. It also neutralizes over-acidity and reduces irritation by coating the lining of the stomach.

Temperature control: Many other cultures see bananas as a "cooling" fruit that can lower both the physical and emotional temperature of expectant mothers. In Thailand, for example, pregnant women eat bananas to ensure their baby is born with a cool temperature.

Seasonal Affective Disorder (SAD): Bananas can help SAD sufferers because they contain the natural mood Enhancer tryptophan.

Smoking &Tobacco Use: Bananas can also help people trying to give up smoking. The B6, B12 they contain, as well as the potassium and magnesium found in them, help the body recover from the effects of nicotine withdrawal.

Stress: Potassium is a vital mineral, which helps normalize the heartbeat, sends oxygen to the brain and regulates your body's water balance. When we are stressed, our metabolic rate rises, thereby reducing our potassium levels. These can be rebalanced with the help of a high-potassium banana snack.

Strokes: According to research in The New England Journal of Medicine, eating bananas as part of a regular diet can cut the risk of death by strokes by as much as 40%!

Warts: Those keen on natural alternatives swear that if you want to kill off a wart, take a piece of banana skin and place it on the wart, with the yellow side out. Carefully hold the skin in place with a plaster or surgical tape

~°~°~°~°~°~°~°~°~°~°~°~°

- To ripen green bananas, wrap them in a wet towel and put them in a brown paper bag.
- When your bananas become too ripe to eat, peel and place them in a plastic bag and freeze them for banana bread or cake.

~°~°~°~°~°~°~°~°~°~°~°~°~°

Tips for Writing a Living Will:

A living will is a legal document that allows you to exercise your right to decide what will happen to you at a time of critical illness or imminent death.
Carefully consider your wishes for the living will.

If you want to authorize someone to make decisions on your behalf, discuss it thoroughly with that person first.

Organize a witness for your living will.

Write in a clear and straightforward manner.

Check and double check your living will text to ensure that nothing is left open to interpretation.

~°~°~°~°~°~°~°~°~°~°~°~°~°

Bird nests: Put Shredded Wheat out for the birds—they can use it to build their nests.

~°~°~°~°~°~°~°~°~°~°~°~°~°

Resume Tips:

Name, Address, Telephone Number and E-mail Address (Optional):

Begin your resume with your real name (not nickname) and a permanent address. Include the area code with your phone number. If you are not at home during the day, make sure an answering machine or voice mail is available for messages.

Objective:

This is the focal point of your resume—the position you are seeking in specific terms. Your objective should be simple yet directly related to your qualifications and accomplishments.

Education:

List your most recent educational experience first. Be sure to include your degree (BA, BS, etc.), major, institution attended, graduation date, minors/concentrations and any other major coursework or projects. Special awards and commendations should be noted.

Work Experience:

Always include the title of your position, name of organization, location (city, province) and dates of employment. Describe your work responsibilities using strong action words. Volunteer work, internships and student teaching should be listed here.

Additional Information:

This is the place for extra information that doesn't fit into other categories, such as special interests, computer knowledge and activities. Multilingual and medically trained people should list their experience here.

References:

You may wish to include on your resume: "References available upon request." Always ask for permission before listing someone as a reference. List three people, including name, title, employer, address, and business and home telephone numbers.

Resume Do's & Don'ts:

The Do's and Don'ts of Resume Writing

Do:

Use action words, such as developed, managed and designed.

Keep paragraphs under seven lines. Since resumes' are often scanned by hiring managers, it has a better chance of being read if it is condensed.

Be honest.

Check thoroughly for grammar and spelling mistakes. It's a good idea to have a friend look it over for unnoticed mistakes.

Use high-quality paper that is white, ivory or another conservative colour.

Use normal margins (1 inch on top and bottom, 1.25 inches on sides). Make sure your resume is clear and visually pleasing.

Make your resume unique. List technical skills, certificates awarded, professional memberships, military experience, travel and community work if it relates to the job you are seeking.

Don't:

Be vague.

Be too focused on job duties. Go above and beyond, listing the new programs you took part in.

Write about inappropriate and unnecessary personal experiences.

Use personal pronouns, such as "I" and "me."

Include copies of transcripts, letters of recommendation or awards.

Include reasons you left your previous job.

Staple your resume.

~°~°~°~°~°~°~°~°~°~°~°~°~°

Eco Office Tips:

- **Get light motion sensors for offices, conference rooms, and bathrooms**. There's no reason for lights to be one when there's no one in the room and let's face it, some of us forget to turn the lights off
- **Shut down your printers, faxes, and computers**. Some people are under the false impression that it's more efficient to leave computers on overnight. This is not true—shut off all the electronics when you leave the office.
- **Get a programmable thermostat**. This device will help you keep your building warm or cool when the people are there and save power and money when the people are away.

~°~°~°~°~°~°~°~°~°~°~°~°~°

Tips on Tipping:

At nearly every step of the traveling process, there are professionals waiting to provide assistance.

Taxi/Limo Drivers: A $2 to $3 tip is usually satisfactory; more if he helps you with your bags and/or takes special steps to get you to your destination on time.

Porters: A standard tip for airport and train porters are $1 per bag; more if your luggage is very heavy.

Hotel Bellman: Again, $1 per bag is standard. Tip when they show you to your room and again if they assist you upon checkout. Tip more if they provide any additional service. *Note: A $5 tip upon arrival can usually guarantee you special attention should you require it.*

Doorman: Typically, a $1 tip for hailing a taxi is appropriate. However, you may want to tip more for special service, such as carrying your bags or shielding you with an umbrella.

Concierge: Tip for special services such as making restaurant or theatre reservations, arranging sightseeing tours, etc. The amount of the tip is generally dependent on the type and complexity of service(s) provided—$2 to $10 is a standard range. You may elect to tip for each service, or in one sum upon departure. If you want to ensure special treatment from the concierge, you might consider a $10-$20 tip upon arrival.

Hotel Maid: Maids are often forgotten about when it comes to tipping because they typically do their work when you are not around. For stays of more than one night, $1 per night is standard. The tip should be left in the hotel room in a marked envelope.

Parking Attendants: Tip $1 to $2 when your car is delivered.

Waiters: 15-20% of your pre-tax check is considered standard. The same applies for room service waiters. Some restaurants will automatically add a 15% gratuity to your bill, especially for large parties—look for it before tipping. If the 15% is added, you need only tip up to another 5% for superlative service.

Cloakroom Attendants: If there is a charge for the service, a tip is not necessary. However, if there is no charge, or extra care is taken with your coat and/or bags, a $1 to $2 tip is appropriate.

Tour Guides/Charter Bus Drivers: If a tip is not automatically included, tip $1 for a half-day tour, $2 for full-day tour, and anywhere from $5 to $10 for a week-long tour. Tip a private guide more.

These are some of the people you are most likely to encounter while traveling. Undoubtedly there will be others. One standard rule in tipping is: *If someone renders special service to you along the way, show your appreciation with a tip.*

Restaurants: It is customary to tip approximately 15% on the total bill before tax, 20% for exceptional service.

Public Behaviour Tips:

Business:

In business situations, a handshake is used upon greetings or introductions. Men usually wait for women to offer their hand before shaking.
An open, cordial manner is usually necessary when dealing with Canadian businesspeople.

Conversation:

Direct—but not too intense—eye contact can be acceptable, especially when you want to convey interest and sincerity. Some ethnic groups, however, look away to confer respect.

The standard distance between two people should be two feet.

Francophones usually are not as reserved as Anglophones. Moreover, they are often more likely to use expansive gestures, stand closer while talking, and touch during a conversation.

Greetings are English expressions similar to those in Great Britain and the <u>United States</u>, such as "good morning", "good afternoon", "good evening", "hi", and "hello." Some young people have recently adopted "hey" as an informal greeting; it is used the same way as "hi", and is not meant to be disrespectful.

"How are you?" is a popular greeting in Canada. This question does not require a literal-minded, detailed answer; a simple "Fine, thank you" will suffice.

When parting, common expressions are "goodbye", "bye", "have a nice day", "good night", and " see you later". "Have a safe trip" is a sincere expression of good wishes and friendly concern.

When someone says "thank you", expected responses are "you're welcome" , "no problem", or "happy to help". The response "Uh huh" is frequently heard in the USA, but may be interpreted as rude in Canada.

Canada is a very open society, exercising maximum social tolerance. Boasting and ostentation, however, tends to be frowned upon or at least regarded with some misgivings.

In public, emotion is kept under restraint. Most Canadians try to be tactful when dealing with other people. For the most part, they will try to avoid arguing or causing scenes in public.

It is considered rude for people to speak in a foreign language in the presence of others who do not understand what is being said. If you are in a group where everyone speaks and understands that language, speaking it in public within that group is acceptable (e.g. while dining together at a restaurant or touring attractions as a group).

Generally, Canadians like to consider themselves as tolerant of religious diversity, but many are uncomfortable with certain outward displays of religion.

Gestures & Body Language:

If you see an acquaintance at a distance, a wave is an appropriate acknowledgement.

If you need to point, use the index finger. Pointing at other people, however, is often considered unacceptable. If you need to point at a person in public, wave your whole hand in their general direction or nod your head toward them.

To beckon someone, ensure that you wave with your fingers curled toward you and that your palm is facing up.

The "O.K." sign, and the "thumbs up" sign are two popular gestures used for expressing approval.

To wave good-bye, move your entire hand facing outward.

If you want to give the "V" for victory sign, do so with the palm facing out. Attempting this gesture with the palm inward may cause offense.

Generally, friends of the same gender do not hold hands. But same gender partners may hold hands or demonstrate affection in public. However, tolerance for public affection between same-gender partners can vary greatly within Canada and within Canadian cities.

Throwing money or credit cards on the counter for an employee in a shop, hotel or restaurant is considered insulting.

Shopping, Banking, & Dining:

The GST (Goods and Services Tax) rebate formerly available to visitors from USA and overseas is no longer available.

Common courtesies such as holding doors open for the person behind you are appreciated and often expected.

People using Automated Bank Machines (ABMs or ATMs) expect the next person in line to stand a few feet behind them.

People routinely line up to pay for items in stores, buy tickets in movie theatres, and board public transportation. Even without a formal line, expect to be served on a "first come, first served" basis. Be patient when waiting to be served. Also, If you are in a place with two cash registers (tills) side by side, don't be surprised to see the line form in between the two. The person at the front of the line (queue) has the choice of whichever till becomes available first. This can give the mistaken impression that there is nobody in line behind the people who are currently being served, so be careful to check for a line forming a little ways back from the cash registers and service area; otherwise, you may unintentionally jump the queue Canadians deeply resent people who push ahead in line.

Most restaurants in Canada don't have a smoking section. It is a non-smoking environment almost everywhere. In an increasing number of Canadian communities, there are by-laws in effect prohibiting smoking in restaurants—and even bars. With the exception of the streets, you will find that smoking is restricted in most public places. Since smoking in restaurants falls under municipal jurisdiction, you will find that the rules vary depending on the city or town that you are in.

On the Road:

Similar to the United States, one should expect to encounter more aggressive driving behaviour in Canada's urban areas, as opposed to rural areas, especially in the Central Canadian provinces of Ontario and Quebec.

Pedestrian behaviour differs depending on the region, with "jay walking" being more common in Central Canada than in the West or East. That being said, only the pedestrians in <u>Montreal</u> rival those of <u>New York City</u>, in terms of seemingly ignoring traffic signals.

Treatment of pedestrians, by drivers, also differs across the country. In Alberta, provincial laws accord right of way to pedestrians at virtually all intersections, and cross walks are very common. Stringent enforcement over the years have made Alberta drivers very cautious, leading to most erring on the side of caution whenever a pedestrian comes into view on a roadway. Jay walking is accordingly fairly rare in Alberta, and can lead to some embarrassment for the jay walker when cars suddenly stop while he or she tries to slip quickly across a city street.

By contrast, a jay walker in Montreal or Toronto arguably takes his life into her own hands, as Quebec and Ontario drivers are not compelled by law to give right of way to pedestrians outside of official cross walks (which often times go unnoticed by many drivers).

On expressways, the left lane is reserved for passing or faster vehicles. Even if they are driving faster than the posted speed limit, slower vehicles are expected to move to the right for vehicles attempting to overtake them. Drivers are also expected to make room (normally by shifting one lane over or slowing down) for vehicles merging onto the expressway. In some provinces, slower vehicles are required by law to keep right; in other provinces, this is just customary.

On the highway, if an oncoming driver turns his headlights on and off before you, he is probably attempting to inform you that you have neglected to turn your lights on (especially if at dusk or at night). However, she may also be attempting to warn you of an approaching traffic hazard or police "speed trap".

At night, if an oncoming driver switches to her high-beam setting and back before you, she is normally attempting to inform you that you have neglected to switch from high—to low-beam with your own car.

Radar and laser detectors may not be used in most of Canada's provinces, although they remain legal in some locations, such as the province of Alberta. The use of automatic traffic speed cameras is widespread in some provinces, such as Alberta, but politically unpopular in other provinces, such as Ontario and BC.

In Canadian Homes:

You will be expected to remove your shoes as soon as you enter most Canadian homes. If you're unsure about this, or uncomfortable, simply ask your host if you should take your shoes off. This is a bit of a hangover from the long Canadian winters, but is practiced all year.

In most Canadian families, at meals you are expected to request items and not to just reach and grab it, e.g. "Please pass the butter".

If you are invited to a Canadian home for dinner, it is normal to bring a small "hostess gift" or contribution to the evening. Flowers, a bottle of wine, or a box of chocolates are typical gifts.

~°~°~°~°~°~°~°~°~°~°~°~°

A Brief Overview on Tipping Abroad:

Argentina

It is customary to leave 10-15 per cent at restaurants. Hotels generally charge around 10 per cent, but where that is not the case then tip housekeeping and porters 3 pesos. Taxi drivers expect between 5-10 percent and other like car-park, toilet attendants, cloakroom and bar staff expect 2 pesos.

Australia

Tipping in Australia is starting to happen more frequently, but is still entirely optional. A 10 per cent tip in restaurants is acceptable. It is not customary to tip taxi drivers but this form of tipping is on the increase as tourism to Australia grows.

Austria

Restaurants charge 12.5 per cent service charge and diners leave a discretionary 1-2 Euros extra. Where service is not included, leave around 10 per cent. Hotels charge 10 per cent and a small extra tip is expected for good service. Taxis expect 10 per cent and cloak staff and toilet attendants expect 1 euro and 50c respectively.

Belgium

Restaurants usually add on 15 per cent but leave a few coins for good service. Where service is not included, 15 per cent tip is expected. Tipping is not the norm in hotels and in taxis just round up the fare. Car park attendants receive 1 Euros, cloakroom staff, 50c, toilet attendants, 25c and bar staff just small change.

British Virgin Islands

Tipping of 15-22 per cent is expected at restaurants and hotels. Taxis get between 2-4 per cent and 10 per cent discretionary tip for bar staff.

Canada

Most service staff in Canada expect something in the 10-20 percent tip range, depending on whether it's French or English Canada, and how good the service is—if the service is really bad, leave a few cents and they should get the message.

Czech Republic

Tipping is not part of the culture here, but in restaurants and taxis just round up the bill.

China

You'll never have to tip anywhere in China. It's the one comfort from the fact that foreigners are generally thought of as filthy rich, and therefore charged a lot more. Most government operated hotels and restaurants prohibit the acceptance of tips, but it is sometimes expected at the bigger hotels and by younger service personnel in the more open cities. Use your discretion.

Cyprus

Expect to be charged 10 per cent at restaurants and hotels plus small tips for porters and housekeeping. Taxis don't expect tips but cloakroom staff and toilet attendants expect 1 euro.

Denmark

Tipping is not generally expected except for exceptional service.

France

In France service must be included in the price of a restaurant bill by law so no need to tip, although it is customary to round your bill to include a little more. At hotels leave a euro or two for housekeeping and porters. This is not true of bars so you should use your discretion if you feel you have got particularly good service or not.

Germany

Service is not generally included at restaurants but a discretionary tip of 10-15 per cent is expected. At hotels housekeeping and porters expect 2-3 Euros. Taxi drivers expect 10-15 per cent tips.

Greece

At restaurants a discretionary charge of 4-8 per cent is expected. At hotels, a discretionary tip of 4-5 per cent is the norm. Taxi drivers do not expect to be tipped.

Hungary

Tips are generally around 8-15 per cent.

Ireland

Tipping is not de rigueur in Ireland, however it is customary to tip of between 12 and 15 per cent in restaurants or hotels, if there is not already a service charge included. If you receive good service then a 10 per cent tip would be about the right amount for taxi drivers, porters and hotel staff.

Italy

No tip is expected in restaurants throughout Italy, as you will normally be charged a copper to (cover charge) on top of your bill. However it will be much appreciated if you have had a good service to leave a bit extra.

Malta

At restaurants expect to pay 10-15 per cent tips. At hotels a discretionary tip of LM5 for housekeeping and for porters and bar staff LM1 is adequate. Taxi drivers expect LM 1-2. Everyone else between 10-50c.

Netherlands

Restaurants charge 10% but where service is not include leave a tip of 10%. At hotels, tip as you please but taxis expect 5 per cent or round up the fare.

New Zealand

Tipping is not part of the culture unless service is exceptional.

Portugal

At restaurants leave around 5 per cent. Hotels tend to charge between 5-19 per cen. Where service is not included leave the concierge and porters 2 euros. Taxi drivers expect 5-10 per cent.

Romania

At restaurants include service at a rate of 5-10 per cent. Where it is not, a tip between 5-10 per cent is expected. Hotels charge around 5% but where it is not included leave housekeeping and porters 100,000-150,000 lei. In taxis, round up the fare and cloak room, car-park and toilet attendants expect between 25,000-30,000 Lei.

Russia

Restaurants charge anywhere between 5-20 per cent service charge but where they don't leave between 10-25 per cent tips. Hotels charge 5-20 per cent but a small tip is expected by porters and housekeeping. Taxi drivers don't expect a tip.

Singapore

According to government notices in the Lion City, tipping is not allowed. Officials encourage tourists not to add to the 10 per cent service charge that many high-end hotels include on the bill. Hotel porters are one exception to the no-tipping rule, as they usually receive a couple of dollars for lugging bags.

Spain

In Spain most restaurants and bars will expect to receive a tip from tourists, although it is really is still a matter of personal discretion. Bills will usually include a service charge in restaurants and as a general rule if you are served a drink in bar at your table you should leave a small tip, as with porters and chambermaids in your hotel.

Sri Lanka

A 10 per cent tip is generally expected. Hotels will charge this amount, but where they don't tip the concierge, bar staff and housekeeping 100Lkr and porters 30LKr. Taxi drivers expect 10 per cent or up to 100LKr for a short journey. Car park and toilet attendants and bar staff expect 50-100LKr.

Thailand

Everything goes in Thailand, and that rule applies to tipping as well. Some places expect it and others don't. In general, the more Westernised the place is, the more likely you'll be expected to leave a gratuity. Cabs are now metered in

Bangkok, so there's no haggling over your fare, but local custom is still to round the fare up to the nearest five baht.

United States

This country is the tipping capital of the world where not tipping can easily offend. Restaurants in the USA usually call for a 15-20 percent tip, which supplements a normally meagre wage. This is true of everyone in the service industry, so the rule is, if someone helps you out, from porter to bar tender it pays to leave a small tip!

~°~°~°~°~°~°~°~°~°~°~°

Choosing a career:

Is choosing career a Simple Job?

In fact, choosing a career is a complicated process and one should give enough time it deserves. Career planning is a multi-step process that involves learning enough about yourself and the occupations, which you are considering in order to make an informed decision.

Can a career counsellor tell me what occupation to pick?

A career counsellor, or any other career development professional, can't tell you what career is best for you. They can provide one with guidance in choosing a career and can help facilitate their decision.

Why I can't make a living from my hobby?

When choosing a career, it makes perfect sense to choose one that is related to what you enjoy doing in your spare time, if you so desire. In addition people tend to become very skilled in their hobbies, even though most of their skills have been gained informally.

Will making a lot of money make me happy?

While salary is important, it isn't the only factor one should look at when choosing a career. Countless surveys have shown that money doesn't necessarily lead to job satisfaction. For many people, enjoying what they do at work is much more important. However, everyone should consider earnings, among other things, when evaluating an occupation.

Once I choose a career, will I be stuck in it forever?

No you'll not be. If you are unsatisfied in your career for any reason, you can always change it. You'll be in good company. Many people change careers several times over the course of their lifetime.

Will my skills go to waste, if I change my careers?

Your skills are yours to keep. You can take them from one job to another. You may not use them in the exact same way, but they won't be useless.

If my best friend or relatives is happy in a particular field, will I be to?

Everyone is different. Six billion people in this world have six billion thoughts. What works for one person won't necessarily work for another, even if that other person is someone with whom you have a lot in common. If someone you know has a career that interests you, look into it, but be aware of the fact that it may not necessarily be a good fit for you.

Is all I have to do is pick an occupation?

Things will fall into place after that choosing a career is a great start, but there's a lot more to do after that. A career action plan is a road map that takes you from choosing a career to becoming employed in that occupation to reaching your long-term career goals.

How can I know more about my preferred occupation?

There are several ways to know about your chosen occupation. You may search several print and online resources about that particular job and learn more about it. You can even ask those who have been working in that particular field from long time.

~°~°~°~°~°~°~°~°~°~°~°~°~°

<u>Personal Safety Checklist:</u>

In the home:

Do you keep doors and windows locked at all times?

Do you have a peephole so that you can see who is outside without having to open the door?

Do you verify a person's identification before opening the door?

If a stranger asks to use your phone, do you refuse to let them into your home and offer to make the call yourself?

Do you, as a woman living alone, use your first initials only in telephone directories, on mailboxes, etc.?

Do you refuse to reveal personal information to anyone on the phone or at your door?

Do you always have your keys ready when approaching your home?

If you return home to find windows and doors tampered with, would you avoid entering and go to a neighbour's house to call the police?

Telephone answering:

Do you teach family members not to give personal or family information to strangers over the phone?

Do you instruct older children who are babysitting or the babysitter to always say that you are at home, but busy and so they will take a message?

Do you record only non-specific messages on your answering machine and avoid messages such as: "We'll be back around 7 o'clock on Sunday"?

Do you use the telephone company's 'Caller ID' feature?

If you have a pager, do you 'Call Forward' your calls from your home to the pager?

If you receive an obscene or crank call, would you hang up immediately, saying nothing?

On the go:

Do you plan in advance the safest route to your destination?

Do you choose busy, well-lit streets?

Do you avoid routes that pass by high-risk areas?

Do you avoid isolated bus stops?

Do you walk facing traffic so you can see approaching cars?

Do you walk near the curb to avoid the element of surprise or someone hiding between shrubs or in a doorway?

Do you stay out of reach if someone in a vehicle asks directions?

Are you wary of approaching strangers?

If you continue to be followed, do you flee to the nearest safe place?

Do you try to get a description of the person and/or vehicle following you?

Do you avoid carrying large sums of money in your purse or wallet?

Do you carry your purse close to your body, without wrapping the straps around your arm or hand?

Do you avoid leaving a purse unattended, even for a moment?

Do you avoid displaying large amounts of cash in public?

In your car:

Do you always lock your car doors while driving?

Do you keep windows rolled up whenever possible?

Do you avoid picking up hitchhikers?

Do you keep your car in good running order to avoid breakdowns in dangerous areas?

Do you look for well-lit areas to park your car?

Do you always lock your car when it is parked?

Do you look around the car before you get out, especially at night or in deserted areas such as underground parking lots?

When returning to your car, do you have your keys in hand?

Do you look in the back seat before getting into the car?

If you are being followed, do you avoid going home and go to the nearest place of safety instead?

~°~°~°~°~°~°~°~°~°~°~°~°~°

When interviewing a potential professional babysitter or commercial daycare centre:

- Do staff have Early Childhood Education certificate?
- Will they encourage parents to visit at any time?
- Do they appear to be warm and friendly?
- Do they have a sense of humour?
- Do they seem to be someone with whom you can develop a relaxed, sharing relationship?
- Do they appear to be someone your child will enjoy being around?
- Do they seem to feel good about herself/himself and the job?
- Do they have child-rearing attitudes and methods that are similar to your own?
- Do they understand what children can and want to do at different stages of growth?

- Do they have the right materials and equipment on hand to help them learn and grow mentally and physically?
- Will they patiently help children solve their problems?
- Do they provide activities that encourage children to think things through?
- Do they encourage good health habits such as washing hands before eating and after using the toilet?
- Will they talk to the children and encourage them to express themselves through words?
- Will they encourage children to express themselves in creative ways?
- Do they seem to have enough time to look after each of the children in her/his care?
- Will they help the children to know, accept and feel good about themselves?
- Do they have previous experience or training in working with children?
- Will they provide a routine and rules that the children can understand and follow?
- Do they have an entrance physical examination and yearly TB test?
- Are they certified in first aid and CPR?
- Do they have a first-aid kit, a fire extinguisher, smoke detectors, covered (child-proof) radiators and heaters?
- Does the child care facility have an up-to-date license, if required?
- Do they have a clean and comfortable look?
- Do they have enough space indoors and out so all children can move freely and safely?

- Do they have enough furniture, playthings and other equipment for all the children in care?
- Do they have equipment that is safe and in good repair?
- Do they have equipment and materials suitable for the ages of the children in care?
- Do they have safety caps on electrical outlets?
- Do they have a safe place to store dangerous items such as medicines, cleaners, poisons, matches, sharp instruments, etc.?
- Do they have an alternate exit in case of fire?
- Do they have a safety plan to follow in emergencies?
- Do they have an outdoor play area that is safe, fenced (or secure) and free of litter?
- Do they have groups of manageable size?
- Do they have a scholarship program, subsidies or sliding fee scale?
- Do they have enough heat, light and ventilation?
- Do they have any pets? If so, are they properly trained or penned, and have they had all their appropriate shots?
- Do they have safe transportation for field trip with seat belts and car seats used?
- Do they have a nap or resting area, depending on ages and needs or the children?
- Do they have cots for children through age five?
- Do they have nutritious meals and snacks that meet your preferences about the types of food you want your child to eat?
- Do they have enough adults to give attention to all of the children in care?
- Are the children able to play quietly and actively indoors and out?

- Are the children able to play alone at times and with friends at other times?
- Are the children able to follow a schedule that meets their need for routine, but is flexible enough to meet the different needs of each child?
- Are the children able to use materials and equipment that help them learn new physical skills, develop muscular control and get exercise?
- Are the children able to learn to get along, to share and to respect themselves?
- Are the children able to learn about their own and others cultures through art, music, books, songs, games and other activities?
- Are the children able to visit nearby places of interest, such as the park, library, fire station or museum?
- Are the children able to play with many different toys and equipment that enable them to use their imaginations? (For example: books, musical instruments)
- Are the children able to choose their own activities for at least part of the day?

Does the person who will be caring for your child:

- Treat your child as capable and fun to be around?
- Have a willingness to adapt toys and activities to the needs of your child?
- Seem to have extra effort and patience to give to your child?

- Have a willingness to work with you and any other agencies or medical personnel involved in the care of your child?
- Have facilities to accommodate your child?

The following questions are unique to infant care:

- Is there a diaper changing area with a washable surface, and is it sanitized regularly?
- Are hands washed before and after feeding and diapering?
- Are bottles, nipples and toys kept clean?
- Are food and formula served at the right temperature?
- Are unused formula and food refrigerated and labelled or discarded when no longer fresh?
- Are babies changed promptly when diapers are wet or soiled?
- Are babies cleaned thoroughly during diaper changes?
- Is a separate crib, portrait or playpen provided for each infant?

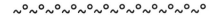

Child Home Safety:

General

- Garbage and recycling materials are stored in covered containers.
- Keep purses closed and out of reach of children, a purse can be the source of medicines and matches.

- Set your home's water heater temperature at no more than 120 degrees to prevent scalds and burns.

Doors

- Decals placed at a child's eye level on sliding glass doors can help to warn them when the doors are closed.
- Buy a special guard to keep a patio door locked to prevent your child from opening it and slipping out. This will also help protect your door from the outside and prevent unwanted entry.
- Be aware that any open door, can pose a hazard.
- Watch for little fingers when closing doors.
- Use safety doorknob covers on doors that you don't want your child to open. Attach a bell to the door so you can hear it when it does open.

Windows

- Install window safety devices and adjust them so they cannot open more than 100 millimetres (four inches).
- Don't leave furniture or anything that can be climbed upon near a window.
- Install safety glass in large windows and French doors so they won't shatter if a child falls into them.
- The U.S. Consumer Product Safety Commission (CPSC) and the Window Covering Safety Council are joining with major manufacturers, importers, and retailers across the United States to warn parents and caregivers that young children can become entangled and strangle in pull cords—for window coverings. CPSC is aware of at least 194 deaths in

the United States since 1981. With the continuing number of strangulation deaths, CPSC is reissuing this warning which was first issued in 1985.

Window covering cords are one of the products most frequently associated with strangulation of children under five. The younger victims, usually between 10 to 15 months of age, typically are in cribs which have been placed near window covering pull cords.

Although a few older children, usually from two to four years old, find cords hanging near the floor, most of these victims become entangled in cords while climbing on furniture to look out the window. Entanglement and strangulation can occur when a child is alone in a room for only a short time. The CPSC and the Window Covering Safety Council urge parents to eliminate the loop in two-corded horizontal blinds, and pleated and cellular shades by using any of the following technical fixes:

- **Horizontal Blinds**

  - Cut the cord above the tassel, remove the equalizer buckle, and add a separate tassel at the end of each cord, or cut the cord above the tassel, remove the equalizer buckle, and add a breakaway tassel which will separate if a child becomes entangled in the loop.

- **Pleated or Cellular Shades**

  - Leave the cord stop near the head rail in place. Cut the cord above the tassel and add a separate tassel at the end of each cord. Warning: When shades are raised, a loop will appear above the cord stop. Keep cord out of the reach of children.

- **Vertical Blinds, Continuous Loop Systems, and Drapery Cords**

  - Install a cord tie-down device. Permanently attach and use the tie-down to floor, wall, or window jamb.

- **General Advice**

  - Keep all window covering cords out of the reach of children. Unless the cords can be completely removed from a child's reach, including when a child climbs on furniture, CPSC recommends against knotting or tying the cords together which creates a new loop for a child to become entangled.
  - Replacement safety tassels are available free of charge at window covering retailers. Consumers can call (800) 506-4636 to find the location of the nearest store or to order free tassels.
  - CPSC also recommends that when you install window coverings, adjust the cords to their shortest length possible. When you order new custom window coverings, specify that you want a short cord.

Electricity

- Cover all electrical outlets that are not in use with safety plugs that snap into the outlets. Children might be tempted to try to insert something into exposed outlets. Check for exposed outlets behind furniture that you may have overlooked.

- Keep fans and other appliances up high, out of children's reach.
- Do not use extension cords unless absolutely necessary. Be sure that the extension cord is rated for the amount of electricity that you will draw through it.
- Shorten all cords with cord shorteners. Shortening extension cords will reduce the risk of tripping.

Halls and Stairways

- Safety gates should be installed at all open stairways if required. If a gate is not provided, place a barrier of some kind in front of the stairway that a child cannot climb over. Accordion-style gates with large V-shaped or diamond-shaped openings should not be used since they can entrap a child's head, causing strangulation. A gate with a straight top or small V's and diamond-shaped openings is safer. Make sure pressure gates are firmly in place and can't be dislodged by the child.
- Place the safety gate bar latch on the side farthest from your child's reach.
- Never leave anything on the stairs that you can trip on while carrying your baby.

Furniture and Accessories

- Put away any unstable or rickety furniture your child could pull over. Fasten to the wall high bookcases or other tall pieces that your child may be able to pull down.

- Keep all drawers firmly closed so your child can't shut fingers in them or climb on them.

The Kitchen

• General Kitchen Safety

- Keep all cleaning products, pesticides, and other volatile substances locked up.
- Use unbreakable dishes for feeding a young child.
- Keep step stools out of reach.
- Clean up spills immediately to prevent slips and falls.
- Keep boxes of plastic kitchen wraps and plastic grocery bags out of your child's reach to avoid suffocation.
- Don't use long phone cords that a child could trip on or wrap around their neck.

• Countertops, Cupboards and Drawers

- Never sit your child on the countertop. Besides the danger of a fall, they can easily reach for items that can harm them.
- Use cabinet and drawer guard latches to keep certain reachable cupboard doors and drawers off limits to your baby.
- Use cord shorteners on appliance cords in order to keep them short and away from where child can pull on them.
- Keep garbage in a tightly covered container, or better yet, behind a securely latched cabinet door.

• **Highchair Safety**

- Be sure the tray is locked and always secure the restraint system.
- To prevent pinching watch your child's fingers and hands as you slide the tray in place.
- Never leave your child alone in a room in a highchair.
- Keep the highchair a safe distance from tables and countertops. A child can tip it over by pushing off with hands and feet.
- Make sure your highchair has the 'CSA' label.

• **Appliances**

- Turn the handles of pots and pans toward the back of the stove or counter. Use the back burners for cooking whenever possible.
- Don't let your child play at your feet while you are cooking.
- Use a stove guard to prevent your child from reaching the stove burners.
- If your child can reach the controls on the front of the stove, try installing stove knob covers.
- Never leave a boiling pot or sizzling skillet unattended on the stove.
- Teach your child that the oven is 'hot' and not to touch.
- Install an appliance latch on appliances such as the microwave, refrigerator and dishwasher.
- Keep the dishwasher closed when not in use. There are many sharp edges that can hurt a young child inside.

- Store appliances, such as electric toasters and can openers, where your child can't reach. A child can be electrocuted if they attempt to plug them in.

The Bedroom

- Ensure that your child cannot become trapped inside the toy box: lids should be lightweight and removable latches should be removed and ventilation holes added hinged lids should include a support that will hold the top open.

The Bathroom

- Never let children lock a bathroom door. Go in the bathroom with young children to assure this doesn't happen. If the door does become locked it should be possible to unlock it by inserting a pin into the hole on the outside of the doorknob. Know where the unlocking pin is. When not in use, keep the bathroom door closed and the toilet seat and lid down. If at all possible, place a guard on the lid to lock the toilet seat.
- Be sure that all medications are stored high and out of reach of children. This also applies to any cleaning supplies, hair sprays, and other personal care items. Consider adding child proof locks to the lower cupboard doors.
- Place adhesive non-slip stickers in the bathtub and shower to prevent falls.
- Use soft, inflated spout covers to save child from bumps and bruises.
- Never leave a child under 5 in a tub by themselves.

Medications

- All medications should be kept in a locked and very secure place at all times. Remember that a high place is not always a secure place and they should be kept out of sight and out of reach.
- Make sure all medicines are in child-resistant containers.
- Don't save old prescription medicines. Flush them down the toilet when you are finished using them.
- Don't tell your child that medicine tastes "like candy" or is good. It's better to have to struggle to get them to take it than to tempt them to take more when they don't really need it.
- Store children's vitamins in a safe place also. Overdosing on vitamins is among the top phone calls received by Poison Control Centres.
- If your child does manage to swallow or eat any medicine, get whatever you can out of the mouth and call 911 immediately. Have the bottle in your hand so you can tell them what was ingested and approximately how much. Keep syrup of ipecac on hand but NEVER use it unless you are advised by the physician or poison control to do so. Keep the Poison Control phone number on hand by every phone in your household in case of an emergency such as this.

The Nursery

- When buying items, look for the CSA certification sticker. This indicates voluntary safety certification for common children's items. Equipment with this certification has passed rigorous safety standards and is as safe as current manufacturing can make it.

- On all items you will consider purchasing, look for lead free paint; sturdy non-tip design; smooth edges and rounded corners; and safety restraint straps.
- Try to avoid rough edges; sharp points; small parts that can break loose; exposed hinges; attached strings, cords or ribbons on items you might consider using.

- **Cribs**

  - Cribs made before September 1986 are dangerous. They do not meet current standards. It is illegal to sell, import or advertise these cribs. Look for a label on the crib that shows when the crib was made, cribs that were made before September 1986 or without a label are not safe for use.
  - Ensure there is a Canadian Safety Association (CSA) or Consumer Product Safety Commission label (CPSC).
  - Bars should be no more than 2-3/8 inches apart with no splinters or cracks in wood.
  - Mattress adjustability with a minimum rail height of 22 inches when the mattress is at its highest position and the rail is at its lowest.
  - Be sure the mattress is firm and fits snugly against the frame. You should not be able to get two fingers between the mattress and the crib sides. Check the crib often to make sure the frame is solid. Tighten loose screws regularly.
  - Health Canada recommends that soft mattresses, pillows, comforters, stuffed toys and bumper pads not be used in cribs.

- When placing the crib in the room, make sure that your child cannot reach lamps, electrical cords, shades or blinds.
- Don't place the crib near a window especially on the second level of a house.
- Never tie the baby in the crib and do not let the baby wear a necklace or a soother on a cord around the neck. Don't leave rattles, teethers or squeeze toys in the crib. They can become wedged in child's mouth causing suffocation.

• Bassinets and Cradles

- A bassinet or cradle should have a wide base and be sturdy and stable.
- Do not use a basket not intended to be a bassinet. Loose wicker can poke and hurt a baby.

• The Changing Table

- Look for a table that is sturdily built, with high sides and a safety strap. Always keep the child fastened and never turn your back, even for a second.
- Keep diaper-changing supplies out of baby's reach.
- If you keep a diaper pail near the changing table, be sure it has a locking lid. If it does not, keep it where your child cannot get at it.

• Infant Seats (also called Bouncer Seats)

- Look for a wide base, non-skid bottom and a crotch and waist safety belt.

- Don't place your child in an infant seat on top of a counter or table.
- Never use an infant seat as a car seat.

- **Infant Swings**

  - Never leave your child unattended in either an infant seat or and infant swing.
  - Use a head support for infants.
  - The two most common types of injuries from swings are entrapment of a child's head when it gets caught between the edge of the backrest and the bars from which the seat hangs and falls, when the back of the seat collapses.

- **Walkers**

  - Walkers are dangerous and have been responsible for many injuries. Use of these devices should be done under very careful supervision. If you have a walker with wheels, the wheels should be removed or discard the walker all together. New style walkers (standers) are designed to be stationary.

- **Playpens**

  - A playpen can inhibit your child's exploration and environmental stimulation so you don't want to place your child in one all day.
  - The sides should be high enough to contain an 18-month-old child (Approximately 20 inches).
  - Never tie a toy across the top of the playpen, it is a strangulation hazard.

- Keep the railing secured tightly; a child can become entrapped in the pocket formed between the floor edge and the mesh siding and suffocate.
- Be sure that your child cannot lower the side of the playpen.

Strollers

- Always engage the stroller brakes when not in motion.
- Don't use a stroller that doesn't have a safety strap. Many injuries occur when children are not securely strapped in.
- Check for a wide sturdy base and a locking device to prevent accidental folding.
- Be sure that your child's fingers are out of the way when folding or closing the stroller.

The Backyard Pool

- Fence your pool inside your yard, so it cannot be entered directly either from the house or the back yard. The fence should be at least four feet high, with spokes and slats not more than three inches apart. If you use chain link fencing, be sure the links are small enough so a child cannot climb on them. Be sure nothing blocks the view of the pool from the house.
- A water activated pool alarm may be necessary if the pool can be accessed directly from the house.
- Install a child resistant spring lock gate, self-closing and self-latching, with the latch at least 54 inches from the ground.
- Install textured concrete or other slip resistant material around the pool.

- Install a phone by the pool, so you won't be tempted to leave your child even for a minute to answer a call.
- Don't use glass of any kind by the pool.
- Use only battery operated radios and televisions by the pool.

- **Common sense pool rules**

- Each family should make their own set of inflexible pool rules and insist that everyone, child or adult, adhere by them.
- Never leave a child alone in a pool. In fact, don't take your eyes off the child. Drowning can occur in a matter of seconds.
- Don't drink alcohol while you are watching children.
- Ensure your child can demonstrate good head control before you take them into the pool.
- Don't allow children under five in a spa or hot tub. Children are more sensitive to stress from high water temperatures.
- Don't trust swimming lessons to protect your child. In a panic, even a good swimmer can forget what to do.
- No rough-housing or running by the pool.
- Don't swim during thunderstorms.
- Never allow riding or wheeled toys of any kind in the pool area. These can easily be ridden into the water.

Safety Outdoors

- Never let an infant or toddler play alone outside. Even a child in a safety harness or napping in a carriage needs to be watched almost constantly.

- Keep swimming or wading pools inaccessible to babies and toddlers. If you have a swimming pool keep it fenced in and keep the doors and windows to the pool area locked.
- Check the play area frequently, watching for broken sidewalks that need repair, loose boards on wooden steps, holes or ditches in the lawn that should be filled.
- Clean areas of all animal droppings.
- Watch for poisonous plants in the backyard and pull up mushrooms and toadstools as soon as they appear.
- Install childproof locks on gates and don't leave anything near the gates that a child could climb on to.
- Keep a constant eye on a child that still puts things in their mouth, stones, twigs and dirt are as attractive as rattles and teethers.
- Make sure outdoor play equipment is safe and sturdily constructed. Place play equipment at least 6 feet away from fences and walls.
- Teach your child about dangers they may find in their play area. Create a vocabulary of warning words (Ouch, Hot, Sharp etc.).
- Keep your child out of the area altogether when the lawn is being mowed. Flying debris can seriously injure a small child.
- Don't leave a hose lying in the sun. Water in it can get hot enough to scald a child.
- Keep children away from a grill at all times, especially when you are cooking on it.

~°~°~°~°~°~°~°~°~°~°~°

Hot Weather Safety Tips:

How to beat the heat

In the summer the combination of high heat, high humidity, and smog can be very dangerous. You need to be **extra careful**, those especially at risk during these weather conditions include:

- The elderly
- People with certain chronic illnesses, such as heart or lung conditions or people unable to move or change position by themselves
- Infants and preschool children
- People who exercise vigorously or are involved in strenuous work outdoors for prolonged periods
- People taking certain medications, for example, for mental health conditions. (Please consult your doctor or pharmacist).

How to avoid heat related illness:

- Drink lots of water and natural juices even if you don't feel very thirsty.
- Avoid going out in the blazing sun or heat when possible. If you must go outside, stay in the shade as much as possible and plan to go out early in the morning or evening when it is cooler and smog levels may not be as high as in the afternoon. Wear a hat.
- Take advantage of air conditioned or cool places such as shopping malls, libraries, community centres or a friend's place.

- Try to spend some time near the lake or waterfront where it is cooler.
- If you don't have air conditioning, keep shades or drapes drawn and blinds closed on the sunny side of your home, but keep windows slightly open.
- Keep electric lights off or turned down low.
- Take a cool bath or shower periodically or cool down with cool, wet towels.
- Wear loose fitting, light clothing.
- Avoid heavy meals and using your oven.
- Avoid intense or moderately intense physical activity.
- Try to take it easy, and rest as much as possible.
- Never leave a child in a parked car or sleeping outside in direct sunlight.
- If you sleep outside during the day, try to sleep in the shade. Remember the sun moves, so try to sleep in a spot that will be shady for a few hours.
- Fans alone may not provide enough cooling when the temperature is high.
- Consult your doctor or pharmacist regarding side effects of your medications.

Get help from a friend, relative, or a doctor if you have the following symptoms of heat illness:

- Rapid breathing
- Weakness or fainting
- More tiredness than usual
- Headache
- Confusion

Friends and relatives can help someone with heat illness by doing the following:

- Call for help.
- Remove excess clothing from the person.
- Cool the person with lukewarm water, by sponging or bathing.
- Move the person to a cooler location.
- Give the person sips of cool water, not ice cold water.

If you become ill, faint, have difficulty breathing or feel confused and disoriented, call your doctor.

In an emergency, call 911.

Summer Safety: Fan Facts

Do . . .

- Use your fan in or next to a window. Box fans are best.
- Use a fan to bring in the cooler air from outside.
- Use your fan by plugging it directly into the wall outlet. If you need an extension cord, it should be CSA (Canadian Standards Association) approved.

Don't . . .

- Don't use a fan in a closed room without windows or doors open to the outside.
- Don't believe that fans cool air. They don't. They just move the air around. Fans keep you cool by evaporating your sweat.

- Don't use a fan to blow extremely hot air on yourself. This can cause heat exhaustion to happen faster.

If you're afraid to open your window to use a fan, choose other ways to keep cool. See the other tips on this page.

Medications and Heat-Related Illness

Some medications make it harder for your body to control its temperature. If you are taking any of the medications listed below, you are at higher risk for heat-related illness, especially if you are doing lots of exercise or heavy work and are not drinking enough water. This is even more true if you are on 2 or more medications.

The list below is based in part on information from the Office of the Chief Coroner. Please note it is not complete. Also, some drugs have different brand names, so check with your doctor, nurse, or pharmacist to be sure.

- chlorpromazine (Thorazine, Largactil) *
- thioridazine (Mellaril) *
- perphenazine (Trilafon) *
- fluphenazine (Modecate, Moditen) *
- thiothixene (Navane) *
- trifluoperazine (Stelazine)
- prochloperazine (Stemetil)
- haloperidol (Haldol)
- clozapine (Clozaril)
- risperidone (Risperdal)
- loxapine (Loxapac, Loxitane)
- fluspirilene (IMAP)
- pimozide (Orap)

- olanzapine
- flupenthixol (Fluanxol)
- zuclopenthixol(Clopixol)
- reserpine (Serpasil, Serpalan)

- Lithium—heavy exercise or heavy sweating in hot weather may change lithium levels, so that you may have too much or too little in your system.

* The medicines starred here may make it easier for your skin to burn. Many other medicines may also cause your skin to burn more easily. To be sure, ask your doctor, nurse or pharmacist. Try to stay out of the sun. If you can't, try to get sunscreen and wear a hat and long sleeves.

Antiparkinson drugs such as:

- benztropine (Cogentin)
- biperiden (Akineton)
- ethopropazine (Parsitan, Parsidol)
- procyclidine (Kemadrin, Procyclid)
- trihexyphenidyl (Artane, Trihexane)
- levodopa (Dopar)
- selegiline (Eldepryl)
- amantadine (Symmetrel, Symadine)

Antidepressants such as:

- amitriptyline (Elavil)
- doxepine (Sinequan)
- clomipramine (Anafranil)
- protriptyline (Vivactil)

- imipramine (Tofranil)
- desipramine (Norpramin)
- nortriptyline (Pamelor)
- fluoxetine (Prozac)
- fluvoxetine (Luvox)
- sertraline (Zoloft)
- paroxetine (Paxil)

If you also take the medicines below, you further increase your risk for heat-illness:

- some antihistamines (eg Benadryl, Chlortripolon)
- over-the-counter sleeping pills (eg Nytol)
- anti-diarrhoea pills (eg Lomotil)

If you are taking any medications regularly, ask your doctor, nurse or pharmacist if you need to be extra careful during hot weather.

~°~°~°~°~°~°~°~°~°~°~°~°

Holiday Safety Tips:

It is natural to get caught up in this busy time of the year, but we ask that you take a moment to look around and check that your family and home are safe during the holidays. Here are some tips to help ensure that everyone stays safe.

- Keep small toys, gifts, and breakables out of reach of infants and toddlers. Children like to place small objects into their mouth which may cause choking and could be fatal. The same also applies to rubber balloons. Balloons may break and the small pieces are enticing for kids to chew on. These pieces are similar in texture to your skin and may also cause a child to choke.

- Be aware that Christmas tree electrical cords may pose a tripping hazard if left on the floor. Keep these and any other electrical cords secure so that a child does not have the opportunity to pull on them.

- Do not leave purses with medications in areas where they can be reached by children. Whether at home or just visiting friends, this is a common way for children to get access to medications.

- Do not piggyback multiple extension cords. Known as an octopus, this is a common cause of electrical fires. Inspect all electrical cords for cracks in the protective sheathing. Worn electrical cords should not be used and need to be thrown out.

- Be aware that candles pose a fire risk if not handled correctly, they may fall over and start a fire. Candles should also be placed away from the edge of tables so they cannot fall off if a child pulls on the tablecloth.

- You may have visitors who have food allergies, especially nut allergies. You need to inform all guests with allergies to ask what is in the food before they enjoy it.

- When decorating for the holidays, be aware that tinsel is a common cause of choking for infants, toddlers, and animals. Dogs and cats are especially fond of this holiday decoration.

- Keep infants, toddlers, and animals away from Poinsettias. Even though it is not poisonous, eating poinsettia leaves may cause vomiting.

- Holly and mistletoe are considered poisonous and should also be kept away from children. If ingested, contact Poison Control.
- Check all carbon monoxide and smoke detectors to be sure they are in working order.
- When driving on snowy or icy roads, keep in mind that it takes longer for vehicles to stop. Reduce your speed on slippery roads and give yourself plenty of room to stop.
- Don't let children hollow out snow banks and play in them. The snow can collapse, trap, and suffocate a child. The same applies to playing on snow banks by the roadside, children could fall in the path of traffic or snow plows.
- When travelling this holiday season, remember to have a safety kit in your car. A first aid kit, booster cables, gloves and hats, non perishable snacks, blanket, and candles would be a great start to protecting yourself while travelling.
- Keep all stairs in your home clear of toys and gifts.
- Be nice, clear your ice. This not only helps pedestrians but also the emergency workers that may be responding to your home or work site.
- Turn off all holiday lights when you go to bed, or when you leave your home.
- Please remember "Don't Drink and Drive", have a designated driver.
- While cooking, try to use the rear burners, this will help to prevent clothing catching on the pots that could cause a spill or burn. Never leave cooking unattended on the stove, children are naturally curious and may injure or burn themselves.

- Always have a first aid kit in your home. Be sure it is stocked and everyone knows where it is.
- Always keep the draw strings for blinds and drapes high and out of reach of children. Children can have their necks become entangled and risk suffocation.
- Have a very safe and happy holiday season.

Travelling Safety Tips:

Here are some tips to help you have a safe and enjoyable holiday.

- Know where you are and where you are going at all times. Carefully plan road trips in advance.
- Do not pick up hitchhikers.
- Keep valuables out of sight, and never leave them in a parked vehicle.
- Leave a copy of your itinerary and proof of citizenship (for example, Canadian birth certificate or certificate of Canadian citizenship) with a family member or friend who can be contacted in an emergency.
- Phone home regularly if you do not have a fixed schedule.
- Keep a separate record of your travellers' cheques, credit cards and medical insurance, and ensure that the information is also available to someone back home.
- Do not carry your passport, tickets, identification documents, cash, credit cards and insurance papers

together. Keep them separate so that in the event of theft or loss you do not lose everything.

- Use the safety deposit box at your hotel. Never leave valuables in your room.

In certain cases, you may wish to register with Foreign Affairs Canada as a Canadian Abroad:

- You are going to be abroad for three months or more.
- You will be spending any time in a country, or a specific area within a country, that is covered by an official Travel Warning.
- You will be visiting a country for less than three months that has security concerns and/or does not have a resident Canadian government office. they will be travelling to a hurricane-prone region during the hurricane season (June 1st to November 30th).
- In co-operation with the Consular Affairs Bureau in Ottawa, Canadian diplomatic offices provide a range of services to assist you during your visit.

The services include:

- advice and support in the event of accident, crime or illness
- communication with relatives and friends
- assistance during natural disasters
- support and assistance in the event of a death
- identification of sources of information on local laws, regulations and facilities;
- in the event of an arrest, seeking equitable treatment, informing relatives and friends, and assistance in making arrangements for a lawyer; in the event of

a conviction, assistance in applying for transfer to Canada under the Transfer of Offenders Treaty

- making arrangements for friends and relatives to transfer funds in emergencies
- interventions with local authorities
- notarial services such as legalization and certification of documents (a fee is charged for these services)
- assistance in locating missing persons
- emergency passport services
- citizenship services

Services are available during normal business hours from the Canadian diplomatic office nearest your location abroad.

My Special Tips

Chapter Two

Kitchen

*@GFIdeas "As a child my family's menu
consisted of two choices: take it or leave it."*

—Buddy Hackett bit.ly/mRYLlh

Homemade chemical-free dryer sheets

If you have a couple of old but clean rags or washcloths that have up until now been languishing in the darkest corners of your closet, it's time to let them see the light. (Cutting up an old flannel or sweatshirt into tidy little squares will also do the trick.)

Whatever basic material you use, place your fabric squares into a re-sealable plastic container with a tight-fitting lid and saturate them with Ecover natural fabric softener (or the chemical-free brand of your choice). There you have instant re-usable fabric softener sheets. If, on the other hand, you prefer controlling your specific ingredients, then all you need to do is spray them with a white vinegar, baking soda and essential oil solution, or, believe it or not, diluted hair conditioner. Just be sure to make it a natural brand.

Homemade plastic-free dryer balls and sachets

The texturized candy-coloured balls that you can purchase from a home supply store look admittedly nifty, but you can easily kick 'em up a notch by crafting your own <u>recycled fabric</u> or <u>felted wool</u> alternatives in a veritable smorgasbord of colors. Practically nothing is off limits—think old panty hose, socks, recycled cotton sweaters, yarn, sweatshirt fleece, etc.

If you don't care so much about their purported wrinkle-reducing capabilities as you do about simply inhaling a dreamy scent, then you'll likely prefer sewing up a few <u>dried herb-filled sachets</u> that can be refreshed occasionally with a few drops of essential oils.

~°~°~°~°~°~°~°~°~°~°~°~°

@GFIdeas "I washed a sock. Then I put it in the dryer. When I took it out, it was gone."

—Rod Schmidt bit.ly/mRYLlh

~°~°~°~°~°~°~°~°~°~°~°~°

When cooking vegetables with strong odours; simmer a pan of vinegar on the stove at the same time.

Or

Add vinegar to the cooking water.

~°~°~°~°~°~°~°~°~°~°~°~°~°

Place slices of lemon rind in a warm oven to dispel unpleasant odours.

~°~°~°~°~°~°~°~°~°~°~°~°~°

Easier dusting: Use soft bristled paintbrushes to dust hard to reach places like telephones and keyboards

~°~°~°~°~°~°~°~°~°~°~°~°~°

All-purpose cleaner and deodorizer: mix baking soda in warm water. Use on a clean rag, it works well for cleaning the inside of fridges, appliances and kitchen countertops.

For cleaning smelly hands after chopping onions or garlic, just rub them on a stainless steel spoon. The steel is supposed to absorb the odour.

Fresh coffee beans can also absorb nasty odours from your hands.

~°~°~°~°~°~°~°~°~°~°~°~°~°

Food Safety Tips:

Chill

It is extremely important to keep cold food cold and hot food hot so that your food never reaches the "temperature danger zone". That is where bacteria can grow quickly and cause food borne illness.**

Storing

- Keep your raw meat, poultry, fish and seafood cold. Refrigerate or freeze them as soon as you get home from the grocery store. Make sure your refrigerator is set at 4ºC (40ºF) or lower and your freezer at -18ºC (0ºF) or lower. This will keep your food out of the temperature danger zone, between 4ºC (40ºF) to 60ºC (140ºF), where bacteria can grow quickly.

- Deli meats can be more risky for people with weakened immune systems to eat. Store deli meats in the refrigerator. Use deli meats within 4 days, preferably 2-3 days after opening; even if this date is different than the best-before date. Best-before dates apply to unopened packages only. Deli-meats sliced at the grocer should also be eaten within 4 days; preferably 2-3 days.

- Store cut fruits and vegetables in the refrigerator.

- You can cool leftovers quickly by placing them in shallow containers. Refrigerate as soon as possible or within two hours.

- Never leave raw meat, poultry, fish, seafood or leftovers out on the counter for longer than two hours. After two hours at room temperature, levels of bacteria in your food can become dangerous. You can't tell if food is unsafe by its smell or taste. When in doubt, throw it out!

Defrosting

- Defrost your raw meat, poultry, fish or seafood in the refrigerator, in a microwave or immersed in cold water.

- Food that has been defrosted in the microwave should be cooked as soon as possible after thawing.
- Don't refreeze thawed food.
- If you are defrosting a large piece of meat, such as a turkey that may not fit easily in the fridge, immerse it in cold water, keeping it in its original wrapping. Change the water often (for example, every 30 minutes) to make sure that the water continues to be cold.
- Immediately wash sinks, kitchen surfaces or containers that come in contact with raw meat, poultry, fish or seafood.

Cook

Proper cooking is the best way to make sure your food is safe to eat. Bacteria such as *E.coli, Salmonella* and *Listeria* are killed by heat.

~°~°~°~°~°~°~°~°~°~°~°~°~°

If you happen to over-salt a pot of soup, just drop in a peeled potato. The potato will absorb the excess salt.

When boiling eggs, add a pinch of salt to keep the shells from cracking.

Mixed up: Hard boiled eggs and fresh eggs—Spin them . . . Fresh eggs won't spin!!

Add vinegar to the water when boiling eggs as the vinegar prevents the shells from cracking.

Drop an egg on the floor? Cover it with salt, then sweep it up. No slimy mess.

Never put citrus fruits or tomatoes in the fridge. The low temperatures degrade the aroma and flavour of these pernickety fruits.

To clean cast iron cookware, don't use detergents. Just scrub them with salt and a clean, dry paper towel.

Will milk curdle if it is allowed to boil? It turns out that this age-old piece of wisdom isn't true, after all. Milk that has been boiled is perfectly safe to consume.

Tomatoes last longer if you store them with the stems pointed down.

To clean an electric kettle with calcium build-up on the heating element, boil a mixture of half white vinegar and half water, then empty.

When storing empty airtight containers, throw in a pinch of salt to keep them from getting stinky.

If you are making gravy and accidentally burn it, just pour it into a clean pan and continue cooking it. Add sugar a little at a time, tasting as you go to avoid over-sugaring it. The sugar will cancel out the burned taste.

Burned a pot of rice? Just place a piece of white bread on top of the rice for 5-10 minutes to draw out the burned flavour. Be careful not to scrape the burned pieces off of the bottom of the pan when serving the rice.

Before you chop chili peppers, rub a little vegetable oil into your hands and your skin won't absorb the spicy chili oil.

If you aren't sure how fresh your eggs are, place them in about four inches of water. Eggs that stay on the bottom are fresh. If only one end tips up, the egg is less fresh and should be used soon. If it floats, it's past the fresh stage.

To banish ants from the kitchen, find out where they are coming in and cover the hole with petroleum jelly. Ants won't trek through the jelly. If they are coming under a door, draw a line on the floor with chalk. The little bugs also won't cross a line of chalk.

Before making popcorn on the stove or in an air popper, soak the kernels in water for 10 minutes. Drain the water, then pop as normal. The additional moisture helps the popcorn pop up quicker and fluffier with fewer "old maids."

Don't store your bananas in a bunch or in a fruit bowl with other fruits. Separate your bananas and place each in a different location. Bananas release gases which cause fruits (including other bananas) to ripen quickly. Separating them will keep them fresh longer.

To keep potatoes from budding in the bag, put an apple in with them.

If you manage to have some leftover wine at the end of the evening, freeze it in ice cube trays for easy addition to soups and sauces in the future.

To clean crevices and corners in vases and pitchers, fill with water and drop in two Alka-Seltzer tablets. The bubbles will do the scrubbing.

After boiling pasta or potatoes, cool the water and use it to water your house plants. The water contains nutrients that your plants will love.

When you clean your fish tank, the water you drain can also be used to water your house plants. The nitrogen and phosphorus in fish droppings make aquarium water a great fertilizer.

When defrosting meat from the freezer, pour some vinegar over it. Not only does it tenderize the meat; it will also bring down the freezing temperature of the meat and cause it to thaw quicker.

The substance in onions that causes your eyes to water is located in the root cluster of the onion. Cut this part out in a cone shape, with the largest part of the cone around the exterior root section.

Taking the top layer off of a onion can also reduce the amount of eye-watering misery.

Toothpaste is a great silver cleaner.

Baking soda isn't as effective a deodorizer for the fridge as that baking soda company would like you to believe. Activated charcoal is much better at absorbing fridge and freezer odours.

Baking soda is an extremely effective cleaner, though. Use it with vinegar to deodorize drains and clean stovetops and sinks.

A favorite tip of thousands of grandmas: when you nick your finger while cutting veggies, wait until the bleeding stops and paint on a layer of clear nail polish. It will keep juices out of the wound and won't fall off into the spaghetti sauce like a bandage.

The jury is still out on what to put in the bag of brown sugar to keep it from going hard: a slice of apple, a piece of bread, and a shard of a terra cotta pot have all been used.

Got a nasty invisible splinter from your kitchen tools? Put a piece of adhesive tape on the area and then pull it off to remove the splinter.

When you burn yourself in the kitchen, just spread mustard on the affected area. Leave it for a while and it will ease the pain and prevent blistering.

For aluminum pans that are looking dull, just boil some apple peels in them. This will brighten up the aluminum and make your house smell yummy.

To keep cookies fresh, savvy grannies like to put some crumpled-up tissue paper in the bottom of the cookie jar.

If your salt is clumping up, put a few grains of rice in with it to absorb excess moisture.

To clean fruit stains off of your fingers, rub them with a fresh, peeled potato. White vinegar can also do the trick.

Keep iceberg lettuce fresh in the fridge by wrapping it in a clean, dry paper towel and storing lettuce and paper towel in a sealed baggie in the fridge.

If your loaf of bread is starting to go stale, just put a piece of fresh celery in the bag and close it back up. For some reason, this restores a fresh taste and texture to the bread.

Always keep an aloe vera plant in your kitchen. It's invaluable when you scrape your arm or burn your finger. Just break off a leaf and rub the gel from the inside on the injury.

When making a soup, sauce, or casserole that ends up too fatty or greasy, drop in an ice cube. The ice will attract the fat, which you can then scoop out.

To reuse cooking oil without tasting whatever was cooked in the oil previously, cook a ¼" piece of ginger in the oil. It will remove any remaining flavors and odours.

If your milk always goes bad before you can finish it, try adding a pinch of salt to the carton when you first open it. It will stay fresh days longer.

Water that has been boiled and allowed to cool will freeze faster than water from the tap. This comes in handy when you're having a party and need ice pronto.

Remove tea or coffee stains from your fine china by mixing up a paste of baking soda, lemon juice, and cream of tartar. Rub it over the stains and they'll come off easily.

If two drinking glasses become stuck together after stacking, it's not impossible to un-stick them. Just put ice in the inner glass and dunk the outer glass in warm water. The warm glass will expand and the cold glass will contract, making the glasses separate easily.

For splinters under the fingernail, soaking the affected finger in a bowl of milk with a piece of bread in it is said to draw out the splinter.

Did grandpa ever give you a drink of cola for an upset tummy? It turns out that this is actually a pretty effective remedy. The sugar and carbonation can soothe many tummy problems—but it can also exacerbate others.

Putting salty bacon on a boil is said to "draw the poison out" of boils.

To help old wooden drawers (without runners) open and close smoothly, rub a candle on the tracks.

A cotton ball soaked in white vinegar and applied to a fresh bruise will reduce the darkness of the bruise and help it disappear sooner.

Drinking cranberry juice and eating blueberries regularly will help stave off urinary tract infections.

~°~°~°~°~°~°~°~°~°~°~°~°~°

Tomatoes added to roasts will help tenderize the meat naturally.

~°~°~°~°~°~°~°~°~°~°~°~°~°

Vegetables: that grow under the ground (potatoes, beets, carrots) should start cooking in cold water. Vegetables that grow above the ground (corn, peas, green beans) should be placed in boiling water.

~°~°~°~°~°~°~°~°~°~°~°~°~°

Washing Dishes: Add a tablespoon of baking soda to your water with your usual dish soap. It will soften your hands while cutting through that nasty grease!

~°~°~°~°~°~°~°~°~°~°~°~°~°

Plump Raisins: If you want plump raisins in your baking, soak them in Coca Cola instead of water. Water leaches out the flavour where Coke adds a spiciness and intensifies the flavour.

~°~°~°~°~°~°~°~°~°~°~°~°~°

Onions without tears: Light a match and blow it out. Put the non burnt end between your teeth while you cut your onion. The sulphur will absorb the fumes.

Or

Always cut the root end of the onion off last.

Or

A good way to cut onions without tears is to cut them near water. Running water works best.

Or

Put them in the freezer for about 5 to 10 minutes before cutting them.

~°~°~°~°~°~°~°~°~°~°~°~°~°

Whipping Cream: Sweeten your whipping cream with confectioners' sugar instead of granulated sugar. It stays firmer.

~°~°~°~°~°~°~°~°~°~°~°~°~°

Soggy Mashed Potatoes: Sprinkle with dry powdered milk for the fluffier mashed potatoes

~°~°~°~°~°~°~°~°~°~°~°~°~°

*"Planting mint around your kitchen window
will help keep flies away."*

~°~°~°~°~°~°~°~°~°~°~°~°~°

Burnt pot: pour some ammonia over burn and place the pot in a plastic bag. Set aside for a day or two, then wipe out.

~°~°~°~°~°~°~°~°~°~°~°~°~°

Need to cut a pie into 5 pieces cut a "Y" then slice each of the two larger sections in half.

~°~°~°~°~°~°~°~°~°~°~°~°~°

Juicier Burgers: add one stiffly beaten egg white to each half kilogram of hamburger.

~°~°~°~°~°~°~°~°~°~°~°~°~°

Is your soup or stew too greasy? Drop an ice cube in the soup. The fat will adhere to the ice. You can do the same with lettuce leaves; just drag them across the soup and the fat will cling to the leaf.

Or

If you have time place the soup in the fridge. The fat will rise to the top and you simply skim it off.

~°~°~°~°~°~°~°~°~°~°~°~°~°

To test if a cake is done, use a strand of uncooked spaghetti, a toothpick or a straw off a corn broom. They won't leave a mark like a knife.

~°~°~°~°~°~°~°~°~°~°~°~°~°

Rinse pasta in fresh tap water after it is cooked. This gets rid of the starchy taste.

~°~°~°~°~°~°~°~°~°~°~°~°~°

Reuses for Coffee Grounds:

- Use them as fertilizer on acid-loving plants like tomatoes and carrots
- Deter cats from the garden by sprinkling around beds or pots
- Mix with mashed avocado for an invigorating face mask
- Scrub your hands with spent grounds after chopping onion or garlic to get the smell off your skin
- Compost them
- Make an anti-cellulite scrub
- Keep them in the fridge or freezer instead of baking soda to eliminate odours
- Repel ants, snails and slugs by sprinkling coffee grounds near the point of entry
- Steep the grounds in water, strain out the grounds and you've got all natural brown fabric dye
- Scour away grease on your pots and pans
- Stick a sachet of dried coffee grounds into a smelly pair of shoes to get rid of the smell
- If you have dark hair; you can massage coffee grounds into your scalp to prevent dandruff. Blondes and red-heads, this is not for you since the grounds can colour roots slightly
- Vermin composters can feed grounds to the worms. Just be careful since grounds are acidic. Too much isn't good for the wigglers
- Use coffee grounds to exfoliate your skin
- To give paper an "aged" look for craft projects quickly dip pages. Soak grounds in some water overnight, then quickly dip tour pages and let them dry before crafting

- Place a layer of grounds in your ashtrays to greatly reduce the smell of old cigarette butts.

~°~°~°~°~°~°~°~°~°~°~°~°~°

Cutting warm brownies makes a MESS! They stick to the knife and you wind up with a scrambled brownie . . . Use a pizza cutter and it just rolls right through the brownies in a clean straight line

~°~°~°~°~°~°~°~°~°~°~°~°~°

Alcohol Substitutes:

Substitute chicken stock for wine in entrees. Substitute ¼-½ teaspoon almond extract for each ¼ cup of Amaretto or almond liqueur requested. Substitute frozen orange juice concentrate and a little orange zest for orange liqueurs. Substitute quadruple-strength coffee for coffee liqueurs.

~°~°~°~°~°~°~°~°~°~°~°~°~°

If your crackers have become soggy, heat in the oven for a few minutes. This works for cereal too.

~°~°~°~°~°~°~°~°~°~°~°~°~°

Brown Sugar:

To keep brown sugar moist, store in an airtight container with a whole orange, lemon, or lime. To soften brown sugar, place in a microwave-proof dish, add a slice of soft white bread or an apple wedge, cover tightly and microwave at 100% power for 30 seconds. Discard the bread or apple and stir. If you're out of brown sugar, try substituting an equal amount of granulated (white) sugar plus ¼ cup molasses (light or dark) for every cup of white sugar.

~°~°~°~°~°~°~°~°~°~°~°~°~°

Butter:

To soften butter, let it stand at room temperature for 10 to 30 minutes (depending on the room's temperature). No time for that? Either slice it or place it between sheets of wax paper and pound with a rolling pin; the larger surface area will allow for faster softening.

Or

Simply grate the butter.

~°~°~°~°~°~°~°~°~°~°~°~°~°

Cheese:

To easily shred cheese, let sit in freezer for 30 minutes. The firmer cheese is less likely to make a melted mess on your grater. To prevent hard edges from forming on older cheese, lightly oil the outsides OR rub with butter before storing.

Cottage cheese will keep twice as long if you store the carton upside down.

Try not to physically touch cheese when cutting because it will mold where your fingers touch.

If cheese has become hard and dry, don't throw it away! Grate it and store in a tightly covered jar for later use in sauces and toppings.

~°~°~°~°~°~°~°~°~°~°~°~°~°

Cottage Cheese, Sour Cream & Yogurt:

Keep them fresher longer by storing carton in the refrigerator upside down.

~°~°~°~°~°~°~°~°~°~°~°~°~°

Curry Powder:

When you use commercial curry powder, combine two or more brands—each has a different mix of spices.

~°~°~°~°~°~°~°~°~°~°~°~°~°

Basic safety steps you should always follow when handling, storing, preparing and shopping for food:

Separate: Make sure to always separate your raw foods, such as meat and egg from cooked foods, fruits, and vegetables to avoid cross-contamination.

Clean: <u>Wash your hands</u>, kitchen surfaces, utensils, and reusable shopping bags with warm, soapy water to eliminate bacteria and reduce your risk of food borne illness.

Chill: Always refrigerate food and leftovers promptly at 4°C (40°F) or below.

Cook: Always cook food to safe internal temperatures. Health Canada recommends that you check this by using a digital food thermometer. Cooked foods are safe to eat when internal temperatures are:

- 71°C (160°F) for ground meat (beef, veal, lamb and pork)
- 74°C (165°F) for leftover food and boned and deboned poultry parts
- 85°C (185°F) for whole poultry

~°~°~°~°~°~°~°~°~°~°~°~°~°

Don't peek into the oven too often while it's on—every time you open the oven door you lose 25°F.

Use less heat by cooking in glass or ceramic dishes. They conduct heat much better than metal dishes; allowing you to lower the oven temperature by 25°F.

Turn the oven off a half an hour before your roast is done. There will be plenty of heat remaining in the oven to finish cooking the roast.

~°~°~°~°~°~°~°~°~°~°~°~°~°

Dry Beans:

Soak beans before cooking to soften them, which reduces cooking time, and to allow some of the gas-generating substances to dissolve into the water, making them easier to digest.

~°~°~°~°~°~°~°~°~°~°~°~°~°

Eggs:

The simplest way to tell is an egg is fresh it to observe it's shell. If it's rough and chalky, it's fresh. If it's smooth and shiny, it's old. You can also place an egg in cold salted water. If it sinks, it's fresh. If it floats, it's old. To tell if an egg is hard boiled or raw, spin it. A hard-boiled egg will spin smoothly. A raw egg will wobble. It is easier to separate eggs when they are cold.

For fluffier omelettes, add a pinch of cornstarch before beating.

Use a funnel to separate eggs expertly.

Pierce the round end of an egg with a pin to keep it from cracking in boiling water.

Put a few drops of vinegar in the water when poaching eggs to keep them from forming "streamers". Try this also if your boiling eggs and they crack.

Beat eggs at room temperature only.

Extra large eggs may cause cakes to fall—use medium or large.

Seven or eight eggs will yield one cup of whites.

~°~°~°~°~°~°~°~°~°~°~°~°

Measuring Corn Syrup, Molasses, and Honey:

Dip measuring cup or spoon either in hot water or brush with oil before pouring in the syrup. This way, you get all that's in the cup to come out.

~°~°~°~°~°~°~°~°~°~°~°~°

Milk:

Rinse the pan with cold water before scalding milk to prevent sticking.

Or

Add a bit of sugar.

~°~°~°~°~°~°~°~°~°~°~°~°

Grill a juicier piece of chicken: Place a piece of banana peel on top of each breast while cooking. The peel will create a barrier that acts like skin helping the meat retain its natural juices.

~°~°~°~°~°~°~°~°~°~°~°~°

Nuts:

To chop or grind nuts fine in a food processor without turning them into nut butter, add 2 or more tablespoons sugar from the recipe. Toasting nuts intensifies their flavour. Fire up a skillet (high temperature) and spread pecans, walnuts, almonds, pine nuts, etc. over its surface. Stir constantly. When the nuts start to turn brown, remove from the heat and reserve for use in salads, pasta, baked goods and more. Keep a constant eye on them during the process—nuts can turn from brown to black in seconds. Nuts can also be toasted in the oven (or a toaster oven). Spread on a cookie sheet, then bake at 400 ºF for 5-10 minutes. Be sure to stir the nuts occasionally while roasting. Broken pieces will toast faster than whole nuts.

~°~°~°~°~°~°~°~°~°~°~°~°~°

Oil For Frying:

To effectively strain debris from used cooking oil, use a coffee filter placed in a funnel.

~°~°~°~°~°~°~°~°~°~°~°~°~°

Rice:

Does your rice dry out when you reheat it? Next time, add 2 tablespoons of liquid for each cup of cooked rice. Cover and heat for a few minutes on the stove or in the oven. In the microwave, cook on high about 1 minute per cup. Fluff it with a fork and enjoy! Perk up white rice by adding chicken broth with a pinch of crumbled dried thyme, marjoram, rosemary, or basil in the cooking water.

~°~°~°~°~°~°~°~°~°~°~°~°~°

Salt:

Kosher salt is best for cooking, while sea salt is best for the table. The taste of sea salt is more potent and the rigid shapes of the grains don't roll off your food as easily. Now that it has become more popular and more widely available, sea salt can be purchased iodized, which I recommend getting. When salting a dish, less is always best. As we know, you can always add more, but never take away. Less salt allows for your guests to season to their own taste.

~°~°~°~°~°~°~°~°~°~°~°

Soy Sauce:

Use light (slightly sweeter) soy sauce for marinades and dressings; use dark (slightly heavier) soy sauce for cooking and sauces.

~°~°~°~°~°~°~°~°~°~°~°

Sugar:

A sack of lumpy sugar won't be if you place it in the refrigerator for 24 hours.

~°~°~°~°~°~°~°~°~°~°~°

Tortillas:

Tough and chewy tortillas? Try spraying tortillas with water (or running them quickly under the faucet), then sautéing them briefly in a lightly greased skillet over medium high heat.

~°~°~°~°~°~°~°~°~°~°~°

Vanilla:

Make your own vanilla by placing 2 split and chopped <u>vanilla beans</u> in 1 litre of vodka or bourbon. Shaking the bottle once a day, let sit for 2-3 months, or until desired color. This also makes great holiday gifts when poured into glass bottles.

~°~°~°~°~°~°~°~°~°~°~°~°~°

Wine:

Don't throw out all that leftover wine. Freeze into ice cubes for future use in casseroles and sauces.

~°~°~°~°~°~°~°~°~°~°~°~°~°

Save energy by boiling part of the water for pasta in a teakettle and adding to the pot. Teakettles boil faster.

~°~°~°~°~°~°~°~°~°~°~°~°~°

Make buttermilk by replacing 1 tablespoon milk with 1 tablespoon lemon juice per cup of milk needed.

~°~°~°~°~°~°~°~°~°~°~°~°~°

To make cake flour out of all-purpose flour replace 2 tablespoons flour with 2 tablespoons cornstarch.

~°~°~°~°~°~°~°~°~°~°~°~°~°

Dropping Cookie Dough—To get cookie dough to drop without sticking, dip the spoon in milk first.

Add 1/3 cup melted butter to ¾ cup milk to make heavy cream. Cannot be used to make whipped cream (cooking or baking only)

~°~°~°~°~°~°~°~°~°~°~°~°~°

If your recipe calls for wine, you can use 2 tablespoons rice wine (or wine vinegar) and add chicken broth to make ½ cup.

~°~°~°~°~°~°~°~°~°~°~°~°~°

1 teaspoon dry herbs equals 1 tablespoon fresh herbs.

~°~°~°~°~°~°~°~°~°~°~°~°~°

¼ cup chopped fresh onion equals 1 tablespoon dried minced onion. (Won't work for sautéing, but is great for meatloaf)

~°~°~°~°~°~°~°~°~°~°~°~°~°

When grating cheese, spray the surface of the grater with cooking spray to prevent the cheese from sticking

~°~°~°~°~°~°~°~°~°~°~°~°~°

Uses for Toothpicks:

Home Improvement Uses

Wood filler: Toothpicks also have plenty of uses outside the kitchen. One of the best and most popular uses is as a make shift but sturdy wood filler. If you have stripped screw holes for hinges, drawer hardware or other spots, you can fill the hole with toothpicks. Dab glue on the end of each toothpick, then slide it in, and break off the end. Once the hole is tightly filled with toothpicks, re-drill the stripped hole.

Touch up furniture and woodwork: A toothpick is the perfect tool for adding paint to small scratches in furniture, woodwork and cabinets. It's smaller, cheaper and neater than a paintbrush, and will only repaint the small crack rather than the surrounding area.

Repair ornaments: A toothpick is also handy for getting glue into small spaces and onto small surfaces, such as figurines, statuettes or ornaments.

Fill small holes: Toothpicks can also hide accidental, exposed nail holes in wood projects. Dab some glue on the toothpick and push it into the hold. Break off the end, then sand flush and add stain or paint if necessary.

Sew buttons: Some sewing experts keep a couple of toothpicks in the sewing kit for sewing on buttons, either by machine or hand. They use the toothpick as a thread shank to create space between the button and the fabric. The space is necessary for the button to fasten properly. Toothpicks are also handy for cleaning and repairing sewing machines.

Mark tape: Avoid searching for the end of the tape roll, then shredding the tape in trying to use the end. Wrap the tape around a toothpick each time you finish using the tape.

Cleaning Uses

Clean brushes: Poke a toothbrush through the bristles of a dog brush or other brush to easily pull out the accumulated hair.

Clean cracks and gaps: Dip a toothpick in rubbing alcohol or other sterile cleaning solution, then use it to scrape out cracks and gaps in furniture and gadgets. It also may be the only way to reach into small spaces and clear out cobwebs and dirt.

Clean the phone: dirt and grime in the receiver holes. The best way to clear out the holes is with a toothpick.

Clean keyboards: Likewise, keyboards have lots of tight, small spaces that are difficult to clean with anything larger than a toothpick.

Wash your hands: After gardening or doing other dirty jobs, it's hard to get all the grime out from under your fingernails, even if you wash your hands thoroughly for 30 seconds with soap and hot water. However, a carefully used toothpick under the nails can quickly take them from dirty too date-worthy.

Crafty Uses

Add sequins and jewels: To neatly attach small sequins, jewels or buttons to a craft project, dab on small amounts of glue with a toothpick.

Stir tiny paint cans: Toothpicks also make great miniature stirrers for the paint containers that go with model kits and other small projects. As noted above, toothpicks also work for applying paint in small, precise spaces.

Finish or fix projects: Toothpicks come in handy before and after the painting stage as well. Dab small amounts of glue onto surfaces for completing or repairing model airplanes or similarly small, detailed projects.

Make doll furniture: Toothpicks can serve as doll-size lamp stands, curtain rods, table legs and much more. Just cut to fit and paint to suit.

Build a remote control yacht: Instead of just accessorizing with toothpicks, you can also make entire craft projects with toothpicks, including a remote control yacht.

Educational Uses

Build a bridge: Toothpicks are also great for the classroom, from elementary school through college. High school and college students struggle annually with the physics, math and engineering challenges of building a toothpick bridge that is structurally sound, and can support significant amounts of weight.

Make a box: There are also lesson plans for a toothpick box, which is both more fun and more functional than a toothpick bridge. However, building a solid box takes careful counting and precise work. As Fat Albert said, "If you're not careful, you might learn something before it's done."

Teach math: Third, math lesson plans involving toothpicks are available for parents and teachers.

Gardening Uses

Plant an avocado: The best way to start an avocado plant from seed is not to plant it in soil. Instead, wash the avocado seed and push three toothpicks into the seed. Then suspend the seed on a glass with water covering the bottom inch of the wide end of the seed. Give it a warm spot out of direct sunlight and keep it watered. After the roots and stem start to grow, plant the bottom half of the seed in rich soil.

Repair a bent stem: A toothpick can often brace a drooping or bent plant stem. Straighten the stem and attach the toothpick with tape. Water the plant and watch for it to grow back to health. Remove the toothpick splint once it is growing again to avoid choking off the stem.

Repair a garden hose leak: Stick a toothpick into the hole in a leaking garden hose. The water will swell the wood and provide a good temporary plug.

Test soil moisture: The toothpick test for cakes sort of works in reverse for houseplants. Push a toothpick into the soil around potted plants. If it comes out clean, it needs water. If it comes out wet and covered with soil, it doesn't need water yet.

Deter cutworms: Experienced green thumbs recommend pushing three toothpicks into the soil close to the stem of a tomato plant or other seedling. This can keep cutworms from curling around the plant and eating it.

Random Uses

Press the reset button: Toothpicks are the perfect size for reaching into the tiny recessed holes that house reset buttons on many gadgets.

Fix broken glasses: If you lose a screw in your eyeglasses, try aligning the screw holes and inserting a toothpick. Break off the end and tape the toothpick in place. You will at least be able to see until you can get them properly fixed.

Light candles: Toothpicks burn slower and longer than matches, so use a match to light a toothpick for lighting candles.

Quit smoking: The act of chewing on a toothpick, particularly a flavoured toothpick, can help with nicotine withdrawal.

Navigate: In a real pinch, a toothpick can help you find which way is north, so you can navigate without a compass. If you hold a toothpick next to a manual wristwatch, it should cast a shadow on the watch. Turn the watch so the toothpick casts its shadow over the hour hand. Find the line halfway between the hour hand and 12 (or 1 during daylight savings time). That line should run north-south.

Make a bookmark: In a pinch, a toothpick can be a handy way to mark your place in a book without folding the page.

Re-enact "Star Wars" or "The Three Musketeers" on a small scale: No list of toothpick uses could be complete without some weaponry. It's no mistake some cocktail toothpicks are shaped like swords. Toothpicks make great miniature make-believe light sabers, swords and javelins.

Make blow darts: If you happen to be stranded in a bar without a weapon and you suddenly need to defend yourself against pirates, put a toothpick in a cocktail straw and you have an effective blow dart. (We do not endorse this or in any way encourage you to do this. If you try this stunt, that's your problem and we're not responsible for your decision. If you decide to test this, do not do it near other people. You really could hurt someone.)

Culinary Uses

Test foods for "doneness": Stick a toothpick into cakes and brownies while baking. If it comes out clean, the baked goods are done. The toothpick test is also a proven but less publicized method for checking barbecued ribs for "doneness." However, heed a few warnings. The toothpick test is not foolproof. Chocolate chips and other melting ingredients can mess up the test. Also, the toothpick test could crack a cheesecake. Finally, resist the urge to open the oven prematurely or obsessively to stick toothpicks in your cakes. Opening the door releases a lot of heat, and could cause problems.

Design icing: Toothpicks are also handy after the cake is out of the oven. The thin tip makes a nice "pencil" for sketching out designs and words on the cake before permanently applying your decorations in icing.

Differentiate foods: At a party or potluck, use differently coloured or labelled toothpicks to mark foods with different ingredients or cooked to different levels. For example, you can mark wheat and gluten-free rolls, or meat and vegetarian dumplings, or rare, medium and well-done burgers.

Make food handles: Speaking of parties, make messy appetizers and desserts easier to handle with toothpicks.

Complete a martini: Toothpicks are also great for adding olives to martinis or fruit to tropical cocktails, or even a fancy way to put an orange or lemon slice in a beer.

Dress a ham: Add flavour and color to a baked ham by pinning pineapples and cherries to the ham with toothpicks. I know from personal experience that real toothpicks are a better option than makeshift splinters of firewood (I was once without toothpicks at a holiday family dinner and actually resorted to splinters of firewood).

Make a fruit bouquet: Use toothpicks and wooden skewers to make edible arrangements of fruit or other treats.

Hold a sandwich together: Restaurants don't spear club sandwiches with toothpicks just to provide a way to get bacon out of your teeth. They also serve a structural purpose in keeping sandwiches and burgers from falling apart. Serve neater sandwiches held together with toothpicks.

Hold together grilled vegetables: Push toothpicks horizontally through onion slices to keep them from falling apart on the grill. You can also use toothpicks to hold together stacks of vegetables and cheese for quickly melting the cheese on the grill. It's best to soak the toothpicks in water for 10 minutes before putting them on the grill.

Use when marinating: Stick a toothpick through garlic cloves or other items you plan to remove from a marinade. It's an easier, safer and more hygienic way to remove the garlic before serving.

Protect the stovetop: To keep pots from boiling over, create a little gap for escaping steam by sticking a toothpick under the lid.

Cook potatoes even faster: <u>Microwaves</u> make quick work of cooking potatoes, but you can cook spuds and other vegetables even faster by suspending them on little toothpick legs. The potato will cook more quickly and evenly on all sides, including the bottom.

Cook sausages: To cook sausages evenly and easily, pair them up with toothpicks. They will be easier to turn over, they won't roll around in the pan, and you only need to turn them once.

Make a dressing dripper: Free-flowing dressings can really heap the <u>calories</u> on an otherwise healthy salad. Instead of removing the entire foil seal on bottled dressing, poke smaller holes in the top with a toothpick, releasing a slower and healthier drip of dressing.

Make a sweet or spicy "snack": Flavoured toothpicks are a good way to satisfy hunger cravings without adding calories. Cinnamon toothpicks and other flavors are widely available, or you can make your own with cinnamon oil.

Get food out of your teeth: this is the primary use of a toothpick. However, some dentists warn against toothpicks, and prefer dental floss for removing material between teeth

~°~°~°~°~°~°~°~°~°~°~°~°

When boiling corn on the cob, add a tablespoon of sugar to help bring out the corn's natural sweetness.

~°~°~°~°~°~°~°~°~°~°~°~°

An oldie, but a goodie—use cooking spray on plastic containers to prevent stains from tomato sauce, marinara, chili, or any sauce that might stain your Tupperware.

~°~°~°~°~°~°~°~°~°~°~°~°

Measuring honey with a spoon is pretty easy but getting it off the spoon is another matter. Rub the spoon in margarine and the honey will come off.

~°~°~°~°~°~°~°~°~°~°~°~°

Always use tongs to turn meat on the grill to avoid piercing the meat. This keeps most of the wonderful juices inside the meat.

~°~°~°~°~°~°~°~°~°~°~°~°

To easily remove burnt food off of a skillet, add a drop or two of dish soap and enough water to cover the bottom of the pan. Then set it on the stove and bring to a boil to remove the offending foods.

~°~°~°~°~°~°~°~°~°~°~°~°~°

Brown sugar will not harden if stored in the freezer.

~°~°~°~°~°~°~°~°~°~°~°~°~°

To keep mushrooms from discolouring, squeeze the juice of one quarter lemon onto a paper towel and wipe each cap with the dampened towel, this also helps clean the mushrooms.

~°~°~°~°~°~°~°~°~°~°~°~°~°

To keep potatoes from budding, place an apple in the bag with the potatoes.

~°~°~°~°~°~°~°~°~°~°~°~°~°

The best time to harvest fruits and vegetables for maximum flavour is in the morning.

~°~°~°~°~°~°~°~°~°~°~°~°~°

Truss poultry with un-waxed dental floss—it won't burn and it's much stronger than thread.

~°~°~°~°~°~°~°~°~°~°~°~°~°

Boil sausages for 8 minutes before frying. They won't shrink and the skin won't break.

Or

Lightly flour them before frying for the same effect.

~°~°~°~°~°~°~°~°~°~°~°~°~°

Food Safety:

- Barbecues and Picnics -

*   Try to plan just the right amount of foods to take. That way, you won't have to worry about the storage or safety of leftovers.
*   When taking foods off the grill, put them on a clean plate, not the same platter that held raw meat.
*   When preparing dishes like chicken or cooked meat salads, use chilled ingredients. In other words, make sure your cooked chicken has been cooked and chilled before it gets mixed with other salad ingredients.
*   It's a good idea to use a separate cooler for drinks, so the one containing perishable food won't be constantly opened and closed.
*   A cooler chest can also be used to keep hot food hot. Line the cooler with a heavy kitchen towel for extra insulation and place well wrapped hot foods inside. It's amazing how long the foods will stay not only warm, but hot. Try to use a cooler that is just the right size to pack fairly tightly with hot food so less heat escapes.

* Wash ALL fresh produce thoroughly. When preparing lettuce, break into pieces—then wash.
* Cook foods to the required minimum cooking temperatures:

    - 165 ºF > Poultry, poultry stuffing, and stuffed meat.
    - 158 ºF > Ground Beef, fish, and seafood.
    - 150 ºF > Pork and food containing pork.
    - 145 ºF > shell eggs and foods containing shell eggs.

* Separate raw animal foods from other raw or ready-to-eat foods during storage and preparation.
* Cool leftovers as quickly as possible. Reheat to 165 ºF before serving again.

* *BY ALL MEANS, REMEMBER THIS:*

Bacteria on food will rapidly multiply when left at a temperature between 45ºF and 140ºF. Avoid this danger zone as much as possible.

~º~º~º~º~º~º~º~º~º~º~º~º

General Shelf Lives For Common Items:

Flour: unopened: up to 12 months. Opened: 6-8 months.

Sugar: unopened: 2 years. Sugars do not spoil but eventually may change flavour.

Brown sugar: unopened: 4 months.

Confectioners' sugar: unopened: 18 months.

Solid shortening: unopened: 8 months. Opened: 3 months.

Cocoa: unopened: indefinitely. opened: 1 year.

Whole spices: 2-4 years. Whether or not opened.

Ground spices: 2-3 years. Whether or not opened.

Paprika, red pepper and chili powder: 2 years

Baking soda: unopened: 18 months. Opened: 6 months.

Baking powder: unopened: 6 months. Opened: 3 months.

Cornstarch: 18 months. Whether or not opened.

Dry pasta: made without eggs unopened: 2 years. Opened: 1 year.

Dry egg noodles: unopened: 2 years. Opened: 1-2 months.

Salad dressing: unopened: 10-12 months.
Opened: 3 months if refrigerated.

Honey: 1 year. Whether or not opened.

Ground, canned coffee: unopened: 2 years.
Opened: 2 weeks, if refrigerated.

Jams, jellies and preserves: unopened: 1 year.
Opened: 6 months if refrigerated.

Peanut butter: unopened: 6-9 months.
Opened: 2-3 months.

Deep-Frying Tips:

* The oil must reach a good temperature to brown
the exterior of the food quickly while cooking it.
That temperature is almost always between 350 °F
and 375 °F. To be sure the oil is right use a frying
thermometer.
* Use canola oil for frying. It is low in saturated fat,
has a high burning point, and does not detract from
the flavour of the food you are frying.
* Avoid crowding food that is deep-fat-fried. The
food must be surrounded by bubbling oil, and you
must keep the temperature from falling too much.
If you add too much food to a small amount of oil,
the temperature will plummet, and the food will
wind up greasy and soggy.

* Never fill the pot more than halfway with oil; this will prevent bubbling over when the food is added.
* Dry food well with paper towels before adding to the pot; it helps reduce splattering.

Make Your Own Spice Mixes:

FIVE SPICE POWDER

1 tsp. Ground cinnamon
1 tsp. Ground cloves
1 tsp. Fennel seed
1 tsp. Star anise
1 tsp. Szechwan peppercorns

ITALIAN HERB SEASONING

1 tsp. Oregano
1 tsp. Marjoram
1 tsp. Thyme
1 tsp. Basil
1 tsp. Rosemary
1 tsp. Sage

CINNAMON SUGAR

7/8 cup Granulated sugar
2 Tbsp. Ground cinnamon

TAMARIND PASTE

1 tsp. Dates
1 tsp. Prunes
1 tsp. Dried apricots
1 tsp. Lemon juice

CHILI POWDER

3 Tbsp. paprika
1 Tbsp. ground cumin
2 Tbsp. oregano
1 tsp. red or cayenne pepper
1/2 tsp. garlic powder

~°~°~°~°~°~°~°~°~°~°~°~°°

Shellfish: you'll find it much easier to open clams and oysters if you wash them in cold water, place in a plastic bag and leave in the freezer for about an hour. After this they'll open easily.

~°~°~°~°~°~°~°~°~°~°~°~°°

Soak a stewing hen in vinegar for several hours before cooking.

~°~°~°~°~°~°~°~°~°~°~°~°°

Thick ketchup moves to slow for you. poke a drinking straw all the way into the bottle, remove, then pour. The straw will admit enough air to start the ketchup flowing.

~°~°~°~°~°~°~°~°~°~°~°~°°

Deep-frying: before heating your fat, add a tablespoon of vinegar to it. Your food will not absorb as much oil, will be crispier and tastier.

~°~°~°~°~°~°~°~°~°~°~°~°~°

Olive oil: will keep better if you add a sugar cube to the jar.

~°~°~°~°~°~°~°~°~°~°~°~°~°

Barbecue Tips:

*   Approximately 30 minutes prior to grilling, prepare the charcoal fire so coals have time to reach medium temperature. At medium, the coals will be ash-covered. To check the temperature of the coals, spread the coals in a single layer. CAREFULLY hold the palm of your hand above the coals at cooking height. Count the number of seconds you can hold your hand in that position before the heat forces you to pull it away: approximately 4 seconds for medium heat. Position the cooking grid and follow recipe directions.
*   Never place meat directly over an open flame. An open flame is an indication of incomplete combustion, the fire will discolour the meat by leaving a black carbon residue on the meat. Actually an open flame has a lower temperature than coals that are glowing red.
*   Whenever barbecuing, use tongs to turn the meat. A fork should never be used. For it will punch holes in the flesh and allow the natural juices to escape and loose flavour and become chewy.

* Tomato and/or sugar based BBQ sauces should be added only at the end of the grilling process. These products will burn easily and are seldom considered an internal meat flavouring. Once added, the meat should be turned often to minimize the possibility of burning.

~°~°~°~°~°~°~°~°~°~°~°~°~°

Stuff a miniature marshmallow in the bottom of a sugar cone to prevent ice cream drips.

~°~°~°~°~°~°~°~°~°~°~°~°~°

Add a little lemon and lime to tuna to add zest and flavour to tuna sandwiches.

~°~°~°~°~°~°~°~°~°~°~°~°~°

Poke a hole in the middle of the hamburger patties while shaping them. The burgers will cook faster and the holes will disappear when done.

~°~°~°~°~°~°~°~°~°~°~°~°~°

For fluffier, whiter rice, add one teaspoon of lemon juice per quart of water. To add extra flavour and nutrition to rice, cook it in liquid reserved from cooking vegetables.

~°~°~°~°~°~°~°~°~°~°~°~°~°

Put a few marbles in the bottom of your double boiler. When they start to rattle, you'll know the water is boiling.

~°~°~°~°~°~°~°~°~°~°~°~°

Two drops of yellow food coloring added to boiling noodles will make them look homemade.

~°~°~°~°~°~°~°~°~°~°~°~°

When separating eggs, break them into a funnel. The whites will go through leaving the yolk intact in the funnel.

~°~°~°~°~°~°~°~°~°~°~°~°

Fresh fish freeze well in a milk carton filled with water.

~°~°~°~°~°~°~°~°~°~°~°~°

Make your own celery flakes. Just cut and wash the leaves from the celery stalks; place them in the oven on low heat or in the hot sun until thoroughly dry. Crumble and store in an air-tight container.

~°~°~°~°~°~°~°~°~°~°~°~°

When picking a melon, smell it for freshness and ripeness. Check to see that the fruit is heavy in weight and that the spot on the end where it has been plucked from the vine is soft.

~°~°~°~°~°~°~°~°~°~°~°~°

Tenderize pot roast or stewing meat by using two cups of hot tea as a cooking liquid.

~°~°~°~°~°~°~°~°~°~°~°~°

222222222222222222222222222

Thaw fish in milk for fresher flavour

~°~°~°~°~°~°~°~°~°~°~°~°~°

Before leaving on a picnic; add frankfurters to your thermos and fill with boiling water. They will be completely cooked by the time you're ready to eat them.

~°~°~°~°~°~°~°~°~°~°~°~°~°

Shelling nuts:

Brazil nuts: bake at 350°F for 15 minutes, or freeze. Then crack and shell.

Chestnuts: slit the flat side, cover with water and boil about 10 minutes. Use a paring knife to peel.

Walnuts: soak overnight in salted water, then crack gently.

~°~°~°~°~°~°~°~°~°~°~°~°~°

Put meat used for stir frying in freezer for 45 minutes—1 hour to make slicing easier.

~°~°~°~°~°~°~°~°~°~°~°~°~°

You can correct greasy gravy by adding a little baking soda to it.

~°~°~°~°~°~°~°~°~°~°~°~°~°

If you need only ½ an onion, save the root half. It will last longer.

~°~°~°~°~°~°~°~°~°~°~°~°~°

Keep popcorn fresh and encourage more kernels to pop by storing in the freezer.

~°~°~°~°~°~°~°~°~°~°~°~°

Lemons stored in a sealed jar of water will produce twice the juice.

~°~°~°~°~°~°~°~°~°~°~°~°

Use paper bags rather than plastic to store lettuce and celery in the crisper. They will stay fresh longer.

~°~°~°~°~°~°~°~°~°~°~°~°

Bread will stay fresh longer if a celery rib is stored with it in the package.

~°~°~°~°~°~°~°~°~°~°~°~°

Pancakes are lighter and fluffier when you substitute club soda for milk in the batter.

~°~°~°~°~°~°~°~°~°~°~°~°

Before opening a package of bacon, roll it. This helps separate the slices for easy removal of individual slices.

~°~°~°~°~°~°~°~°~°~°~°~°

Drain deep fried foods on brown paper grocery bags as opposed to paper towels to retain crispness.

~°~°~°~°~°~°~°~°~°~°~°~°

Whenever possible, warm your dinner plates slightly in the oven before serving so the meal stays a little bit hotter.

~°~°~°~°~°~°~°~°~°~°~°~°~°

To make lighter and fluffier mashed potatoes, add a pinch or two of baking powder to the potatoes before whipping.

~°~°~°~°~°~°~°~°~°~°~°~°~°

Cookies will spread if your dough is too pliable by allowing butter to get too soft. If your cookies are spreading too much, try refrigerating the dough for a couple of hours before baking.

~°~°~°~°~°~°~°~°~°~°~°~°~°

Cookie dough can be frozen up to three months in an airtight container or refrigerated three to four days.

~°~°~°~°~°~°~°~°~°~°~°~°~°

Check cookies at minimum baking time.

~°~°~°~°~°~°~°~°~°~°~°~°~°

Let cookies cool completely before storing. Store different types of cookies in separate containers so they'll keep their original flavour and texture.

~°~°~°~°~°~°~°~°~°~°~°~°~°

Marinate red meats in wine to tenderize.

~°~°~°~°~°~°~°~°~°~°~°~°~°

Marinate chicken in buttermilk to tenderize.

~°~°~°~°~°~°~°~°~°~°~°~°~°

Use margarine instead of butter to panfry or sauté.
Butter burns quickly.

~°~°~°~°~°~°~°~°~°~°~°~°~°

Instead of adding raw garlic to sauces, sauté the garlic first
for a milder flavour.

~°~°~°~°~°~°~°~°~°~°~°~°~°

Thaw frozen meat and poultry in the refrigerator and not
on the kitchen counter where bacteria can grow.

~°~°~°~°~°~°~°~°~°~°~°~°~°

A simple way to sharpen kitchen shears: cut a piece of steel wool.

~°~°~°~°~°~°~°~°~°~°~°~°~°

Don't just keep dental floss in your medicine cabinet. Keep
some in the kitchen. It's a great tool. Unflavoured dental floss
is often better than a knife to cleanly cut all kinds of soft foods,
soft cheese, rolled dough, layered cake and cheesecake.

~°~°~°~°~°~°~°~°~°~°~°~°~°

When using spaghetti, 8 ounces of uncooked pasta makes
4 cups cooked.

When using all-purpose flour, one pound flour is the equivalent to 4 cups.

When using dried beans and peas, 1 cup dry beans or peas makes 2 1/2 cups cooked.

When using rice, keep 1 cup of uncooked long-grain white rice makes 3 cups cooked.

When using granulated sugar, one pound sugar is the equivalent to 2 cups.

~°~°~°~°~°~°~°~°~°~°~°~°~°

If guests are coming and you're behind making dinner, throw some onions on to sauté and your kitchen will smell wonderful and homey.

~°~°~°~°~°~°~°~°~°~°~°~°~°

Oven Spill-over:

As soon as the spill-over occurs, pour on a mixture of 5 parts salt and one part cinnamon. The salt absorbs the spill; the cinnamon prevents a burned smoky smell. After the oven cools, lift out the salt mixture with a metal spatula and wipe with a damp sponge.

~°~°~°~°~°~°~°~°~°~°~°~°~°

Burned Pans:

Sprinkle with baking soda and dribble with just enough water to moisten. Allow to sit for several hours. The burned stuff will lift right out.

~°~°~°~°~°~°~°~°~°~°~°~°

Garbage Disposal:

To freshen the garbage disposal, sprinkle a few tablespoons of baking soda down the drain, drop in two ice cubes and turn it on. Flush with hot water.

~°~°~°~°~°~°~°~°~°~°~°~°

Oven Racks:

Place racks the bathtub with 1/2 cup dishwasher detergent and several inches of warm water. Allow to soak for 45 minutes. Just rinse. No scrubbing needed.

~°~°~°~°~°~°~°~°~°~°~°~°

Use toaster ovens for small meals. A toaster oven uses 1/3 as much energy as a full-sized oven.

~°~°~°~°~°~°~°~°~°~°~°~°

<u>Poached Eggs:</u>

One trick to make the eggs stay somewhat contained is to take a ring from a Mason jar and place it in the pan. Drop the egg over the Mason jar ring and let it settle in the ring, then turn off the heat and cover.

~°~°~°~°~°~°~°~°~°~°~°~°~°

Plastic Melted on Toaster:

Nail polish remover will remove this easily.

~°~°~°~°~°~°~°~°~°~°~°~°~°

Coffee Grinder:

Grind up a cup or so of rice in a coffee grinder to clean the grinder and sharpen its blades.

~°~°~°~°~°~°~°~°~°~°~°~°~°

Homemade Oxy-clean Recipe:

Mix one cup hot water, 1/2 cup baking soda, and 1/2 cup hydrogen peroxide. Just soak the clothing in it for 20 minutes to overnight and then wash as usual.

~°~°~°~°~°~°~°~°~°~°~°~°~°

Place a dryer sheet and warm water in crusted pots and pans overnight. Then use the dryer sheet to wipe clean.

~°~°~°~°~°~°~°~°~°~°~°~°~°

Golden crispy fried fish:

Your fish will be perfectly fried if you put it in a little milk before flouring it. Also, put it into the pan when the oil is very hot, but not smoking. You will love the crispy coating.

~°~°~°~°~°~°~°~°~°~°~°~°

Blender and Mason Jar: With most blenders a Mason jar will fit the base. Screw it on and grind your product right in the jar. Remove and put on the lid, store away or use.

~°~°~°~°~°~°~°~°~°~°~°~°

If you buy sour oranges:

After buying oranges you find to be a bit sour for your taste. Cut them in quarters and toss them in a little salt. Although you won't believe this. Doing this will remove the acidity that is so unpleasant and they won't taste salty.

~°~°~°~°~°~°~°~°~°~°~°~°

Set up a family charging station:

With the host of electronic devices that surely every member of the family has, the house can turn into uncontrolled cord chaos. Set up a power strip near the door where everyone can easily drop their phone or computer for a charge when they come into the house.

~°~°~°~°~°~°~°~°~°~°~°~°

Diaper saver: cut a diaper in half and use them inside a cloth diaper

~°~°~°~°~°~°~°~°~°~°~°~°

My Special Tips

Chapter Three

Household

"Don't let the past steal your present"
—Cherralea Morgen

For a cheap and convenient dusting tool, wet two socks and place one on each hand. Dust twice as fast and forget throwing away old socks.

~°~°~°~°~°~°~°~°~°~°~°

Painting tips:

- **Bag and tag hardware in clear storage bags.** As you disassemble the room for painting, drop all the switch plates into one medium plastic bag. Separate hardware for each window, door, and curtain into its own bag and mark its location in the room. Once all the hardware has been bagged, place the bags into one large bag with the room name on it, then stick the bag on the windowpane of the room with blue tape.

- **Pull the masking tape while the paint is fresh**. Remove the masking materials within 45-60 minutes after the paint is applied and set to prevent surface tear up. The idea of masking tape is to protect surfaces from the paint, but when you slop the wet paint over the sealed masking tape, and let the paint cure to hard, the paint film bonds to both the wall and the masking tape. Removing the tape after the paint dries also removes paint from the wall or trim work.

- **Use rubber cement to cover hardware**. Instead of removing door hinges and handles, clean them with rubbing alcohol, then mask them with two coats of rubber cement. The cement peels right off when finished.

- **Clean water-based paint from brushes and paint pads in 10 seconds**. Simply remove excess paint from the brush or pad. Mix together ½ cup of fabric softener for each gallon of water, then dip a brush into the mixture, swish briskly through the water, and count to 10. Dry the brush using a paintbrush spinner. Spin the brush in a wet waste bucket. Rub the tool dry with a small towel.

- **For quick touch-ups, pour a small amount of paint into a clean shoe polish bottle**. The pad is perfect for small jobs. Label the bottle with the room and color, snap on the lid to store.

- **To strain lumpy paint, use an old nylon stocking**.

- **The little trick to an easier paint job**. Prevent annoying drips by hot gluing a paper plate to the bottom of the can. The plates will capture the stray drips and go wherever you go. Discard the paper plate when you are finished.

~°~°~°~°~°~°~°~°~°~°~°~°~°

Place lamps in the corners of rooms—they'll give off twice as much light

~°~°~°~°~°~°~°~°~°~°~°~°~°

A leaky toilet can go unnoticed. To check for leaks, add enough food coloring to the tank to brighten the water. After 30 minutes, look to see if the dye has leaked into the bowl.

~°~°~°~°~°~°~°~°~°~°~°~°~°

Did you know that one drip per second from a hot water tap wastes 175 gallons of water a month? Away cheaper to fix!!

Showers use less water than baths . . .

~°~°~°~°~°~°~°~°~°~°~°~°~°

You can save enough water to make 1000 cups of tea by taking a quick 5 minute shower instead of taking a bath!

~°~°~°~°~°~°~°~°~°~°~°~°~°

During winter keep shades on your south facing windows open during the day and closed at night

~°~°~°~°~°~°~°~°~°~°~°~°~°

Choose toys that are labelled lead-free and PVC-free.

~°~°~°~°~°~°~°~°~°~°~°~°

To remove mold from deck or patio furniture wash it down with full strength apple-cider vinegar. Let sit 2 hours and rinse.

~°~°~°~°~°~°~°~°~°~°~°~°

To remove black heel marks, try lighter fluid or a pencil eraser.

~°~°~°~°~°~°~°~°~°~°~°~°

Add a bit of vinegar to your dish water. This will cut the grease, allowing you to use a cheaper brand of detergent.

~°~°~°~°~°~°~°~°~°~°~°~°

Use silver polish to remove crayon marks from vinyl tile or lino.

~°~°~°~°~°~°~°~°~°~°~°~°

Dust talcum powder into the cracks of squeaky wood floors.

~°~°~°~°~°~°~°~°~°~°~°~°

A light bulb broken in the socket can usually be removed with a potato (cut in half).

~°~°~°~°~°~°~°~°~°~°~°~°

If red wine spills on your carpet, try removing it by sponging with white wine or club soda.

~°~°~°~°~°~°~°~°~°~°~°~°

To remove grease spots from wallpaper, make a paste of cornstarch and water. Apply to the spot, let dry, then brush off.

or

cover the spot with blotting paper and press with a warm iron. Repeat with new paper until the grease is gone. This works with cellophane tape also.

~°~°~°~°~°~°~°~°~°~°~°~°

Cover burns in furniture with mayonnaise, let it stand for awhile, then wipe off with a soft cloth.

~°~°~°~°~°~°~°~°~°~°~°~°

White rings on furniture can be removed with a paste of cigarette ashes and butter.

~°~°~°~°~°~°~°~°~°~°~°~°

Remove light stains from bathtubs and sinks with a cut lemon.

~°~°~°~°~°~°~°~°~°~°~°~°

To remove stains from a toilet bowl drop a denture tablet in the bowl prior to going to bed.

Or

Make a paste of lemon juice and borax. Flush to wet the bowl, and then apply the paste. Let stand for a couple hours, scrub and flush.

~°~°~°~°~°~°~°~°~°~°~°~°~°

If a plastic container has picked up an unpleasant odour, crumple a black and white page of newspaper into the container, cover tightly and leave overnight.

~°~°~°~°~°~°~°~°~°~°~°~°~°

The least expensive fridge deodorizer—two charcoal briquettes.

~°~°~°~°~°~°~°~°~°~°~°~°~°

Paint Spatters: Small paint splatters on windows can be removed by applying polish remover to them and wiping off.

~°~°~°~°~°~°~°~°~°~°~°~°~°

Washing Paintbrushes: Use fabric softener in the final rinse water when washing paintbrushes to keep then soft and pliable

~°~°~°~°~°~°~°~°~°~°~°~°~°

Recycled doors make great tables and beautiful headboards

~°~°~°~°~°~°~°~°~°~°~°~°~°

Quick fix for a missing cork: microwave an unscented taper candle for 3 seconds to soften the wax, cut an inch off the bottom and stick in the neck of the wine bottle. The makeshift stopper and seal the bottle until the next time you want a glass of wine. Pull it out as easily as a regular cork.

~°~°~°~°~°~°~°~°~°~°~°~°~°

Use Empty toilet paper roll to store appliance cords in. It keeps them neat and you can write on the roll what appliance it belongs to

~°~°~°~°~°~°~°~°~°~°~°~°~°

For icy door steps in freezing temperatures: get warm water and put Dawn dishwashing liquid in it. Pour it all over the steps. They won't refreeze.

~°~°~°~°~°~°~°~°~°~°~°~°~°

Keep that nasty dust off your TV and computer screens!!! After using your dryer sheet with your laundry, run it over your screens. The anti-static left in the dyer sheet repels dust and dirt.

~°~°~°~°~°~°~°~°~°~°~°~°~°

To clean the oven cheaply and easily:
After supper; Leave the oven at 250 F for about 20 minutes, then turn off. Fill an oven-proof container with about ¼ of ammonia and place it on the top rack. Put a tray of boiling water on the bottom rack. In the morning, open the door and let the oven air for a few minutes. Your oven will wipe clean with a damp cloth.

~°~°~°~°~°~°~°~°~°~°~°~°~°

Frosted Windows:

Want to make your windows "frosted" for more privacy? Add 1 tablespoon of Epsom Salt to 1 cup beer. Brush on the window! Let dry. To remove the frost, wash off with ammonia! This is really neat. Just remember to cover any wood or furniture nearby, because this drips!

~°~°~°~°~°~°~°~°~°~°~°~°~°

Pots and Pans:

Here's an easy way to clean a burnt pot, without using too much "elbow grease"—shake cream of tartar into the pan, fill with water and bring to a boil. After a few minutes, wipe clean.

~°~°~°~°~°~°~°~°~°~°~°~°~°

Store your plastic wrap in the fridge to keep it from sticking to itself.

~°~°~°~°~°~°~°~°~°~°~°~°~°

Direct customer input is a powerful thing:

Done right, a phone call or a well-written letter
can have real impact on the way a product is packaged.
Be polite, but be very specific. Say where you were,
what you saw, and why you didn't buy.

~°~°~°~°~°~°~°~°~°~°~°~°~°

Clean ruffled or pleated lamp shades with a baby's hair brush. The bristles are soft and will not shag or harm the shade.

~°~°~°~°~°~°~°~°~°~°~°~°~°

Take a crack at these eggshell reuses:

1. Compost for Naturally Fertilized Soil

Eggshells quickly decompose in the <u>compost pile</u> and add valuable calcium and other minerals to the soil in the process.

2. Nontoxic Pest Control in the Garden

Scatter crushed eggshell around your plants and flowers to help deter plant-eating slugs, snails and cutworms without using eco-unfriendly pesticides. Also, deer hate the smell of eggs, so scattering eggshells around the flowerbed will help keep Bambi away from your begonias.

3. Less Bitter Coffee

Add an eggshell to the coffee in the filter, and your morning coffee will be less bitter. The spent coffee grounds, eggshell and bio-degradable filter are then conveniently ready for the compost pile.

4. Splendid Seedling Starters

Fill biodegradable eggshell halves with potting soil instead of using peat pots to start seedlings for the garden. And an egg carton on the windowsill is the perfect way to start a dozen tomato seedlings in shells before transplanting to the garden in the spring.

5. Eco-friendly Household Abrasive

Shake crushed eggshells and a little soapy water to scour hard-to-clean items like thermoses and vases. Crushed eggshells can also be used as a nontoxic abrasive on pots and pans.

6. Eggy, Crafty Projects

"Blow out" the inside of a raw egg and paint/decorate the hollow shell to make your Faberge eggs or other craft projects. Pieces of egg shell (plain or dyed) are also used in mosaic art projects.

7. Clever Jello and Chocolate Moulds

Carefully fill "blown out" eggshells (above) with jello or chocolate to make unique egg-shaped treats; peel away the eggshell mold before serving, or serve as is and let your guests discover the surprise inside.

8. Natural Drain Cleaner

Keep a couple of crushed eggshells in your kitchen sink strainer at all times. They trap additional solids and they gradually break up and help to naturally clean your pipes on their way down the drain.

9. Membrane Home Remedies

The super-thin membrane inside the eggshell has long been used as a home remedy for a wide range of ailments, from healing cuts to treating ingrown toenails.

10. Treat Skin Irritations

Dissolve an eggshell in a small jar of apple cider vinegar (takes about two days) and use the <u>mixture</u> to treat minor skin irritations and itchy skin.

11. Egg on Your Face

Pulverize dried egg shells with a mortar and pestle, then whisk the powder in with an egg white and use for a healthful, skin-tightening facial. Allow the face mask to dry before rinsing it off.

12. The Fuel of Tomorrow?

Just when your brain was totally fried by all my ingenious reuses for eggshells, researchers at Ohio State University recently discovered that eggshells might be the key to producing <u>affordable hydrogen fuel</u>. I've heard of walking on eggshells, but maybe someday we'll be driving on them too.

~°~°~°~°~°~°~°~°~°~°~°~°~°

Clean pewter by rubbing with cabbage leaves

~°~°~°~°~°~°~°~°~°~°~°~°~°

To remove unpleasant odours from your cutting board, cut a lemon or lime in half and rub with the cut end.

~°~°~°~°~°~°~°~°~°~°~°~°~°

Over 50% of dust inside of your home is brought in from outside!

~°~°~°~°~°~°~°~°~°~°~°~°

For badly soiled work clothes, add ½ cup ammonia to the wash water.

~°~°~°~°~°~°~°~°~°~°~°~°

To keep socks from tangling the rest of your wash load, place in a net bag and tie loosely before adding to the washer.

~°~°~°~°~°~°~°~°~°~°~°~°

240,000

Number of plastic bags consumed worldwide every 10 seconds

~°~°~°~°~°~°~°~°~°~°~°~°

Here are some ways to get rid of insects and other pests without spending a lot on expensive products.

1. For garden pests, make a mixture of 1 tablespoon liquid dishwashing soap and 1 cup of cooking oil. Mix about 3 tablespoons of this concentrate with a quart of water in a pump bottle and spray on plants.

   Another recipe for insect control: soak citrus rind (lemon, orange, grapefruit) in water for a few days. Pour the water into a pump bottle and spray on plants.

2. Sprinkle cayenne pepper around plants to keep cats away.

3. Cucumber peel on a kitchen shelf will deter ants. You can also try washing or spraying your cabinets with vinegar and water.

4. Basil is a natural insect repellent. Keep a pot in your kitchen. Take a few leaves along with you on a picnic and put them out on the table to keep the flies away.

5. Bay leaves in your pantry will keep pests away. A bay leaf in a container of flour, cornmeal, or cereal will keep weevils out.

6. Plant peppermint around your house. It will keep ants out and it repels mice also.

7. Also cinnamon sprinkled around your foundation is said to keep ants out.

8. Coca-Cola—Pour Coca-Cola into jar lids and set them in and around your garden. Both snails and slugs are attracted by the sweet soda, but the acid will destroy them when they slither into the lid.

Or

Beer—Take a Frisbee or a plant saucer and dig a shallow hole in your garden. Place the saucer inside, leaving about 1/8 of an inch above the ground. Pour beer into the saucer, and place a roof tile or something similar over the saucer to shade it. The alcohol breaks down the body tissue of the snails and slugs, and they won't make it out again. Empty the saucer and refill it with fresh beer every couple of days.

9. Mint teabags can be used in your clothing drawers or in your closet to repel moths.

~°~°~°~°~°~°~°~°~°~°~°

Companion Planting:

To Repel Ants: Catnip, Mint

To Repel Aphids: Catnip, Chives keep aphids away from tomatoes, grapes, Dill, Garlic keeps aphids off roses. Chervil keeps aphids off of lettuce, Coriander, Mint, Nasturtiums deter woolly aphids, Peppermint, Petunia, not all aphids, Rue

To Repel Asparagus Beetle: Petunia

To Repel Bean Beetles: Rosemary

To Repel Beetles: Hemp, Sage

To Repel Black Fly: Rhubarb keeps black fly off beans

To Repel Cabbage Moth: Hyssop, Mint deters white cabbage moth, Oregano repels cabbage butterfly from broccoli, cabbage and cauliflower. Peppermint deters white cabbage moth, Rosemary, Sage, Summer Savoury

To Repel Cabbage Worm: Borage, Clover, Geranium, Thyme

To Repel Carrot Fly: Garlic, Leeks, Rosemary, Beetles
To Repel Chinch Bug: Soybean

To Repel Cucumber Beetle: Nasturtiums, Oregano to repel cucumber beetle from cucumber, Radish

To Repel Fish Moth: Rue

To Repel Fleas: Lavender, Mint, Pennyroyal (poisonous to cats)

To Repel Flea Beetles: Catnip, Hyssop, Peppermint, Mint, Rue, Sage repels black flea beetles

To Repel Flies: Basil, Rue

To Repel Gopher: Gopher Purge

To Repel Hornworm: Borage, Opal Basil

To Repel Japanese Beetle: Catnip, Chives, Garlic, Geranium, Rue in roses and raspberries, Soybean

To Repel Japanese Rust Fly: Chives

To Repel Leafhoppers: Petunias

To Repel Mexican Bean Beetle: Petunia

To Repel Mice: Catnip, Mint deters rodents

To Repel Moles: Gopher Purge

To Repel Mosquitoes: Basil

To Repel Moths: Costmary, Lavender

To Repel Nematodes: Marigolds, Chrysanthemums, Dahlias

To Repel Onion Maggot: Rue

To Repel Potato Beetle: Coriander, Horseradish, Lamium

To Repel Root Maggots: Garlic

To Repel Rust Fly: Radish

To Repel Slugs: Chervil, Rue

To Repel Snails: Garlic, Rue

To Repel Spider Mites: Coriander, Dill, Rhubarb keeps red spider mites away from columbines.

To Repel Squash Bug: Nasturtiums, Radish protects from squash borers.

To Repel Thrips: Basil

To Repel Tomato Worms: Petunia

To Repel Weevils: Catnip

To Repel Whiteflies: Nasturtiums

~°~°~°~°~°~°~°~°~°~°~°~°

Remove ink by mixing tartar and lemon juice into a paste, smear over stain let sit for an hour and wash in cool water

~°~°~°~°~°~°~°~°~°~°~°~°

My Special Tips

Chapter Four

Personal Care

Tips to keep bugs from biting:

Protect your child by their delicate skin with lightweight, long sleeved clothing. Insects may be attracted to floral prints. Choose light, solid coloured fabrics.

Mosquitoes are usually most active at dusk and just before dawn, avoid playing outside during these peak hours.

Keep your windows and door screens in good repair. When possible keep your child protected indoors or behind mosquito netting.

If eating outside, use an outdoor fan to blow away mosquitoes.

To reduce mosquito breeding near your home, plant scented geraniums, lemon thyme, marigold, tansy, citrosa plants, sweet basil and/or sassafras.

Eliminate common mosquito breeding sites such as sources of standing water (old tires, pools, plastic pots, buckets, garbage cans or clogged roof gutters). Change water in birdbaths every other day.

Make your yard friendly for natural predators such as ladybugs, bats, dragonflies, praying mantis, spiders and many birds. Stock a pond with goldfish or freshwater minnows.

Use yellow light bulbs (non-attractive to bugs) in outdoor fixtures.

Fragrances attract insects. Avoid using scented products (such as soap or shampoo) on your child or yourself.

Choose safe bug repellent products

Tips for Soothing Bug Bites:

Herbal Household Remedies

Tea Tree Oil: If you are stung, remove stinger if there is one. Apply tea tree oil liberally in a circular motion surrounding the entry point. Be gentle touching the entry point. Let dry and the pain and swelling should ease in a couple minutes. Re-apply if necessary.

Baking Soda: Mix baking soda with water to form a paste. Remove stinger if present and apply the paste. Cover with a gauze, bandage and or tape. Leave on for ½ hour or until pain is gone.

Onion: Relieve the itch from bug bites with an onion. The sulphur in onions neutralizes the chemicals that cause the itch. Simply slice a yellow onion in half and rub one of the cut sides on the bite. The itching should stop immediately. Refrigerate the onion in a sealed container to use again if the itching resumes. Make a fresh slice before reapplying it.

Vinegar: good for spider bites too. Soak a cotton ball in vinegar and place it over the bite. The soaked cotton ball can be held in place with a band aid.

~°~°~°~°~°~°~°~°~°~°~°~°

Relieve Teething Pain:

Fold a washcloth into a small triangle, dip one corner in water, and place in the freezer for a few hours. Once it's frozen, let your baby grasp the dry end of the cloth—or hold it for them—while they gnaws on the frozen corner.

~°~°~°~°~°~°~°~°~°~°~°~°

Bleach Smell: To remove bleach smell from hands (and that slimy feeling) pour a little vinegar or lemon juice over your hands then rinse.

~°~°~°~°~°~°~°~°~°~°~°~°

Paint Remover For Skin: Apply cooking oil to skin to remove paint.

~°~°~°~°~°~°~°~°~°~°~°~°

Removing Gum From Hair: Apply petroleum jelly or peanut butter to the spot and work through the hair.

~°~°~°~°~°~°~°~°~°~°~°~°

Paint remover For Skin: Baby oil will remove most oil-based from skin.

~°~°~°~°~°~°~°~°~°~°~°~°~°

Ink Remover from Skin: Remove ball-point ink from skin with margarine and damp cloth.

~°~°~°~°~°~°~°~°~°~°~°~°~°

Broken Lipstick: Hold a match under the broken ends until they melt enough to adhere to each other. Cool in the refrigerator.

~°~°~°~°~°~°~°~°~°~°~°~°~°

Removing Dead Skin: Rib a bit of Miracle Whip salad dressing into your skin and let it stand a moment. Rub vigorously and dead skin is quickly removed. However, this only works using Miracle Whip, not mayonnaise

~°~°~°~°~°~°~°~°~°~°~°~°~°

Natural Facial: A good and inexpensive facial to try: mash half an avocado, spread thickly on face and remove with warm water 20 minutes later.

~°~°~°~°~°~°~°~°~°~°~°~°~°

Another Easy Facial: Apply a paste of instant oatmeal and water to face. When it dries and feels tight, rub off with fingers, removing dead skin.

~°~°~°~°~°~°~°~°~°~°~°~°

Vinegar for Skin: The natural ph-balance will be restored to your skin by adding cider vinegar to a bowl of warm water and splashing it on your face. Allow to air-dry.

~°~°~°~°~°~°~°~°~°~°~°~°

Health Spa Secret: After washing your face, rub a small amount of petroleum jelly into wet skin. Keep wetting face until the jelly does not feel greasy. This is a little-known secret that many health spas use

~°~°~°~°~°~°~°~°~°~°~°~°

Squeaking Shoes: If your shoes squeak, try applying linseed oil to the soles.

~°~°~°~°~°~°~°~°~°~°~°~°

Cuticle Treatment: Apply a mixture of equal parts of castor oil and white iodine to your cuticles every night.

~°~°~°~°~°~°~°~°~°~°~°~°

Soothe Itchy Mosquito Bites:
Gently roll a liquid or solid antiperspirant over the swollen, irritated welts. Wait five minutes, then reapply if the bites are still itchy.

~°~°~°~°~°~°~°~°~°~°~°~°

Surgeon's Secret: Apply odourless castor oil around eyes nightly. Plastic surgeons use this n their patients after surgery

~°~°~°~°~°~°~°~°~°~°~°~°

Insect Bite Remedies: Try one of the following for relief of insect bites: apple cider vinegar applied to the affected area; a paste of baking soda and water allowed to dry bites; or a paste of meat tenderizer

~°~°~°~°~°~°~°~°~°~°~°~°

Skin Treatment: A wonderful relief for sunburn pain is the application of mint-flavoured milk of magnesia to the skin. It is also good for applying to oily skin before bed.

~°~°~°~°~°~°~°~°~°~°~°~°

Hair Shiner: These hair rinses will remove soap film and shine hair-for blondes—rinse water containing s few tablespoons of lemon juice. For burettes and redheads a few tablespoons of apple cider vinegar in the rinse water

~°~°~°~°~°~°~°~°~°~°~°~°

Sticking Bottle Tops: Rub petroleum jelly inside the cap of bottles of nail polish to prevent them from sticking.

~°~°~°~°~°~°~°~°~°~°~°~°

Homemade Deodorant: Heat in a double boiler until a smooth cream forms: equal parts of baking soda, petroleum jelly and talcum powder. This homemade deodorant can be kept in small jars and used like a regular cream deodorant

~°~°~°~°~°~°~°~°~°~°~°~°

Ease Diaper Rash:

Instead of cleaning your baby's bottom with pre-moistened wipes, hold them over the sink and let warm water wash over their inflamed skin. Then dry them off using a blow-dryer set on cool.

~°~°~°~°~°~°~°~°~°~°~°~°

*"Never throughout history has a man
who lived a life of ease left a name worth remembering. "*

—*Theodore Roosevelt*

~°~°~°~°~°~°~°~°~°~°~°~°

Sticking Perfume Bottles: If the top on a bottle of perfume stick, put the bottle in the refrigerator until it is cold, then twist the stopper back and forth to prevent future sticking.

~°~°~°~°~°~°~°~°~°~°~°~°

Tweezing Eyebrows: If you wear eyeglasses, it may be hard to tweeze eyebrows. Try turning your glasses upside down before tweezing.

~°~°~°~°~°~°~°~°~°~°~°~°

Earring Allergy: If costume jewellery earrings cause your ears to break out, try washing earrings in rubbing alcohol and putting several coats of clear nail polish on part of the erring that touches your ear

~°~°~°~°~°~°~°~°~°~°~°~°~°

Baking Soda Uses: For a mouthwash: 1 teaspoon dissolved in 1/2 glass of water; for toothpaste, use full strength on your toothbrush; for burns, apply a past of baking soda and water; for cleaning rough knees and elbows, a paste of soda and water.

~°~°~°~°~°~°~°~°~°~°~°~°~°

Squeeze out every last bit of toothpaste; submerge the tube in a glass of hot water for 1 minute. The warmth will expand the tube and loosen any trapped toothpaste enough to give you one last round till you get a new tube the next day.

~°~°~°~°~°~°~°~°~°~°~°~°~°

Soft Hands: Rinse hands in vinegar water after hand washing clothes or dishes.

~°~°~°~°~°~°~°~°~°~°~°~°~°

Quick Shampoo: When you don't have time to wash your hair, sprinkle talcum powder on only areas, with a towel, and brush out.

~°~°~°~°~°~°~°~°~°~°~°~°~°

Calorie Counter: Rather than write down calories and food eaten during the day, use a pocket calculator to count calories. You'll know how close you are to your daily limit.

~°~°~°~°~°~°~°~°~°~°~°

Treat a Sting:

Immediately scrape off the stinger with the edge of a credit card or a very dull knife. Wash the area with soapy water, then hold an ice cube on it for a few minutes.

~°~°~°~°~°~°~°~°~°~°~°

Symptoms of Diabetes:

Type 1 Diabetes

- Frequent urination
- Unusual thirst
- Extreme hunger
- Unusual weight loss
- Extreme fatigue and Irritability

Type 2 Diabetes*

- Any of the type 1 symptoms
- Frequent infections
- Blurred vision
- Cuts/bruises that are slow to heal
- Tingling/numbness in the hands/feet
- Recurring skin, gum, or bladder infections

* Often people with type 2 diabetes have no symptoms

~°~°~°~°~°~°~°~°~°~°~°

Remove a splinter painlessly: tape a piece of banana peel, white side down, over the wound and leave for 30 minutes. The enzymes in the peel will seep into the skin and encourage the splinter to move to the surface for easy plucking.

~°~°~°~°~°~°~°~°~°~°~°~°~°

Baggy Stockings: If your nylon stockings sag and bag, dip your hands in warm water and rub your hands up your legs, starting at the ankle for a better fit.

~°~°~°~°~°~°~°~°~°~°~°~°~°

Stopping Runs: To stop runs in stockings, spray with hair spray or rub with a wet cake of soap.

~°~°~°~°~°~°~°~°~°~°~°~°~°

Give Medicine to a Baby or Toddler:

Place your child in an <u>infant</u> seat or have another person cradle them in a similar position, then let them have several licks of an ice pop or ice cube. Now quickly squirt the medicine into the side of their mouth, between their cheek and gums. *Cold numbs your child's tongue and cheeks, making them less sensitive to taste and less likely to spit the medication back up.*

~°~°~°~°~°~°~°~°~°~°~°~°~°

Static Electricity: To eliminate clinging dresses, run a wire coat hanger between your slop and dress.

~°~°~°~°~°~°~°~°~°~°~°~°~°

Steam Out Wrinkles: To remove wrinkles from a dress or other garment, hang it in the bathroom while taking a shower and steam will remove some of the wrinkles.

~°~°~°~°~°~°~°~°~°~°~°~°

Tired Eyes: Fresh cucumber slices applied to closed eyelids with freshen and revive tired eyes

~°~°~°~°~°~°~°~°~°~°~°~°

Quick-drying Nail Polish: Nail polish will dry quickly if you put your handed in the freezer compartment of the refrigerator for a minute

~°~°~°~°~°~°~°~°~°~°~°~°

Inexpensive Rouge: Combine the last of your lipstick with your lipstick with cold cream for a lovely rouge.

~°~°~°~°~°~°~°~°~°~°~°~°

Shoe Polishing: Keep a pair of old worn-out gloves in your shoe-polishing kit to avoid getting shoe publish under your fingernails

~°~°~°~°~°~°~°~°~°~°~°~°

Beach Sand: Sprinkle talcum powder on body and feet and rub lightly with a towel to remove any traces of beach sand

~°~°~°~°~°~°~°~°~°~°~°~°

Blemish Remedy: Rub baby power or cornstarch on facial blemishes to dry them up without driving skin.

~°~°~°~°~°~°~°~°~°~°~°~°~°

Biting Insects: To make yourself less appealing to insects wear light coloured clothing.

~°~°~°~°~°~°~°~°~°~°~°~°~°

Lint removal: Add a cup of white vinegar to final rinse cycle

~°~°~°~°~°~°~°~°~°~°~°~°~°

Poison Ivy:

Wearing gloves and using liquid dishwashing soap and water, immediately wash any area that came in contact with the plant. Rinse thoroughly with clean water, pat dry. If a rash develops, apply a cool, damp washcloth to the area. *Liquid dish soap, which is detergent-based, will wash away the plant oil and help prevent absorption into the skin. Soaking in cool water or using cold compresses alleviates itching.*

~°~°~°~°~°~°~°~°~°~°~°~°~°

Mosquito bites: To minimize or avoid mosquito bites take B vitamins (B Complex). Flying insects will be turned off by the smell and taste of your blood.

~°~°~°~°~°~°~°~°~°~°~°~°~°

"What's in a name? That which we call a rose
by any other name would smell as sweet."

—*William Shakespeare*

Hydrogen Peroxide: A Simple Trick to Beat a Cold

Amazing results have been seen in 12-14 hours when putting a few drops of 3% hydrogen peroxide in each ear to fight a cold or flu. Add the drops in one ear; wait for the bubbling to stop, drain and repeat in the other ear.

ACNE, BLACKHEADS, AND PIMPLES:

- Dab a small amount of toothpaste (paste, not gel) on pimples before bed; this helps dry out the pimples.
- Mix equal amounts of lemon juice and rose water, apply to face with a cotton ball, and allow to sit for 30 minutes before rinsing. 15-20 days of this application helps cure pimples and also helps to remove blemishes and scars.
- Apply fresh lemon juice on the affected area overnight. Wash off with warm water next morning.
- For acne that hasn't seemed to respond to anything, steep 2-3 teaspoons dried basil leaves in 1 cup boiling water for 10-20 minutes, cool, and apply to affected area with a cotton ball.

ANEMIA:

Avoid drinking tea (regular, not herbal varieties) and coffee immediately after meals, as the tannin present in these interferes in the absorption of iron from the food.

- Drink a cup of herbal tea mixed with ¼ cup blackstrap molasses each day. This provides 80% of the iron needed in one day.
- Foods high in iron: lean beef, lean pork, skinned poultry, shellfish, fish, liver, organ meats, egg yolks, pinto, kidney, lima, navy, chick peas, black-eyed peas, lentils, split peas, green peas, spinach, kale, collards, beet greens, chard, broccoli, raisins, prunes, figs, dates, dried peaches, dried apricots, nuts, peanut butter, whole grain breads.
- Your body absorbs iron from meats easier than fruits and vegetables. To aid in the absorption of iron from fruits and vegetables, eat them with a good source of vitamin C.

ARTHRITIS:

- A daily serving of fresh fish or fish oil capsules helps to give relief of arthritis and other joint pains.
- 3-4 walnuts eaten daily, on an empty stomach, will help.

ASTHMA:

- Mix 1 teaspoon honey with ½ teaspoon cinnamon and take it at night before going to bed.

- Avoid taking aspirin, as this may invoke an asthma attack.

BAD BREATH:

- Boil some cinnamon bark in a cup of water. Store it in a clean bottle in your bathroom. Use it as a mouthwash frequently.
- Parsley leaves are rich in chlorophyll, nature's own deodorizer. Chew some leaves regularly and your breath will remain fresh.
- You can chew some cardamom seeds to sweeten your breath.

BLADDER INFECTION:

Take a bag of fresh or frozen cranberries and boil them in water (they will fall apart). Cool and drink. Don't add sugar! This remedy is also useful for people with kidney problems.

BLADDER STONES:

Boil 2 figs in 1 cup of water. Drink daily for a month.

BRUISES:

Slice a raw onion and place over the bruise. Do not apply this to broken skin.

COLD AND FLU:

Here is a delicious recipe for a cold and flu soup: Sauté 6 crushed cloves of garlic in 1 teaspoon vegetable oil until golden. Pour in a quart of beef or chicken stock and bring to a boil. Reduce heat and whisk in 2 egg whites. Beat together 2 egg yolks and 2 tablespoons distilled white vinegar; pour this mixture into the soup. Season with salt and pepper and top with croutons, if desired.

CONSTIPATION (IN ADULTS):

- Eat a few black licorice sticks.
- Take apple pectin.
- Make sure you're getting enough Folic Acid in your diet.
- Drinking ginger tea will help start a bowel movement.

CONSTIPATION (IN SMALL CHILDREN):

Soak 6-8 raisins in hot water. When cool, crush well and strain. When given routinely even to little infants, it helps to regulate bowel movement.

COUGHS AND ASTHMA:

Steep 3-4 cloves of garlic in a cool, dark place for 2 weeks. Use several drops at a time, several times a day for coughs or asthma. Garlic is an exceptional cleanser for the body and has antimicrobial action similar to other antibiotics.

DAMAGED, DRY HAIR:

A nourishing conditioner for dry or damaged hair which can be used for all hair types: Separate the white of an egg from the yolk, whip it to a peak. Add 1 tablespoon water to the yolk and blend until the mixture is creamy. Then mix the white and yolk together. Wet your hair with warm water, remove the excess moisture, and apply the mixture to your scalp with your fingertips. Massage gently until the froth is worked into your scalp, then rinse the hair with cool water. Keep applying the mixture until it is used up and then rinsed until all of the egg is washed away.

DANDRUFF:

Pour distilled white vinegar onto the hair, as close to the scalp as you can manage; massage into the scalp; and allow to dry for several minutes before washing as usual. Repeat daily until the dandruff disappears, usually within a few days.

DARK CIRCLES AROUND EYES:

Make a paste out of 1 teaspoon tomato juice, ½ teaspoon lemon juice, a pinch of turmeric powder, and 1 teaspoon of flour. Apply around eyes. Leave on for 10 minutes before rinsing.

DEPRESSION:

¾ cup of cooked spinach a day is enough to give dramatic relief from depression if you are deficient in B vitamins.

DIARRHEA:

Eat boiled sweet potatoes seasoned with salt and pepper before bedtime to cure chronic diarrhoea.

DRY SKIN:

Combine 1 cup oatmeal, 1 cup warm water, 1 tablespoon vanilla extract, and ½ cup baking soda in a blender or food processor until you have a smooth paste. Pour this paste under the running water while drawing the bath. Very soothing to dry, itchy skin.

EARACHE:

Steep 1-2 teaspoons chamomile flowers in boiling water for 10-15 minutes. Strain out the water, and apply the hot flowers in a cloth for alleviation of the earache.

ECZEMA:

Rub a whole nutmeg against a smooth stone slab with a little water and make a paste. Apply on affected parts. (Note: It is believed by some rural, old fashioned practitioners that instead of water, one's own early morning saliva can be used for better results.)

ENERGIZER:

Simmer 1 cup honey and 3 cup water together slowly. Allow 1 cup of the water to evaporate. Strain off the top surface, and put the remaining liquid into a stoneware crock or dark bottle. Put a towel over it so it can breathe, yet be free of dirt. Place in a cool place. You can add cinnamon, clove, or the juice of 2 lemons, if you like.

EYE PROBLEMS:

Simmer 1 cup water and 1 teaspoon honey for 5 minutes. Dip a cloth in the liquid and apply to the closed eye.

FACIAL CLEANSER:

Mix 2 tablespoons cornstarch, 2 tablespoons glycerine, and ½ cup water until smooth. Heat in a small pan placed in a water bath inside another pan. Heat until thick and clear; it will have the consistency of pudding. Do not boil. Cool completely, Use in place of soap to cleanse your skin. (If mixture is too thick, you may thin it by adding a little water, 1 tablespoon at a time, until you reach the desired consistency.)

FATIGUE:

Take a glass of grapefruit and lemon juice in equal parts to dispel fatigue and general tiredness after a day's work.

GUM IN HAIR:

Soak the gum-coated hair in Coke® and it should wipe out easily.

HAIR LIGHTENER:

To lighten hair, use ¼ cup chopped fresh rhubarb to 2 cups boiling water. Cool, strain, and apply as a rinse.

HANG-OVER:

Eat honey on crackers. The fructose in the honey will help to flush out the alcohol in your system.

HAY FEVER:

Steep 1 teaspoon fenugreek seed in 1 cup water, covered, for 10 minutes. Drink 1 cup a day to help hay fever symptoms.

HEADACHE:

Eat 10-12 almonds, the equivalent of two aspirins, for a migraine headache. Almonds are far less likely to upset the stomach.

HICCUPS:

- Breath in as deeply as you can, then exhale as hard as you can; repeat 10 times; when exhaling the last time, keep the air pushed out, not taking another breath for as long as you can stand. This normally works the first try, but repeat if necessary. Be sure to sit down when doing this.
- This is a remedy only feasible when sitting at a bar. Have the bartender fill a small glass with club soda. Light a match and drop it, then drink the water quickly (being careful not to drink the match).
- Drink ½ glass water, slowly.
- Keep a teaspoon of sugar in your month and suck slowly.
- Suck 2-3 small pieces of fresh ginger.
- Take a large mouthful of water without swallowing, plug both ears, and slowly begin to swallow the water. Unplug your ears and you're hiccup free
- Eat a heaping teaspoon of peanut butter all at once.

HICKEY:

- Coat area liberally with lotion. Rub with the back of a cold spoon vigorously for as long as you can stand to, changing out spoon for new cold one every 10 minutes. Recommended time for this treatment is 45-60 minutes. Why it works: a hickey is a bruise; the discoloration of a bruise is caused by blood accumulating under the skin from broken capillaries; this remedy breaks up the old blood so it can be reabsorbed by the body more quickly, therefore diminished the discoloration.

- Rub white toothpaste over the hickey, allow to dry, and later, wipe it off with a warm facecloth. After a few applications, the hickey will be faded. Do not use gel toothpaste.

INSECT BITES:

Mix water with cornstarch into a paste and apply. This is effective in drawing out the poisons of most insect bites and is also an effective remedy for diaper rash.

MORNING SICKNESS:

Mix 1 teaspoon each fresh juice of mint and lime, and 1 tablespoon honey. Take 3 times a day.

MOSQUITO BITES:

Apply lime juice diluted with water on bites with cotton ball.

MUCUS IN COUGH:

Pour 1 cup boiling water over ½ teaspoon each of ginger, ground cloves, and cinnamon. Filter. Sweeten with 1 teaspoon honey and drink.

MUSCLE CRAMPS:

Apply clove oil on the affected body parts.

NAUSEA:

Boil ½ cup of rice in 1 cup of water for about 10-20 minutes. After it is boiled, drain the water into a cup and sip at the rice water until symptoms are gone.

OBESITY:

- Mix lime juice with honey and water; drink a glass of this every morning.
- Mix 3 teaspoons lime juice, ¼ teaspoon black pepper, 1 teaspoon honey, and 1 cup water; drink a glass a day for 3 months.
- Mix 1 teaspoon lime juice with 1 cup water and drink each morning.
- Eat a tomato before breakfast.

OILY SKIN:

For oily skin, mix ½ cup cooked oatmeal, 1 egg white, 1 tablespoon lemon juice, and ½ cup mashed apple into a smooth paste. Apply to face and leave on 15 minutes. Rinse.

OVERWEIGHT:

Effective at getting rid of fat, drink up to 3 cups of green tea daily. Regular tea can also be used with a lesser effect.

PAIN RELIEVER:

Mix 3 tablespoons of honey in boiled water and drink. Honey has natural pain-relieving powers.

SMELLY FEET:

Soak feet in strong tea for 20 minutes every day until the smell disappears. To prepare your footbath, brew two tea bags in 2 ½ cups of water for 15 minutes and pour the tea into a basin containing two litres of cool water.

SMOKING HABIT:

Lick a little salt with the tip of your tongue whenever you feel the urge to smoke. This is said to break the habit within 1 month.

SORE THROAT:

Mix 1 teaspoon lime juice and 1 tablespoon honey. Swallow tiny amounts slowly 2-3 times a day.

SPLINTERS:

- Lay scotch tape over the splinter and pull off.
- Soak the area in vegetable oil for a few minutes before removing with tweezers.

STOMACH ACHE:

A simple cure for a stomach ache is to dissolve 1½ teaspoons ground cinnamon in 1 cup warm water, cover and let sit for

15 minutes, then drink it like tea. This remedy can also ease diarrhoea and flatulence.

STOMACH ACIDITY:

- Drink coconut water 3-4 times a day.
- Have a plateful of watermelon and/or cucumber every hour.

SUNBURN:

Mix 2 teaspoons tomato juice and ¼ cup buttermilk. Apply to affected area. Rinse after ½ hour.

TOOTHACHE & MOUTH PAIN:

To ease toothache or other mouth pain, make a tea by boiling 1 tablespoon fresh peppermint in 1 cup water and adding a little salt. Peppermint is an antiseptic and contains menthol, which relieves pain when applied to skin surfaces.

VARICOSE VEINS:

Take 2-3 tsp. black strap molasses orally daily. This also treats all kinds of circulatory ailments.

VOMITING AND NAUSEA:

- Sucking a piece of ice controls vomiting.
- Eat ½ teaspoon ground cumin seeds.
- Cinnamon and sliced ginger work by interrupting nausea signals sent from the stomach to the brain. If you are an herbal tea drinker, simply sprinkle

cinnamon on the tea and drink. To make ginger tea, simmer a few slices of ginger in hot tea water.

WARTS:

Try taping a slice of garlic to the wart. Be sure to first protect the surrounding skin with petroleum jelly.

WEAK NAILS:

To strengthen and shine nails, combine 2 teaspoons salt, 2 teaspoons castor oil, and 1 teaspoon wheat germ oil and mix thoroughly. Pour into bottle. Shake before using. To use, rub a small amount into your nails. Leave on 3-5 minutes and tissue off. Follow up with more plain castor oil, if desired.

WRINKLES & SKIN FRESHENER:

- Combine 2 tablespoons vodka, 1 tablespoon fennel seeds, and 1½ teaspoons honey. Stir well and allow to sit for 3 days. Strain mixture. Use full strength or add 2 tablespoons water to dilute. Use a cotton ball to apply to face as a toner.
- Apply coconut oil on the portions of skin and face where wrinkles set in and gently massage every night at bed time.

YELLOW TEETH:

Mix salt with finely powdered rind of lime. Use this as toothpowder frequently.

~°~°~°~°~°~°~°~°~°~°~°

Heal paper cuts: With Chap Stick. Rub on paper cuts to stop the pain immediately & heal the cut.

~°~°~°~°~°~°~°~°~°~°~°~°~°

Shelf Life of Makeup?

It's unlikely you'll go blind from using 2-year-old mascara.

- **Concealer** Up to 12 months.
- **Powder** 2 years.
- **Cream & gel cleansers** 1 year.
- **Pencil eye liner** Should be sharpened regularly. Will last up to 3 years.
- **Eye_shadow** Will also last up to 3 years. *Extra tip:* A dark eye shadow can double as eyeliner, in fact, most makeup artists swear by eye shadow used as eyeliner.
- **Brushes** Wash every 2-3 months in a mild detergent.
- **Sponges** Wash weekly and discard monthly.
- **Foundation** Check the ingredients: A water-based foundation will last up to 12 months, oil-based will last up to 18 months. You may find you need two different shades of foundation each year: One for summer when your skin is naturally darker and one for winter when you're lighter. *Extra tip:* If your water-based foundation dries out before its expiration date, simply add a few drops of alcohol-free toner and shake to mix it in.
- **Lip liner** Up to 3 years. Extra tip: Skip the push-up lip liners.
- **Lipstick** Some experts say 1-2 years. Others say up to 4 years. What everyone agrees on is that if it

smells rancid, throw it out, it's spoiled. *Extra tip:* If you store lipstick in the refrigerator, it will last longer. Bonus tip: Want your lipstick to last longer during the day?

- **Mascara** This product expires the fastest: Throw out after 4 months. *Extra tip:* If you don't want your mascara to expire faster than its fresh date, don't pump the wand in and out—you're only exposing the product to drying air.
- **Nail Polish** Up to 12 months, depending on the quality and how many times you take it on a plane

~°~°~°~°~°~°~°~°~°~°~°~°

Safeguard:

Keep a wide-mouth jar with a tight fitting lid near the sink. Place rings and other jewellery in the jar when washing and cleaning.

Frostbite:

If (1) there is frostbite but no sign of hypothermia and (2) immediate medical care is not available, proceed as follows:

- Get into a warm room as soon as possible.
- Unless absolutely necessary, do not walk on frostbitten feet or toes—this increases the damage.
- Immerse the affected area in warm—not hot—water (the temperature should be comfortable to the touch for unaffected parts of the body).
- Or, warm the affected area using body heat.

For example, the heat of an armpit can be used to warm frostbitten fingers.

- Do not rub the frostbitten area with snow or massage it at all. This can cause more damage.
- Don't use a heating pad, heat lamp, or the heat of a stove, fireplace, or radiator for warming. Affected areas are numb and can be easily burned.

∼°∼°∼°∼°∼°∼°∼°∼°∼°∼°∼°

Sandy kids: a great way to remove wet sand, especially from children's feet and legs is to use baby powder. Simply sprinkle on sandy areas and brush off.

∼°∼°∼°∼°∼°∼°∼°∼°∼°∼°∼°

My Special Tips

Chapter Five

Clothing

"Don't find fault with what you don't understand"

~°~°~°~°~°~°~°~°~°~°~°~°

Paint Remover: Mix equal parts of turpentine and ammonia to remove even harden paint from clothing.

~°~°~°~°~°~°~°~°~°~°~°~°

Long-lasting Buttons: Coat the center of buttons with clear nail polish and they'll stay on longer.

~°~°~°~°~°~°~°~°~°~°~°~°

Stuck Zippers: If a zipper sticks, run a bar of soap over it and it will slide easily.

~°~°~°~°~°~°~°~°~°~°~°~°

Removing Makeup Smudges: Makeup smudges may be removed from clothing with a slice of bread.

~°~°~°~°~°~°~°~°~°~°~°~°

Collar Rings: To remove stains from collars, rub heavily with chalk, which will absorb oil. Several applications may be required. Launder as usual.

~°~°~°~°~°~°~°~°~°~°~°~°

Make visible hem stitches vanish: dip a clean rag into a mixture of equal parts distilled white vinegar and water. Lay the hem on top of the damp rag and go over the stitches with a hot iron until they disappear. The vinegar's acetic acid will soften the material, while the steam will expand the fibres to their original condition.

~°~°~°~°~°~°~°~°~°~°~°~°

Blood Stains: Apply meat tenderizer to stained area. Add warm water to make a paste. Wait 15 to 30 minutes and sponge with cool water. Pre-soaking may be necessary before laundering.

~°~°~°~°~°~°~°~°~°~°~°~°

Ball Point Ink Stains: Spray hair spray on the stain, then rub with clean dry cloth. The ink should disappear. Repeat, if not removed. This method works especially well on polyesters.

~°~°~°~°~°~°~°~°~°~°~°~°

Fresh Smelling Closet: Put cloves, pine needles or mothballs in an old stocking and hang in your closet.

~°~°~°~°~°~°~°~°~°~°~°~°

Remove Grease from Suede: Dip a-clot in vinegar and sponge leather, then dry. Use a Swede brush to restore nap.

~°~°~°~°~°~°~°~°~°~°~°~°

Renew frayed shoelaces: Trim off frayed pieces and dip the ends in clear nail polish. Let dry thoroughly.

~°~°~°~°~°~°~°~°~°~°~°~°

To take static out of a dress or skirt: Run a wire coat hanger between your dress and nylon slip or stockings. The wire will draw out most of the electricity

~°~°~°~°~°~°~°~°~°~°~°~°

Use a mixture of vinegar and water to clean salt off shoes and boots

~°~°~°~°~°~°~°~°~°~°~°~°

Blood stains on clothes? Not to worry! Just pour a little peroxide on a cloth and proceed to wipe off every drop of blood. Works every time!

~°~°~°~°~°~°~°~°~°~°~°~°

To keep fabrics from bleeding, add 2-3 teaspoons of salt to wash and rinse cycles.

~°~°~°~°~°~°~°~°~°~°~°~°

Got a stubborn string knot, shoelace, thread, etc.? Dust the knot with talcum powder, it will easily come undone.

~°~°~°~°~°~°~°~°~°~°~°~°~°

Pre-wash Spray:

½ Cup household ammonia
¼ Cup baking soda
½ Cup white vinegar
½ gallon water

After mixing this solution, put part of it in a smaller spray bottle to keep handy by the washing machine when doing laundry. Spray liberally onto clothes where needed.

~°~°~°~°~°~°~°~°~°~°~°~°~°

Stuck zipper :

Rub a small amount of candle wax onto the area of the zipper closest to the stuck zipper pull. Work the zipper until you work it free.

Zipper won't stay up:

Use a safety pin, loop it through the small opening that is found at the tip of almost every zipper pull, and secure the zipper to your waistband. Be sure to attach the pin with the sharpest side facing outward to avoid becoming pinched.

Loose hem:

Use a strip of tape (the heavier the fabric, the stronger the tape) to secure the hem until you have more time to sew it up. If you will be wearing the outfit for a long period of time, try to use adhesive backed Velcro.

Clothing pulls:

Use a small needle with a large eye to thread the pull to the underside of the garment. Secure it with clear nail polish, especially if it is long in length. Try to use a smaller needle for finer fabrics.

Run in your pantyhose:

Use a small dab of clear nail polish to stop the run from getting any larger.

~°~°~°~°~°~°~°~°~°~°~°~°~°

Safe Storage of Different Types of Clothing:

Leatherandsuede should be stored in a closet that is cool and well ventilated. The garments are best covered with white muslin that's been washed. Supple leather garments should be laid flat and padded well with white tissue.

Rayon should also be stored flat. If the garment has to be hung, pad it with white tissue and cover it with clean, white muslin.

Linen garments should be rolled. If you feel you must fold them, be sure to refold often to avoid fabric from becoming permanently creased. Always cover with white muslin that's been washed.

Knittedandsilk fabrics should always be stored flat. If you feel you must hang these garments, be sure to pad well with white tissue and cover it with clean, white muslin.

Garments made of *metallicfabric* should be rolled with clean, white muslin or tissue paper separating each layer.

Fur garments need to be stored in a cool, dark place. Cover fur with clean, white muslin. However when storing fur, professional cold storage is best.

Wool should be thoroughly cleaned, padded and wrapped in white tissue. Add mothballs to the storage area to prevent moth damage.

More Storage Tips:

- When storing garments, use a chemical desiccant to absorb moisture and prevent mildew. Do not let the desiccant touch the garments. Examples of chemical desiccant are calcium chloride or silica gel.
- Reduce dampness in closets by tying pieces of chalk together and hanging them from a support post or from the ceiling.
- If the weather in your area is cool and dry, be sure your storage areas are well ventilated.

- Always store garments loosely so they can breathe and air can circulate. Never use fabric finish or starch on garments that are to be stored.
- Protect clothing from wood acid by lining dresser drawers with an acid free shelf paper or quilted fabric. Never use wallpaper remnants or gummed shelf paper. The backing will attract insects to your clothing.
- Always clean garments that are to be stored. Insects are attracted to drink, food and perspiration.
- Areas where garments are stored should be dark and clean. Light fades colors and attracts insects.
- Never store clothing in a cold basement or hot attic. Extreme temperatures damage clothes.
- Cotton, linen, silk and wool are all natural fibres. Always store these in a well ventilated area.
- To rid garments of wrinkles when they come out of storage, put them in the dryer on the fluff or air cycle that has no heat.
- When adding mothballs to a storage area, place them in an old sock so they don't touch the garments.
- The beauty in cedar is its natural resistance to insects, especially moths. With a cedar-lined closet there will be no more need for toxic (and awful smelling) mothballs. One thing to remember though is that cedar will have to be lightly sanded periodically, in order to release its fragrance which is what maintains its bug deterrent factor.

"If you want to repel moths, other insects, odours and moisture, you should line your closet with cedar or invest in cedar hangers".

<u>My Special Tips</u>

Chapter Six

Pets

"The difference between friends and pets
is that friends we allow into our company,
pets we allow into our solitude."

—*Robert Brault*

~°~°~°~°~°~°~°~°~°~°~°~°

To remove burrs crush with a pair of pliers and work oil into the tangle. The burrs should then brush out easily.

~°~°~°~°~°~°~°~°~°~°~°~°

If you don't want your cat up on the upholstery, put a few mothballs in the cushions.

~°~°~°~°~°~°~°~°~°~°~°~°

"A house is not a home without a pet."

—*Anonymous*

~°~°~°~°~°~°~°~°~°~°~°~°

Put fresh pine needles under your dog's bed to keep fleas away.

~°~°~°~°~°~°~°~°~°~°~°~°~°

When your dog makes a mess, first blot the excess moisture with paper towels. Then sponge with vinegar and blot again. Pour club soda over the spot, cover with a paper towel and weigh down with a heavy flat object. When the towel is wet, replace it with a dry one and repeat until the spot is dry. This method works for cat messes also. But sprinkle on a bit of ammonia—cats hate the smell and will never go on that spot again.

~°~°~°~°~°~°~°~°~°~°~°~°~°

Fresh urine stains: Blot with an ammonia solution, then with a detergent solution. Rinse with warm water. If it has been on for more than 24 hours, blot with a vinegar solution and then the detergent solution.

~°~°~°~°~°~°~°~°~°~°~°~°~°

Vomit: scrape up as much as possible. Blot with a detergent solution. If a stain remains use an ammonia solution.

~°~°~°~°~°~°~°~°~°~°~°~°~°

Doggy Paws: When the pads become shiny and their foot pads get worn down, soak them for 20 minutes in Coca Cola. This prevents the pads from getting too much wear

~°~°~°~°~°~°~°~°~°~°~°~°~°

Itchy Pooch: Dab some apple cider vinegar onto the spot. That should take the itch away.

~°~°~°~°~°~°~°~°~°~°~°~°

"My little dog.a heartbeat at my feet."

—Edith Wharton

~°~°~°~°~°~°~°~°~°~°~°~°

Doggy Breath: If doggy breath is a problem for your pet, just mix some parsley in with his food once a day

~°~°~°~°~°~°~°~°~°~°~°~°

Constipation: When your dog gets constipation you can give it 1-2 teaspoons of pumpkin, not the pie filling just the pure pumpkin. It will regulate their system.

~°~°~°~°~°~°~°~°~°~°~°~°

Baking soda works wonders for pet odours. Sprinkle ¼-½ cup of baking soda onto the carpet and vacuum it up. Repeat every time you replace your vacuum bag.

~°~°~°~°~°~°~°~°~°~°~°~°

Get rid of pet hair on upholstery effortlessly by wiping the furniture with a slightly dampened sponge.

~°~°~°~°~°~°~°~°~°~°~°~°

*"An animal's eyes have the power
to speak a great language."*

—*Martin Buber*

~°~°~°~°~°~°~°~°~°~°~°~°~°

$4,000

Cost of recycling 1 ton of plastic bags

~°~°~°~°~°~°~°~°~°~°~°~°~°

For a safe, fun road trip:

- **Make sure your pet is fit for traveling.** Older pets in particular, or those who have medical conditions, should be examined by a vet prior to travel. If your pet shouldn't travel, or doesn't enjoy it, find a responsible and trusted kennel or pet-sitter.
- **Take frequent rest stops** so that you and your pet can stretch your legs and take a bathroom break. Pets have been known to escape out the car door, so be sure he is securely restrained before opening the door.
- **Keep your pet in the back seat.** It's safer for both you and him, and will help to prevent him from distracting the driver or getting in the way in case the driver needs to perform some emergency manoeuvring.

Please don't allow your pet to ride in the open bed of a pickup truck, even if leashed—many dogs have jumped or been thrown from the truck and suffered serious injury and even death.

- **Consider the use of a restraint** such as a kennel or a pet seat-belt. It will offer extra protection in case of an accident, as well as prevent nervous or excitable pets from distracting the driver.

- **Don't let your pooch hang his head out the window.** Flying debris can be kicked up from tires or it can fall off the car or truck in front of you. Any of this may hit your pet and can cause injury.

- **Offer water regularly.** Pets can become dehydrated, just like we can. Keep a supply of cool water and a dish in the car. You can even freeze small containers of water for travel.

- **Keep your pet comfortable.** In cold weather, pets should have adequate warmth at all times and thus should not be left alone in the car for extended periods. In warm weather, be aware that even a few minutes in a hot car can cause serious damage. It can even be fatal! Consider alternatives such as having a picnic instead of eating in a restaurant, or take turns staying with your pet if he cannot accompany you on an activity.

~°~°~°~°~°~°~°~°~°~°~°~°

To dry bathe your dog or cat, sprinkle your pet's coat with baking soda, then give the coat a good rubdown with your hands. Next, use a gentle brush to spread the baking soda throughout the coat until the baking soda is gone. And since it is nontoxic, there's no need to worry if your pet takes a liking to its taste.

~°~°~°~°~°~°~°~°~°~°~°~°

Fishy Fish Tank:

When it's time to clean out the fish tank, clean the inside of the glass with plain non-iodized salt by sprinkling it onto a damp sponge and scrubbing. This will remove hard water deposits or other build-up on the glass. Rinse everything well before returning the fish to the tank.

~°~°~°~°~°~°~°~°~°~°~°

"There is no psychiatrist in the world like a puppy licking your face."

—*Ben Williams*

~°~°~°~°~°~°~°~°~°~°~°

<u>Pet Travel Checklist:</u>

- **Medications.** Before you leave, consult with your vet. Ensure your pet is in good physical health before you travel. Pick up refills of any medications your pet will need while you are away . . . and find out whether or not there are any concerns about the area to which you are traveling. For example, common medications include flea and tick control, and heartworm pills.
- **Kennel or carrier.** Some places ask that you kennel your pet if you are going out and leaving him in the room. The kennel is also a safe way for your pet to travel. Please don't let your dog ride loose in the back of a pickup truck; he could fall out and suffer serious injuries. Be sure the crate is well-padded!

- **Food and water bowls.**
- **Food (and even some water)!** Keeping your pet on the same diet that he's accustomed to will help to prevent the dreaded "messy butt" or vomiting. If your pet has a sensitive stomach, you may also want to bring water.
- **Can opener**—if your pet likes canned food.
- **Stain remover/cleaning supplies** . . . just in case! Please be courteous and clean up as much pet hair, etc. as you can. A good quality lint brush or pet hair roller is always useful!
- **Plastic bags, or litter box/scoop** so that you can clean up after your pet.
- **Grooming tools**—including a comb and/or brush, nail clippers, pet shampoo, and anything else your pet may need. *Do not groom your pet inside your accommodation. Do it outdoors, away from other guests and rooms, and clean up immediately.*
- **Extra towels**—for wiping those muddy paws and wet or dirty bodies!
- **Collar and leash(es).** Consider bringing an extra leash just in case one of them breaks.
- **Comfortable bedding.** Bring along whatever your pet is accustomed to, and what smells like "home".

~°~°~°~°~°~°~°~°~°~°~°

"No heaven will not ever Heaven be;
Unless my cats are there to welcome me."

—Anonymous

~°~°~°~°~°~°~°~°~°~°~°

My Special Tips

Chapter Seven

Garden

"Even a mistake may turn out to be the one thing necessary to a worthwhile achievement."

—*Henry Ford*

FYI: Ants prefer not to walk through baby powder!

Natural Insecticide: Add onions and garlic to a jar of water, let it stand for a week, and spray plants with it.

~°~°~°~°~°~°~°~°~°~°~°

Weeds in your Garden: Spray or pour apple cider vinegar on weeds and they will be done for the next day. But do not pour or spray on or around any plant you do not wish to destroy.

~°~°~°~°~°~°~°~°~°~°~°

Reuse empty plastic bottles by cutting them in half, fill one half with soil and plant seedlings, fit the other half back over the top and you have a mini greenhouse.

~°~°~°~°~°~°~°~°~°~°~°~°~°~°

*"Did you know you can make pesticide for plants
by boiling water and adding Rosemary? Works great on ants
and other pests."*

~°~°~°~°~°~°~°~°~°~°~°~°~°~°

*"Every gardener knows
that under the cloak of winter lies a miracle . . .
a seed waiting to sprout,
a bulb opening to the light,
a bud straining to unfurl.
And the anticipation nurtures our dream."*

—Barbara Winkler

~°~°~°~°~°~°~°~°~°~°~°~°~°~°

*"Did you know that Vaseline around a garden pot
can detour snails, slugs?"*

~°~°~°~°~°~°~°~°~°~°~°~°~°~°

Less than 1 percent

Amount of plastic bags that are recycled

~°~°~°~°~°~°~°~°~°~°~°~°~°~°

Dog pee kills grass: Twice a day put one tablespoon of tomato juice in with your dog's food. The harmful acid in the pee is neutralised, which means that the grass is not killed. (This does not harm the dog!)

~°~°~°~°~°~°~°~°~°~°~°~°

Slugs & snails: Tempt them away from plants with the skins of oranges and grapefruits.

Or

Spray WD-40 on pots—they don't like crawling through it!

~°~°~°~°~°~°~°~°~°~°~°~°

Ants: Treat them with a sprinkling of one part sugar with one part Borax crystals.

~°~°~°~°~°~°~°~°~°~°~°~°

Garden tools: The late fall is the time to time to oil and clean the lawn mower and other machinery. Brush on clean engine oil or lightly spray with WD40

~°~°~°~°~°~°~°~°~°~°~°~°

Take a bucket into the shower with you to use the water for the garden. You can then feel no guilt whatsoever when you use it for watering your plants

~°~°~°~°~°~°~°~°~°~°~°~°

"When leaves show their undersides, a sure thing the rain betides"

<u>Seed Bombs—Guerrilla Gardening:</u>

<u>Seed Ball Recipe:</u> 5 parts dry clay

3 parts dry organic compost
1 part seed
1-2 parts water

Mix ingredients into a sticky conglomerate. Roll the seed ball mixture into balls 1-2 inches in diameter. Be prepared to get messy! Set aside to dry on cookie sheets for a few days before storing or using.

Seed balls are great for reclaiming derelict areas making them ideal spaces for guerrilla gardening. Seed balls can be placed wherever by tossing, placing or sling shot into empty or neglected areas.

Enjoy the results!!

Tips/Facts on wildflower gardening:

If you have a large area, fill in grasses to discourage weeds, and to give it a wild look.

Since the garden would include perennials, which take a year to bloom at the start of the garden, over seeding helps to balance the garden. Do this whenever you see an imbalance in the garden, either due to bad weather or other such causes.

While designing your garden, check for the specific points:

- the blooming period.
- the height it grows up to

- the sowing depth
- the growing time
- the color to formulate a color scheme

~°~°~°~°~°~°~°~°~°~°~°

Keep cutworms away from seedlings with the cardboard centers of toilet paper rolls. Cutworms, which are moth caterpillars, creep along the soil surface, eating tender stem bases of young seedlings and cutting sprouts off at the roots.

Or

Place a small stick close to the tender stem so the cutworm can't wrap around the plant.

~°~°~°~°~°~°~°~°~°~°~°

*"Winter'sdone,andApril'sintheskies,
Earth,lookupwithlaughterinyoureyes!"*

—CharlesG.D.Roberts

~°~°~°~°~°~°~°~°~°~°~°

Use <u>newspaper</u> covered with straw between garden rows to eliminate weeds and retain moisture. This dynamic duo works more efficiently together than either one alone. At the end of the growing season, roto-till the paper and straw into the soil to decay.

~°~°~°~°~°~°~°~°~°~°~°

"When dew is on the grass, rain will never come to pass."

Deer Resistant Perennial Plants:

Achillea_(Yarrow)

Yarrow is such a garden workhorse. It's drought tolerant. It repeat blooms. It makes a nice cut flower. And it's deer resistant. The old adage that deer don't like plants with fuzzy leaves, gray leaves or scented leaves applies here.

Ajuga_(Bugleweed)

Ground covers don't often get respect and Ajuga basically grows itself, so it really gets taken for granted. But there are many really nice newer cultivars of Ajuga that are worth taking a look at. They come with colourful foliage, so once the spectacular burst of blue is gone in the spring, you still have great foliage. Many Ajugas can spread to the point of annoyance, but if you have room to let them roam, it's a great, deer resistant plant.

Astilbe

A word of caution: Deer don't particularly like Astilbe, but groundhogs love it. However aside from groundhogs, Astilbe have very few problems. They don't need staking or deadheading. They're fine in sun or partial shade. And there are varieties that bloom at different times in the season, to extend your bloom.

Campanula_(Bellflower)

Bellflowers look so delicate with the pastel coloured, bell-shaped blossoms. For the most part, bellflowers can look after themselves. Many varieties will self-seed throughout your garden, making them ideal cottage garden plants. And the deer don't seem nearly as enchanted with them as gardeners are.

Coreopsis_(Tickseed)

Coreopsis has been a garden staple for years, but the introduction of buttery yellow Coreopsis 'Moon-bean' made it a garden favorite. Unfortunately 'Moon-bean' is rather short lived and can be temperamental. But plant breeders have continually developed new varieties of Coreopsis with hardier constitutions and still boasting deer resistant.

Echinacea_(Coneflower)

You'll notice I didn't say purple coneflower. It's hard to find a garden without purple coneflowers in it. They're dependable favourites. But coneflowers have moved way beyond purple with the introduction of orange, red, burgundy and russet coneflowers. These new varieties are also deer resistant. The main drawback to using them is they are still so expensive to purchase and they've haven't been fully tested in a wide range of gardening situations. Still, they are hard to resist.

Lavendula_(Lavender)

You don't need to be told that lavender is deer resistant. The real surprise may be how adaptable lavender is. Cooler climates may never get their lavender to grow into a hedge, but it will return year after year. And tropical climates who can provide regular water will be able to enjoy it too. Seems like only the deer will have to do without lavender.

Nepeta_(Catmint)

Catmint may call every feline in the neighbourhood to your garden, but it won't impress the deer. Some varieties can be weedy and self-seed aggressively, but if you stick with some of the newer cultivars, you'll have vivid blue color most of the season. Shear it back after the first flowering and wait for it to burst into bloom again. Just keep the cats from rolling all over it.

Perovski_(Russian_Sage)

Russian Sage is often suggested as a lavender alternative, but I think you should grow Russian Sage for its own merits. The foliage isn't just gray, fuzzy and scented, it's lacy and attractive. The flowers start out a soft pale blue and just keep getting more vibrant as they mature and open fully. And the only maintenance is a pruning in the spring.

Platycodon_(Balloon_Flower)

Balloon Flower is a plant many people remember from their childhood. Those expectant puffs that suddenly pop open into lavender blue flowers were too tempting to resist helping along. If you've outgrown the need to pop balloon flower buds, you'll be happy to know that they are perfectly capable of opening on their own and they are quite deer resistant, too.

Solidago (Goldenrod)

If you still think of goldenrod as a weedy plant that makes you sneeze, think again. Something this hardy had to be cultivated and it was, many times. There are now some spectacular goldenrods that are well behaved enough to invite into your garden. What's especially nice about goldenrod is how late in the season it blooms. Just when you think the garden is done for the year, golden showers burst forth.

Stachys_byzantina_(Lamb's_Ear)

Lamb's ear, another gray, fuzzy-leaved plant that deer avoid, is often forgotten by gardeners. Lamb's ear isn't going to be a show stopper in your garden, but it sure makes for a nice edge. And the silver gray leaves have an almost glowing quality. Usually soft pastel colors disappear at a distance, but lamb's ear demands to be noticed, except by deer.

Deer Resistant Spring and Early Summer Flowering Bulbs:

ALLIUM

Ornamental onions are among the most deer resistant flowering bulbs. The most commonly know alliums have pom pom like blossoms on top of single, straight stalks. There is, however, a fair amount of variation in the species. Allium schubertii looks like a fireworks sparkler. Others, like Allium unifolium and Allium bulgaricum are bell shaped. You can find alliums in almost every color and height and their bloom times vary throughout the season. Allium are also rodent resistant.

- Height: Varies (4"-4')
- Bloom Time: Late Spring—Early Summer
- Exposure: Full Sun
- Zones: 4-9

CROCUS

The bright colors of crocus are a welcome sign that the soil is starting to warm. Crocus will even bloom in the snow. This versatile little spreader can be used as a ground cover or as an accent. Plant a few by your mail box to make the walk down to collect your mail worth it.

- Height: 4"
- Bloom Time: Early Spring
- Exposure: Full Sun to Partial Shade
- Zones 3-9

DWARF IRIS (Iris reticulata)

You get the familiar iris flower on a low growing, spreading plant that blooms early in the season. What's not to like. You can find Iris reticulata in blues, purples and white. They all blend extremely well with other spring bloomers.

- Height: 4-6"
- Bloom Time: Early Spring
- Exposure: Full Sun to Partial Shade
- Zones: 5-9

EARLY STARDRIFT (Puschkinia libanotica)

Another of spring's blue offerings, this time in a pastel powder blue. Puschkinia makes a nice addition to the border, but it also works well when allowed to naturalize and spread.

- Height: 4-6"
- Bloom Time: Early Spring

- Exposure: Sun to Partial Shade
- Zones 3-7

Fritillaria

Fritillaria add a touch of drama to your spring garden. From the dramatic, loud colours of 'Crown Imperial', to the speckles of 'Guinea Hens' (Fritillaria meleagris), the deep purple of Fritillaria persica, the bi-colors and the creamy white 'Ivory Bells", Fritillaria will be noticed. They look exotic, but they are fuss-free, easy growers. Fritillaria are also rodent resistant.

- Height: Varies (10-24")
- Bloom Time: Mid-Spring
- Exposure: Full Sun to Shade
- Zones: 4-9

GLORY OF THE SNOW (Chinodoxa forbesii)

Similar to Scilla siberica, Glory of the Snow works best as a ground cover or naturalized in the lawn. Each bulb provides multiple blue, star-shaped blossoms with white centers, that start to bloom as the snow is melting.

- Height: 4-8"
- Bloom Time: Early Spring
- Exposure: Full Sun to Partial Shade
- Zones: 3-9

GRAPE HYACINTH (Muscari)

Sweet fragrance and a brilliant blue color have made Grape Hyacinth long standing favourites. This is the perfect little bulb for massing under trees that haven't yet leafed out. And it doesn't take many bulbs to rapidly spread into a mass planting.

- Height: 4-7"
- Bloom Time: Mid-Spring
- Exposure: Full Sun to Partial Shade
- Zones: 3-9

LILY OF THE VALLEY (Convallaria majalis)

These aren't really bulbs, they're rhizomes with buds on them, called pips. But Lily of the Valley are often grouped in with the spring bulbs because they bloom early and then disappear for the season and they like to spread and naturalize. More to our point, the deer don't like them. And the fragrance of Lily of the Valley can fill the air. The common variety is dainty white bells, but there is also a pink Lily of the Valley.

- Height: 6-12"
- Bloom Time: Late Spring
- Exposure: Partial Shade
- Zones: 3-7

SCILLA, SQUILL or STAR OF HOLLAND (Scilla siberica)

These little charmers work best when allowed to naturalize in the lawn. They surprise you every year with a carpet of dazzling blue. If you find yourself looking out the window, searching for signs of spring, scilla won't disappoint.

- Height: 4-6"
- Bloom Time: Early Spring

- Exposure: Sun to Partial Shade
- Zones 1-9

SNOWDROPS (Galanthus nivalis)

They look like snowdrops and they bloom while the snow is still dropping. If Galanthus has a drawback, it's that it can't take any heat. But just like crocus, Galanthus lets us know that ground is warming. Plant them near a door or walkway for the best view.

- Height: 4-6"
- Bloom Time: Very Early Spring
- Exposure: Sun
- Zones: 3-9

WINTER ACONITE (Eranthis cilicica)

With its upturned petals and down turned foliage, Eranthis can form a thick clump fast. The yellow flowers generally bloom at the same time as Scilla and dwarf iris and make a nice complement.

- Height: 2-4"
- Bloom Time: Early Spring
- Exposure: Full Sun to Partial Shade
- Zones: 4-7

~°~°~°~°~°~°~°~°~°~°~°~°~°

*"QueerthingshappeninthegardeninMay.
Littlefacesforgottenappear, andplantsthoughttobedead
suddenlywaveagreenhandtoconfoundyou"*

—*W.E.Johns*

~°~°~°~°~°~°~°~°~°~°~°~°~°

Perennial Vegetables anyone can grow:

Asparagus

Grows best in full sun and non-soggy, somewhat sandy soil. I like it cut into one-inch pieces and stir fried raw with sesame oil and a little sliced ginger (top with toasted sesame seeds). Or, brush with olive oil and crushed garlic and grill whole spears on the bar-q.

Bamboo Shoots

We have a good-sized stand of bamboo that was on the property when we moved here, so I guess bamboo will be my contribution to the lineage of Yeager Roots. Not all varieties of bamboo shoots are edible (or tasty), so do your homework first. We boil ours to remove the bitterness, then sauté them in butter and a little sherry or sweet vermouth for flavour. Also, be advised that many varieties of bamboo are highly invasive and can be toxic if eaten in large amounts.

Bunching Onions

This is a variety of onion that grows in clumps and multiplies on its own, and they are hardy in the ground even in fairly cold climates. The bulbs themselves are fairly small and pinkish in color. I like to pickle them as something a little unusual for the relish tray . . . or in the martini glass.

Garlic

As the saying goes, "If your lover doesn't like garlic, get a new lover." Garlic is a healthful perennial, although it's often grown and harvested as an annual. I like to rub a whole head of unpeeled garlic with olive oil, wrap it in <u>aluminum foil</u>, and stick it in the oven or on the grill for an hour or so when I'm cooking something else; squirt the warm, creamy pulp of each clove onto a cracker or piece of bread for a heavenly appetizer.

Horseradish

As long as you harvest just the side roots, horseradish taproots will continue to produce a new harvest every year. To use as a condiment, clean and peel roots; cut into small chunks, and grind in a blender or food processor with a little water to the desired consistency. Add 1/2 teaspoon of salt for each cup of blended horseradish, and 2 or 3 tablespoons of white vinegar; seal and store in the refrigerator.

Kale and Collard Greens

Perennial varieties will grow in many climates, and are among the healthiest of all vegetables. I eat greens at least once a week, and find that the secret is to not overcook them. Chop greens into half-inch strips and plunge into a pot of boiling, salted water for 10-15 minutes; remove and dress with butter/ olive oil, vinegar/lemon juice and salt or feta cheese. And you thought you didn't like greens. (Kale is a super food.

Radicchio

Think you can't grow any perennial vegetables in your garden? Don't be radicchio! Seriously, radicchio (aka "Italian chicory") will come back every year in most climates if you don't dig it up for blanching, as some chefs do. I like to add young, raw leaves to spice up a tossed salad, or grill older bunches (brushed with olive oil) to remove some of the bitterness.

Rhubarb

Prefers colder climates, well-drained soil, and part-shade. Strawberry-rhubarb pie is hard to beat, but I also like to make rhubarb sauce instead of apple sauce: Cook two cups of inch-long pieces of cut up rhubarb stems in one-half cup of water until totally broken down, then add sugar and cinnamon to taste.

~°~°~°~°~°~°~°~°~°~°~°

Got seeds? A Seed_Savers_Exchange isn't just about vegetables; there's an affiliated Flower and Herb exchange, too. Got flowers?

~°~°~°~°~°~°~°~°~°~°~°

Pest problems!!

Home grown herbs are wonderful in sauces and salads; they also keep away many common garden pests. Use this guide for planting herbs next to specific vegetables:

Basil by tomatoes, asparagus

Mint, sage, dill, thyme by cabbage, cauliflower, broccoli and brussel sprouts.

Onions and garlic by carrots and beets.

Carrots by marigolds, sage, thyme and rosemary

Horseradish by potatoes

Marigolds, anise and coriander anywhere in the garden.

Dust a little talcum powder around your plants to keep rabbits and flea beetles away.

Spray soapsuds around your plants to keep most insects away.

~°~°~°~°~°~°~°~°~°~°~°~°

Organic Fungicide:

- A strong brew of chamomile or cinnamon tea. Use it to water and/or mist your seedlings.
- A splash 1 tablespoon of 3% solution of hydrogen peroxide/ qt. water as a seedling mist.
- A dusting of cinnamon on the soil surface.

~°~°~°~°~°~°~°~°~°~°~°~°

How to Prevent Damping Off:

- Damping off is a term used for seedling death by any of a handful of fungal diseases, including several root rots (Pythium, Phytophthora) and molds (Sclerotinia or white mold, Botrytis or gray mold).
- Use a sterile <u>potting mix</u>, rather than soil from your garden. Outdoor soil can harbour fungus spores.

- Start with clean pots. If reusing pots, sterilize in 1 part beach to 10 parts water.
- Plant your seeds at the proper depth. Don't bury the plant's crown.
- Don't crowd your seedlings. Be sure to leave room between them for air circulation.
- Water seedlings from the bottom.
- Top potting mix with a thin coating of sand or gravel, to keep the surface relatively dry.
- Don't over water your seedlings or leave them sitting in water.
- If possible, create a breeze by placing a small fan nearby and tuning it on periodically each day.
- Give your seedlings plenty of heat and light, so they germinate and grow quickly. Damping off only affects seedlings.
- Remove any affected plants or trays of plants immediately.

"Wind in the east, good for neither man nor beast."

Hard Working Gardeners:

Homemade Salt Scrub

Wide-mouth, shallow Mason jar
¾ cup coarse sea salt
¼ cup sesame or olive oil
2 tablespoons dry lavender blossoms
1 teaspoon baking soda

Add salt to Mason jar. Sprinkle baking soda and lavender and dry blend. Add in oil, mix thoroughly. Once the mixture is blended, store in the fridge for up to six weeks.

How to use the salt scrub:

Remove jewellery, scoop a palm-sized amount onto your hand and rub the mixture over both hands gently for 15 seconds to exfoliate the dirt. Follow up with a quick soap rinse and your favourite moisturizer.

~°~°~°~°~°~°~°~°~°~°~°~°

Chopsticks and Popsicle sticks make terrific splints for leaning plants

~°~°~°~°~°~°~°~°~°~°~°~°

Compost Tea:

Compost tea is very good for the garden, offering nutrients, beneficial bacteria and micro organisms.

The general guideline is 32 litres of compost or manure per large garbage can of water. Let it steep for a few days and then apply to plants. You can make a large tea bag by placing compost in a burlap bag.

~°~°~°~°~°~°~°~°~°~°~°~°

Over watering is the number one cause for perennial death

~°~°~°~°~°~°~°~°~°~°~°~°

Getting plant seeds for little or no cost:

- **Saving the seeds from store-bought produce.** It's amazing how often this works and yet how few people do it.

- **Seed swaps.** Various clubs and cliques of gardening enthusiasts hold "<u>seed exchanges</u>" or "seed swaps," in which a group of like-minded individuals get together to trade seeds.

- **Saving the seeds from the plants we planted last year.** We always try to let at least one plant of each type "bolt" and go to seed, so we can save its seeds and start the cycle all over again the following year.

- **Get old packets of seeds for free or cheap, then plant more than you need, taking into account the fact that only half of the seeds at most will ever sprout.**

- **Seed sales at discount stores.** If you're lucky, you can catch the right moment when some discount supermarkets drastically lower the prices of already-cheap seed packets as they approach their expiration date.

- **Buying expired and old seed packets at garage sales for very little money.** Old seed packets don't crop up too often at sales, but when they do, you can often get them for ten cents or twenty-five cents a packet.

~°~°~°~°~°~°~°~°~°~°~°~°~°

Sunflower and marigold seeds from dead plants can be dried out, then placed in a glass jar with a lid. In the spring, you can start new plants by placing in a pot or long-length planter and covering with plastic.

~°~°~°~°~°~°~°~°~°~°~°~°~°

Plant your garden with flowers and features that attract birds, butterflies and other beneficial insects and animals. They help to naturally protect your garden from pesky insects. Ladybugs eat soft bellied bugs like aphids and praying mantises eat leaf hopping bugs like grass hoppers and Japanese beetles. Releasing nematodes will take care of the grubs that destroy your lawn. Make sure you plant in layers to attract the right visitors into your garden!

~°~°~°~°~°~°~°~°~°~°~°~°~°

High Yield Vegetables:

Indeterminate Tomatoes, so named because the vines keep getting bigger and producing new fruit until they are felled by frost.

Non-Hybrid Pole Beans. Like indeterminate tomatoes, old-fashioned pole beans keep growing and producing 'til frost—assuming you keep them picked.

Zucchini. Everything they say about avalanches of zucchini is true, especially of hybrid varieties, none of which unfortunately is as delicious as <u>Costata Romanesco</u>.

Swiss Chard. Plants hold without bolting from spring through fall in all but the hottest summer areas

Garlic. You plant it in the fall, after most of the garden chores are over; you can get a lot of it into a small space; and it's beyond simple to plant: Just separate the garlic cloves, shove 'em into the prepared soil, root end down and mulch the bed with straw.

Tall varieties of **Snow Peas and Sugar_snaps** squeeze onto the list because they're so easy to pick and prepare

~°~°~°~°~°~°~°~°~°~°~°~°~°

Planting Garlic:

Growing garlic starts with knowing when to plant it. But planting itself is incredibly easy:

In mid-fall plant garlic bulbs in loose, very fertile soil that's as weed-free as possible. Insert cloves root side down about 8 inches apart in all directions (if space is limited, you can squeeze by with 6), burying the tips about two inches down. Green shoots will come up; mulch around them with straw. Hard freeze will come and kill the shoots. Draw the mulch over the whole bed.

In spring, pull the mulch back when the new shoots emerge. Give them a shot of mixed fish emulsion and liquid seaweed. Keep them weeded. Water only if the soil is dry two or more inches down, being sure to avoid pouring water into the crowns of the plants.

Harvesting Garlic:

When to harvest garlic depends on the type. Garlic varieties are divided into early, midseason and late, but what that means depends not only on your climate zone but also on your climate in the growing year. Heat speeds 'em up, cold slows 'em down, and although the harvest window is wide if you plan to eat the garlic fresh, it's narrow if you want to ensure maximum storage life.

The bulbs are ready when most of the lower leaves have browned. The upper ones will still be green. If you've ever grown onions, it's easy to assume garlic is the same and you should wait until all the leaves have fallen over. Bad idea. By the time all the leaves are dead the bulbs will have split; they won't have the leaf sheaths they need to form wrappers and it's likely fungus disease will have found a way in.

"Lift the bulbs" is usually used to describe moving things like daffodils, but it's also a good way to think about harvesting garlic. Those heads are more delicate than they seem and any cut or bruise will shorten storage life.

Try to choose an overcast day when the soil is dry. Loosen the soil with a digging fork, inserting it well away from the heads, then lift them out of the row and place them in a flat carrier.

Curing Garlic:

Let the whole plants dry in a single layer somewhere out of the sun where it's warm but not hot. When the outer skin is papery, brush off as much dirt as possible and clip the roots. Rush this a bit if you're braiding garlic stems; if you wait until they're *completely* dry they tend to crack and break.

The finished garlic will still be on the dirty side compared to anything commercial. We leave it that way until we want to use it because further cleanup can shorten storage life

Plants for common birds:

Highbush blueberry: *Vaccinium corymbosum* (shrub) attracts 30 species of birds including: American Robin, Eastern Bluebird, Scarlet Tanager, Eastern and Spotted Towhees, Gray Catbird, Northern Mockingbird, Brown Thrasher and Northern Cardinal.

Eastern red Cedar: *Juniperis virginiana* (tree)—attracts many birds including Cedar Waxwing, Northern Mockingbird, Brown Thrasher, Gray Catbird, Cedar Waxwing, Ruffed Grouse, American Robin, Morning Dove, Purple Finch, Common Crow, Northern Flicker, Downy Woodpecker, Evening Grosbeak, Yellow-bellied Sapsucker and Eastern Bluebird.

Southeast:

Arrowwood Viburnum: *Viburnum denyayum* (shrub) attracts species including Eastern Bluebird, Northern Flicker, Gray Catbird and American Robin.

Southern Magnolia:*Magnolia grandiflora* (tree)—attracts species including Eastern Kingbird, Northern Mockingbird, Northern Flicker,Red-belled Woodpecker and Wood Thrush.

Central Plains and Prairies:

Big bluestem:*Andropogon gerardi* (graminiod/ grass) provides cover for at least 24 species of songbirds and nesting site or seeds for Grasshopper, Henslow;s and other sparrows as well as nesting sites for Sedge Wren and Western Medowlark.

Gray Dogwood: *Cornus racemosa* (tree)—Used by many species including Northern Cardinal, Downy Woodpecker, Northern Flicker and Eastern Bluebird.

Western Mountains and Deserts:

Mesquite: *Prosopis grandulosa v. Torr* (Western Honey Mesquite, tree) attracts species including Curved—bill Thrasher, Gambel's Quail and White—winged Dove

Rocky Mountain Juniper: *Juniperus scopulorum* (shrub) attracts Cedar Waxwings, Northern Mockingbird and Evening Grosbecks as well as other species.

Pacific Coast:

California Wax Myrtle: *Myrica californica* (shrub) attracts Northern Flicker, Chestnut-backed Chickadee, Yellow-rumped Warbler, Tree Swallow, California Towhee and Spotted Towhee among others.

California Live Oak: *Quercus agrifolia* (tree) attracts Oak Titmouse, Western Scrub Jay, Stellar's Jay, Chestnut-backed Chickadee and about 30 other species of birds.

~°~°~°~°~°~°~°~°~°~°~°

Grow a tropical lemon tree in a container:

- It's important to choose the right size container for your tree. For a 2-3 year-old tree, we recommend at least a 5 gallon pot to start with. Make sure the pot has a drain hole in the bottom, and begin with a bottom layer of stones and rocks to ensure proper drainage. Add a good quality peat-moss based growing mix that is sandy and slightly acidic, which is preferred by citrus. Put in just enough soil so the root ball is barely covered and make sure the trunk remains above the soil line to avoid rotting.

- Select an area on your patio that receives full sun; these trees need plenty of light, so a southern exposure is best. If possible, the area should be somewhat protected from fierce winds as well.

- Consistent watering is fundamental to the success of a container-grown lemon tree. Citrus trees require soil that is moist but never soggy. When the surface of the soil becomes dry it's time to water, but never allow your lemon tree to sit in standing drainage water.

- Feed your tree at regular intervals with a water-soluble fertilizer, specifically suited to container-grown tropical citrus trees.

- Occasional pruning may become necessary to maintain desired size and shape. Well-pruned trees have stronger branches and will produce a more generous crop of lemons.

~°~°~°~°~°~°~°~°~°~°~°~°~°

Garden Remedies:

Massage away the pain of a headache:

¼ cup almond oil
20 drops of rosemary oil
20 drops of lavender oil
30 drops of peppermint oil

Mix thoroughly and gently massage temples and forehead with the mixture. Place a small amount near your nostrils and inhale this relaxing scent. This should bring relief for most headaches. If the pain persists; massage the back of your neck and fleshy area between your thumb and index finger as well. *Notify your doctor of any headaches that are unusual.*

Cold and Flu Thyme:

Add one grated onion and two tablespoons of thyme leaves into two cups of boiling water. Let steep for ½ hour. Strain and add lemon.

Bee balm for a clear complexion :

Pour boiling water over bee balm leaves and let steep. Apply to skin externally. Bee balm has an aromatic fragrance.

Onion Juice for Asthma:

Onions contain compounds that relax the bronchial muscles and prevent spasms. You will need to mix 2 ounces of onion juice and 2 ounces of carrot juice with 2 ounces of parsley juice. Drink twice a day. *This is to be used in conjunction with the supervision of a physician. Proper medical treatment is suggested.*

Sage for Fever:

Boil sage leaves (approximately 1 tablespoon to a cup of boiling water). Cover, and steep approximately ten minutes. Drink ½ cup no more than 3 times throughout the day.

Lemon juice and honey can be added for flavour. *Pregnant or breastfeeding women should avoid sage.*

Rosemary Toothpowder:

Rosemary has antibacterial effects. You can burn the stems of rosemary and grind the coals into a powder. Brush teeth with this powder. *This won't do anything for your breath but you can eat parsley to neutralize mouth odour.*

Keep nasty colds and flu bugs at bay:

Make an effort to ensure you are getting enough vitamin C on a daily basis. For a daily cup of prevention try drinking a cup of this tea. Soak two cups of rose hips in eight cups of water overnight. Strain; then heat liquid till warm, drink as tea. Add a teaspoon of honey (optional)

Listing of Sea Buckthorn Health Benefits:

Sea buckthorn, a plant which produces the orange-coloured sea buckthorn berry, and is grown primarily in the mountainous and colder regions of China, Russia and Canada, is rapidly becoming popular throughout the world for the hundreds of potential benefits it provides, both nutritionally and medicinally. Whether taken internally, in the form of a juice, tea or supplement, or applied topically to the skin in oil, lotion or cream form, sea buckthorn is beginning to earn a reputation as a "super fruit" for its ability to both heal and prevent a wide array of illnesses and conditions.

- **Acne**: The anti-inflammatory agents in sea buckthorn, such as quercetin and salycins, together with the immune boosting fatty acids mentioned above, work in harmony to help address the 3 main culprits of acne: immune system, hormone imbalances and chronic inflammation.

- **Anti-aging**: Rich in vitamin A and vitamin E, sea buckthorn can help reduce the appearance of wrinkles and retard premature skin maturation.

- **Chemotherapy**: The flavonoids in sea buckthorn can help cancer patients recover more rapidly from the effects of radiation and chemotherapy treatment.

- **Cardiovascular benefits**: Sea buckthorn is rich in unsaturated fatty acids, including omega-3, omega-6, omega-7 and omega-9 oils, which experts believe can significantly help improve heart health and drastically reduce a person's risk for heart attacks and strokes.

- **Cell repair and rejuvenation**: Studies show that sea buckthorn can aid significantly in the repair and rejuvenation of the body's cellular structure.

- **Cerebral health**: The fatty acids, flavonoids and carotonoids found in sea buckthorn not only help reduce the risk of stroke, they promote overall brain health and memory.

- **Cholesterol control**: The flavonoids and essential fatty acids in sea buckthorn help to increase the good cholesterol (HDL) in your blood and reduce your risk of conditions such as coronary heart disease and stroke. Also, phytosterols reduce the amount of cholesterol that you take in during meals.

- **Fatigue**: Sea buckthorn is rich in many important vitamins such as vitamin C and vitamin E, and can help reduce some of the more common symptoms of fatigue such as low energy and muscle tension. Sea buckthorn may even help promote a more restful night's sleep.

- **Gastrointestinal health**: Sea buckthorn seed oil is an effective treatment for gastric ulcers as it normalizes the output of gastric acid and helps to reduce inflammation in the stomach and other gastrointestinal organs.

- **Hair**: The oils and fatty acids contained in sea buckthorn can improve overall hair health and lends itself to a healthy and natural-looking shine. In addition, preliminary trials seem to indicate a correlation between the use of sea buckthorn and a reduction in the onset of premature hair loss.

- **Hypertension or high blood pressure**: Extracts from all parts of sea buckthorn—bark, juice, leaves and oil—can be effective in treating high blood pressure. It's essential fatty acids help to lower blood pressure, and some research suggests that increasing flavonoids (which are abundant in sea buckthorn) intake also benefits hypertension.

- **Immune system**: Sea buckthorn is rich in vitamin C which can help boost the immune system and helps to fight off disease.

- **Liver**: Clinical trials have shown that sea buckthorn can help normalize liver enzymes and immune system markers in those with inflammation or cirrhosis of the liver, and may help prevent the harmful effects of many substances high in toxicity.

- **Menopause:** Sea buckthorn is a natural lubricant and helps to relieve vaginal dryness that may occur during menopause.

- **Skin diseases**: Several studies have investigated sea buckthorn's ability to treat conditions such as acne, dermatitis, eczema, skin lesions and rosacea. Its skin-healing abilities are due to its high essential fatty acid, flavonoids, protein, and vitamin content.
- **Sun Block**: Sea buckthorn naturally absorbs the sun's harmful UV rays which can cause skin damage and may lead to skin cancer.
- **Triglycerides**: Sea buckthorn helps to lower these blood fats that can also contribute to heart disease and stroke.
- **Ulcers:** This fruit improves the health of mucous membranes in the gastrointestinal tract. Research involving rats indicate that the seed and pulp oils can prevent and cure gastric ulcers, possibly because of its phytosterols.

  - **Vitamin C** (300-1600mg/100g)
  - **Vitamin E** (162-255mg/100g)
  - **Vitamin A** (11mg/100g)
  - **Vitamin B1** (0.04 mg/I00g)
  - **Vitamin B2** (0.56 mg/I00g)

- **Wound and burn healing and skin rejuvenation**: Palmitoleic acid, which is just one of the fatty acids produced by sea buckthorn, is a naturally occurring substance in the skin. Thus, sea buckthorn has proved very effective in the treatment of wounds, burns dermatitis and even cancers of the skin.

~°~°~°~°~°~°~°~°~°~°~°~°~°

"It is the month of June,
The month of leaves and roses,
When pleasant sights salute the eyes
And pleasant scents the noses."

—*Nathaniel Parker Willis*

~°~°~°~°~°~°~°~°~°~°~°~°~°

Never throw away the water eggs have been boiled in as it's full of minerals. After cooling the water, feed it to your house plants. They love it and will grow at a much faster rate!

Or

Cold tea is great food for your house plants.

~°~°~°~°~°~°~°~°~°~°~°~°~°

<u>Goji berries health benefits:</u>

- decrease in the incidence of stroke, heart attack, cancer, Parkinson's disease, and Alzheimer's disease.
- increase in the metabolic rate—resulting in increased weight loss.
- increase in sexual activity, libido, and performance.
- stronger bones, healthier blood, increase in eyesight, less mood variability.

Goji Tea:

¼ cup goji berries
16 ounces water

Stir goji berries into water and cover container. Let stand overnight. Pour off water and enjoy a nutrient rich, slightly sweet tea.

~°~°~°~°~°~°~°~°~°~°~°~°

Thyme, rosemary, betony, sage, horehound, hyssop, lavender and savory are all part of the mint family

~°~°~°~°~°~°~°~°~°~°~°~°

Flowering Clematis Vines:

- **Site Selection**—Clematis vines can live for decades, so it's important to pick a site both you and your vine will be happy with for the long term. Most varieties prefer full sun or a minimum of 6 hours of good bright sunshine every day.
- **Soil**—These climbers may like their heads in the sun, but their roots should be firmly planted in a well-drained soil rich in organic matter such as compost or rotting manure.
- **Watering**—During the first growing season, keep the soil moist at all times, but never waterlogged. Once established, the Clematis Vine will only need to be watered during extended dry spells.

- **Fertilizing**—These flowering vines require some serious feeding and will benefit from a good organic fertilizing program. When spring growth appears, sprinkle about 2 inches of rotted manure over the topsoil. Feed again after flowering has finished with bone and blood meals. During the summer, saturate the soil monthly with a fish emulsion solution.
- **Pruning**—To encourage vertical growth, trim the horizontal branches back to just one pair of leaves. To encourage horizontal growth, snip off the vertical stem just above a node at the desired height.

~°~°~°~°~°~°~°~°~°~°~°~°

Have your roses last a lot longer by adding a capful of hydrogen peroxide to the water and repeat as you change the water often. Don't forget to cut the stems on a slant under running water.

~°~°~°~°~°~°~°~°~°~°~°~°

Window boxes: to keep rain from splattering dirt on windows put a layer of gravel on top

~°~°~°~°~°~°~°~°~°~°~°~°

"In summer, the song sings itself."

—*William Carlos Williams*

~°~°~°~°~°~°~°~°~°~°~°~°

Rid your garden of aphids: cut up two or three banana peels then dig a 1 inch deep hole in the ground at the base of the plant. Aphids and ants find the high potassium concentration in banana peels unappealing.

~°~°~°~°~°~°~°~°~°~°~°~°

Raspberries:

Raspberries are a member of the rose family

Some cultures consider the raspberry to be love-inducing

They are not just red: There are also black, purple and gold raspberries.

The average raspberry has 100-120 seeds

Unripe raspberries do not ripen after they are picked.

Raspberries are one of the power foods along with Saskatoons and apples.

Benefits:

Helps keep your metabolic rate high with high levels of the trace mineral manganese.

One of the top 10 antioxidant rich fruits and vegetables.

Has twice the ORAC value (antioxidant) of oranges or apples and higher than blueberries.

Contains elegiac acid, a natural substance which is an anti-carcinogenic (cancer preventing).

High in vitamin C: One cup provides over half your daily requirement

Has more fibre than most fruits. One cup of raspberries provides 8 grams of dietary fibre

The seeds are rich in vitamin E, omega-3 fatty acids and have a natural SPF (sun protection factor) of 25-50.

Naturally have no cholesterol and no sodium.

One cup has only 64 calories with a low—glycemic index

Raspberry leaf tea is commonly used during pregnancy to combat nausea due to morning sickness.

The sugars in raspberries are natural and healthy.

~°~°~°~°~°~°~°~°~°~°~°

*"Someone's sitting in the shade today
because someone planted a tree a long time ago."*

—*Warren Buffett*

~°~°~°~°~°~°~°~°~°~°~°

Avoid storing potatoes with onions because; when close together, they produce gases that spoil both.

Planning a Garden:

Look for the high ground

- Locate the highest point on your property and site the garden on the slope below the hill so that the tops of plants or trees are lower than the crest of the hill. This prevents wind injury and keeps crops from drying out.

Air drainage

- Air flows just like water, from a high point to a low point. Adequate airflow drains cool air away from the crops, and breezes will dry dew off of plants relatively quickly, which helps prevent plant diseases.

Water drainage

- Gardeners can easily check drainage rates by digging a small hole and pouring a bucket of water into it. If the water has not percolated into the soil in 10 to 15 minutes, drainage is poor. If a small section of the garden has poor drainage, mark off that space for building a natural pond or for crops in the mint or watercress families, which like marshy areas.

Perennials need northern exposure

- If you are planting perennial crops, sitting them to the north ensures fewer episodes of freezing and thawing while also delaying growth during the spring frost period. If the garden is in an area that gets hot and cold during the winter, the soil will heave. This will cause roots to rip and the plants to dry out.

Annuals need southern exposure

- Gardens facing south will receive sun earlier and warm more rapidly, which is perfect for vegetables that require early planting or annual flowers such as impatiens and pansies.

Protection from wind

- Many plants, particularly perennials, are sensitive to wind. It is recommended installing a simple or decorative snow fence. The slats in the fence will slow air flow. The fence also allows snow to drift higher onto the garden, which acts as a highly effective insulator.

Check tree species

- Black walnut or butternut trees contain a chemical compound called juglone, which may cause nearby plants to wilt. Garden plants should not be placed within these trees' canopies or root zones.

Check for pH and fertility

- Testing should be done if the land selected for the garden obviously has not been cultivated. Simple soil test kits are available—more—at cooperative extension offices and garden centers. When you submit your test, tell the lab what type of crops you are planting. If they know the crops to be planted, they can give a very specific recommendation for fertilization.

Look for persistent or perennial weeds

- Before cultivating the garden, look for persistent weeds such as purslane, quack grass, thistles or galinsoga. You still can plant there, but you have to address the major weed problems before planting. Frequent shallow cultivation, covering with black plastic film or use of an appropriate herbicide will help keep weeds manageable.

No splendor in the grass

- If the site was once turf, sod or meadow, there may be grass pests such as webworms or grubs beneath the surface. These pests will cause problems with many plants. They can be controlled with an insecticide or with an organic treatment containing milky spore for the grubs, although milky spore must be used over several years.

Is there an adjacent lawn?

- If there is turf grass near the site, make sure weed-and-feed products have not been applied recently. Any product containing the herbicide dicamba can leach through the soil to kill plant roots, particularly those of perennial flowers, trees and shrubs.

Keep land idle

- A small amount of land should be left unplanted to help with crop rotation. All crops will attract insects, weeds and diseases that specifically affect them. By rotating crops into new soil areas, you can minimize these problems.

~°~°~°~°~°~°~°~°~°~°~°

Finish with a pergola bench:

Every garden deserves a place where visitors can sit and admire the beauty. Make yours a working part of your green landscape! A pergola bench offers seating area, storage underneath, and a growing area for plants that love to climb.

~°~°~°~°~°~°~°~°~°~°~°

A nice mix of plants that will make bees happy:

Lavender—looks and smells lovely
Rosemary—Smells great, and you can trim it back to use in recipes whenever you want. Rosemary is an easy plant to care for.

Sunflowers—Nothing happier than a big, sunflower face.

Butterfly Bush—These are beautiful and easy to care for.

Strawberries—Where ever you plant these, the bees will be happy

Lawn Care:

Do the right thing at the right time. Follow an appropriate lawn care calendar for the type of climate you have. For example, don't cut the grass too early in the season—wait until it is dry—and don't cut the grass too short at the end of summer if you are unlikely to see much more warm or dry weather.

Get the right tools and machinery. Appropriate tools and a good quality lawn mower with sharp, adjustable blades are essential and can make your lawn care a whole lot easier and more effective. Other useful tools include a wire rake, a garden fork and an edge trimmer if you have a large lawn.

Choose the right grass type. If your lawn is used a lot, for example by the kids or the dog, you need a hardwearing mix of grasses. For an ornamental lawn, you can choose finer grasses. Again, your choice of a grass type should also be determined by the climate in your part of the world and how much sun and shade the lawn gets.

Tips on keeping Houseplants healthy:

Fertilize your houseplants: spread some compost over the top of the soil. As you water, the compost will work its way down into the soil.

Allow the soil to dry out between watering: Because they are in pots, houseplants are prone to over-watering. Their roots will rot, and you will see yellow leaves on the plant if they are over-watered.

When you do water, do so thoroughly: Make sure the water comes out of the drainage hole at the bottom of the pot. Rainwater is ideal, or you can use filtered or bottled water, or the water from a dehumidifier. If all you have is tap water, let it sit overnight in an open container before pouring it on your plants.

Aerate the soil by gently poking and stirring it. Potted plants' soil can get hard and compacted if it is not loosened by aeration. This also helps prevent root rot.

Re-pot your houseplants periodically: As their roots grow, they will need larger containers. They may also need fresh soil from time to time. You can also trim the roots of some species instead of moving them to larger containers.

Make sure your plants are getting enough light. South or east-facing windows are best. Turn your plants if you see them slanting toward the light source. If you don't have enough natural light, invest in a grow light. Hang it over the plants and keep it on for 8-12 hours a day.

Be very gradual if you move your houseplants outdoors during warm weather and back indoors when it gets cold. As the weather cools, start by putting the plants indoors only at night. Then, put them inside for a few hours each day, increasing the time the plants are indoors every few days. As warmer weather comes on, start by moving plants outdoors during the day for a few hours at a time.

Essential Oils:

When working with oils, most are not applied "neat" (meaning "straight" or undiluted), except to skin that is tough (palms of hands, bottoms of the feet). Always apply with care. If an oil starts to sting or burn, rub a carrier oil (olive, almond, sesame seed, jojoba, etc) over it and the burning will stop.

Angelica (Angelica archangelica) (Electromagnetic Freq: 85 MHz) (73% monoterpenes) Relieves nervous exhaustion and stress, revitalizes tired mind and provides mental drive. Invigorates the lymphatic system, increases perspiration, cleansing system of toxins. Aids indigestion, flatulence, dyspepsia, colic. Stimulates appetite. Urinary antiseptic. Provides use as expectorant in colds, bronchitis, pleurisy. Used to relieve asthma, and restore sense of smell. General tonic to the lungs. Said to encourage production of estrogen thereby helping with painful periods (this may be more so with the Asian species). Said to control uric acid and may be beneficial to rheumatic conditions, arthritis, gout, and sciatica. Useful for headaches, migraines, inflammation, and toothache. Also a remedy to neutralize snake bites.

Basil (Ocimum basilicum) (75% phenylpropanoids) can be relaxing to muscles, including smooth muscles (those not subject to our voluntary control, such as the heart and digestive system). It may also be used to soothe insect bites when applied topically. Beneficial for mental fatigue, basil may help stimulate and sharpen the sense of smell.

Bergamot (Citrus bergamia) has been used in the Middle East for hundreds of years for skin conditions associated with an oily complexion. It soothes insect bites and may serve as an insect repellent. It has about 300 chemical constituents that contribute refreshing, mood-lifting qualities. Bergamot is responsible for the distinctive flavor of Earl Grey Tea. Benefits nervous and digestive system.

Cedar, Red Canadian (Thuja plicata) was used traditionally by the Canadian Natives to help them enter a higher spiritual realm. They used it to stimulate the scalp and as an antiseptic agent.

Cedarwood (Cedrus atlantica) (98% sesquiterpenes) was recognized historically for its calming, purifying properties and is used to benefit the skin and tissues near the surface of the skin. It also helps calm nervous tension, and benefits the digestive system. The oil with the highest percentage of sesquiterpenes, Cedarwood supplies oxygen to tissues and erases DNA damage; just another weapon in our battle against cancer.

Chamomile, Roman (Chamaemelum nobile) may help calm you and relieve restlessness and tension. It is used cosmetically in Europe for the skin.

Cinnamon Bark (Cinnamomum verum) (73% phenylpropanoids) is among the most antiseptic essential oils with a high antioxidant rating. It has been produced in Sri Lanka for over 2,000 years. Invigorates and rejuvenates mind and body.

Cistus or Labdanum (Cistus ladanifer) comes from a rose that has a soft honey-like scent. Cistus has been studied for its effect on the regeneration of cells.

Clary Sage (Salvia sclarea) supports the cells. It contains natural estriol, a phytoestrogen. Relaxing, sweet scent, used as a toning and sedating scent/oil especially for women. Also seems to help digestive and glandular problems.

Clove (Syzygium aromaticum) (90% phenylpropanoids) is one of the most antiseptic essential oils. Eugenol, its principal constituent, is used synthetically in the dental industry for the numbing of gums. Most powerful of the antioxidants and a wonderful aid to the immune system. Also repels ants.

Coriander (cilantro) (Coriandrum sativum) oil has been researched at Cairo University for its effects in supporting pancreatic function. It also has soothing, calming properties.

Cypress (Cupressus sempervirens) (28% monoterpenes) is one of the oils most used to support the circulatory system.

Dill (Anethum graveolens) oil has been researched at Cairo University for its supportive effects on pancreatic function. It is used in European hospitals.

Elemi (Canarium luzonicum) is distilled from the gum of a tree originating in the Philippines. It has been used in Europe for hundreds of years in salves for skin and is included in celebrated healing ointments such as baume parlytique. Elemi was used by a 17th-century physician, J. J. Wecker, on the battle wounds of soldiers. It belongs to the same botanical family (Burseraceae) as frankincense (Boswellia carteri) and myrrh (Commiphor myrrha). Elemi is highly regarded today for soothing sore muscles, protecting skin, and stimulating nerves.

Eucalyptus Dives High in phellandrene and low in eucalyptol. This species has different, more specific antiseptic action than other eucalyptus oils. It is excellent for skin or topical application. Avoid direct inhalation.

Eucalyptus Globulus Contains a high percentage of the compound eucalyptol, a key ingredient in many antiseptic mouth rinses. Often used for the respiratory system, eucalyptus has been investigated for its effect on insects in a study called "Laboratory Evaluation of a Eucalyptus-based Repellant Against Four Biting Arthropods," published in Phytotherapy Research. Has a pungent, camphor-like aroma used traditionally to expel mucus and fortify the respiratory system. DO NOT use with children under 5 or asthmatics.

Eucalyptus Polybractea Well suited for topical application or diffusing. This species is highest in the antiseptic compound eucalyptol (about 80 percent) and has one of the strongest antiseptic actions among the eucalyptus oils. AVOID DIRECT INHALATION.

Eucalyptus Radiata One of the most versatile of the eucalyptus oils, is suitable for topical use, diffusing, and even direct inhalation. Relatively gentle and nonirritating. This antiseptic oil has been studied extensively by Daniel Penoel, M.D.

Fennel (Foeniculum vulgare) is antiseptic and stimulating to the circulatory and respiratory systems.

Fir (Abies alba) has been researched for its antiseptic abilities.

Fir, Douglas (Pseudotsuga menziesii) has antiseptic properties and helps soothe sore muscles.

Frankincense (Boswellia carteri) (40% monoterpenes) (8% sesquiterpenes) is considered a holy anointing oil in the Middle East and has been used in religious ceremonies for thousands of years (. . . presented unto him gifts; gold, and frankincense, and myrrh. Matthew 2:11). It was well known during the time of Christ for its anointing and healing powers. Frankincense is now being researched and used therapeutically in European hospitals. High in sesquiterpenes, it is stimulating and elevating to the mind and helps in overcoming stress and despair as well as supporting the immune system. Comforting, centering, and elevating; long associated with spirituality, the sesquiterpenes help to erase DNA damage and supply oxygen to tissues (excellent for cancer patients).

Galbanum (Ferula gummosa) (80% monoterpenes) is referred to in the book of Exodus (And the Lord said unto Moses, take unto thee sweet spices, stacte, and onycha, and galbanum; these sweet spices with pure frankincense: of each shall there be a like weight. Exodus 30:34). Galbanum was used for both medicinal and spiritual purposes. It is recognized for its antiseptic and body-supporting properties. When combined with other oils such as frankincense

(Boswellia carteri) or sandalwood (Santalum album), galbanum's electrical frequency increases dramatically.

Geranium (Pelargonium graveolens) has been used for centuries for skin care. Its strength lies in the ability to revitalize tissue. It is excellent for the skin, and its aromatic influence helps release negative memories. Also used for glandular and reproductive systems, with some benefits to the nervous system. Used by skin care specialists in restoring balance between oily and dry skin and hair.

Ginger (Zingiber officinale) (59% sesquiterpenes) is used to combat nausea, vomiting, or dizziness associated with motion sickness and has been studied for its gentle, stimulating effects.

Goldenrod (Solidago canadensis) supports the circulatory system, urinary tract, and liver function. It has relaxing and calming effects.

Grapefruit (Citrus x paradisi) works as a mild disinfectant. Especially helpful for the urinary system, and when trying to lose weight. Benefits the nervous system during stressful situations. Diffuse for a refreshing, uplifting aroma. Like many cold-pressed citrus oils, it has unique fat-dissolving characteristics.

Helichrysum (Helichrysum italicum) (Electromagnetic Freq: 181 MHz) has been studied in Europe for regenerating tissue and improving skin conditions, nerves, and circulation. It is best known for its effect on bruises, wounds and other injuries, as well as for reducing pain. Also, known as an excellent cell regenerator and helps reduce formation of scar tissue.

Hyssop (Hyssopus officinalis) (70% monoterpenes) is another Biblical oil, noted for its antiseptic properties. (Purge me with hyssop, and I shall be clean: wash me, and I shall be whiter than snow. Psalms 51:7) It has been studied for supporting the respiratory system.

Idaho Tansy (Tanacetum vulgare) stimulates a positive attitude and a general feeling of well being. This oil has been used extensively as an insect repellant. It is believed it may help numerous skin conditions and tone the entire system.

Jasmine (Jasminum officinale) is an "absolute" extracted from the flower and is an essence rather than an essential oil. It is good for sensitive skin and can also be uplifting and stimulating. Considered an aphrodisiac for centuries, Jasmine supports the nervous system and is helpful for women going through menopause.

Juniper (Juniperus osteosperma and/or J. scopulorum) (Electromagnetic Freq: 98 MHz) (42% monoterpenes) may work as a detoxifier and cleanser that also benefits the skin. It has also been used to support proper nerve function.

Laurus Nobilis An essential oil used for fragrance in cosmetics and perfumes. Ancient Greeks and Romans used leaves of the laurel tree to crown their victors. Both leaves and berries were used to improve appetite and calm digestion. Laurus nobilis has antiseptic properties.

Lavender (Lavandula angustifolia) (Electromagnetic Freq: 118 MHz) is the most versatile of all essential oils. Therapeutic-grade lavender has been highly regarded for the skin. The French scientist Rene Gattefosse was the first to discover these properties when he severely burned his hands in a laboratory explosion. Lavender has also been clinically evaluated for its relaxing effects. It may be used to cleanse cuts, bruises, and skin irritations. The fragrance is calming, relaxing, and balancing—physically and emotionally. Makes an excellent rub for sprains, strains, and sore muscles (used in a carrier oil) and goes well mixed with Tea Tree Oil (Melaleuca). Can be taken internally (1 to 3 drops in a cup of water) for headaches and even migraines. A few drops for a gargle works really peachy.

Ledum (Ledum groenlandicum) has been used for years in folk medicine. As a tea, ledum soothed stomachs, coughs, and hoarseness. It was also believed to stimulate the nerves.

Lemon (Citrus limon) has antiseptic-like properties and contains compounds that have been studied for their effects on immune function, lymphatic, circulatory, and digestive systems. Is antibacterial and may serve as an insect repellent as well as being beneficial for the skin. Diffuse or add a few drops to a spray bottle to deodorize and sterilize the air. Add two drops to soy or rice milk for purification or combine with peppermint (Mentha piperita) to provide a refreshing lift. Use for removing gum, oil, or grease spots. Add to food or soy or rice milk as a dietary supplement or flavoring. CAUTION: Citrus oils should NOT be applied to skin that will be exposed to direct sunlight or ultraviolet light within 72 hours.

Lemongrass (Cymbopogon flexuosus) is used for purification and digestion. Research was published in Phytotherapy Research regarding topically applied lemongrass and its properties.

Marjoram (Origanum majorana) is used for supporting the muscles and the respiratory system. It assists in calming the nerves and is antiseptic.

Melaleuca (Alternifolia) Highly regarded as an antiseptic essential oil. Has high levels of terpinenol, which is the key active constituent. Famous for its beneficial effects on immune system; excellent disinfectant and cleaners. Tea tree oil has been highly praised for a wide variety of healing uses. Some people find the oil irritating when used full strength and need to dilute it with oil, but many people use it straight on athlete's foot, insect bites, arthritis pain, burns, cuts, nail fungus warts and sprains. You might wish to first test your sensitivity. If a rash develops using a small amount, you can dilute with a carrier oil (olive, almond, etc) Diffuse or apply topically. Safe for use on children and pets.

Melaleuca (Ericifola) (formerly known as Australian Rosalina) is a relatively unknown essential oil with antiseptic and calming properties. This variety of melaleuca oil is exceptionally gentle and nonirritating to the skin and is used by the well-known essential oil researcher Daniel Penoel, M.D., to support the respiratory system. Diffuse or apply topically on location or to the temples, wrists, throat, face, and chest. For a whole body massage, dilute four to eight drops in 30 ml of carrier oil. Add several drops to bath water.

Melissa (Melissa officinalis) (Electromagnetic Freq: 102 MHz) Uplifting, mood enhancing, Melissa officinalis is also called lemon balm because of the lemony smell of its leaves. It is a costly essential oil because of the large volume of plants needed to produce small quantities of oil. Beware of inexpensive offerings of melissa, since it is often adulterated with lemongrass and citronella. Melissa Essential Oil is excellent for restoring a calm and relaxed feeling. It relieves occasional nervous tension and has been found helpful for the relief of occasional sleeplessness. Melissa is often used as a digestive aid and helps with occasional heartburn, gas, bloating, and feelings of fullness. True therapeutic-grade Melissa is highly effective and greatly valued.

Mountain Savory or Winter Savory (Satureja montana) has been used historically as a general tonic for the body.

Myrrh (Commiphora myrrha) (62% sesquiterpenes) is an oil referenced throughout the Old and New Testaments (A bundle of myrrh is my well-beloved unto me. Song of Solomon 1:13). The Arabian people used it for many skin conditions, such as wrinkled, chapped, and cracked skin. Is has one of the highest levels of sesquiterpenes, a class of compounds that has direct effects on the hypothalamus, pituitary, and amygdala, the seat of our emotions. Myrrh is widely used today in oral hygiene products. It is emotionally strengthening and empowering; prized since ancient times; antiseptic, anti-bacterial, anti-viral, anti-fungal, and anti-inflammatory; has traditionally been used for aging skin (not for use during pregnancy). Like Frankincense, this is an excellent weapon in your arsenal to battle cancer.

Myrtle (25% monoterpenes) has been researched by Dr. Daniel Penoel for its effects on hormonal imbalances of the thyroid and ovaries. It has also been researched for its soothing effects on the respiratory system. Myrtle may help with chronic coughs and respiratory tract ailments. Apply topically, diffuse, or use in a humidifier. Suitable for use on children.

Neroli Fresh, floral aroma brightens spirits and clears the mind. Supports the body under stress and enhances skin tone.

Nutmeg (Myristic fragrans) helps support the adrenal glands for increased energy. Historically, it has been used to benefit circulation and muscle aches and pains. It also helps to support the nervous system and may assist in overcoming nervous fatigue. Apply topically mixed with Massage Oil Base. Add to food or soy or rice milk as a dietary supplement or flavouring.

Orange (Citrus sinensis) brings peace and happiness to the mind and body. It has been recognized to help a dull, oily complexion. Diffuse or apply topically on location, or add to food or soy or rice milk as a dietary supplement or flavoring. CAUTION: Citrus oils should NOT be applied to skin that will be exposed to direct sunlight or ultraviolet light within 72 hours.

Oregano (Origanum compactum) (60% phenylpropanoids) is highly damaging to many kinds of viruses and was recently shown in laboratory research conducted at Weber State University, Ogden, Utah, to have a 99 percent kill rate against in vitro colonies of Streptococcus pneumoniae, even when used in 1 percent concentration. (S. pneumoniae is responsible for many kinds of lung and throat infections.) It is antibacterial, antiviral, containing 31 known anti-inflammatories, 28 antioxidants, and 4 potent COX-2 inhibitors. Apply topically neat to bottom of feet. Mix with Massage Oil Base if applied elsewhere on the skin. May be used undiluted in Raindrop Technique. Add to food or soy or rice milk as a dietary supplement or flavoring. DO NOT use with children under 5.

Patchouli (Pogostemon cablin) (71% sesquiterpenes) is very beneficial for the skin and may help prevent wrinkled or chapped skin. It is a general tonic and stimulant, helps the digestive system, fighting candida (yeast) infections, and benefits the nervous and glandular systems. It has antiseptic properties and helps relieve itching.

Pepper, Black (Piper nigrum) (74% sesquiterpenes) is a stimulating, energizing essential oil that has been studied for its effects on cellular oxygenation. It has been used for soothing deep tissue muscle aches and pains.

Peppermint (Mentha piperita) (Electromagnetic Freq: 78 MHz) (45% monoterpenes) (25% phenylpropanoids) is one of the oldest and most highly regarded herbs for soothing digestion. Jean Valnet, M.D., studied peppermint's effect on the liver and respiratory systems. Other scientists have also researched peppermint's role in affecting impaired taste and smell when inhaled. Dr. William N. Dember of the University of Cincinnati studied peppermint's ability to improve concentration and mental accuracy. Alan Hirsch, M.D., studied peppermint's ability to directly affect the brain's satiety center, which triggers a sense of fullness after meals. It is beneficial to the sinuses and muscular system, and especially useful for women during monthly cycles or menopause. Diffuse. Massage on the stomach or add to water or tea for supporting normal digestion. Apply to bottom of feet to cool off on a hot day. Rub on temples for a calming effect, or place several drops on the tongue as an invigorating pick-me-up. A wonderful flavoring and preservative. Avoid contact with eyes, mucous membranes, or sensitive skin areas. DO NOT apply neat to a fresh wound or burn.

Petitgrain (Citrus aurantium) is an oil derived from orange leaves, has antiseptic properties and re-establishes nerve equilibrium.

Pine (Pinus sylvestris) (30% monoterpenes) was first investigated by Hippocrates, the father of Western medicine, for its benefits to the respiratory system. In 1990 Dr. Penoel and Dr Frachomme described pine oil's antiseptic properties in their medical textbook. Pine is used in massage for stressed muscles and joints. It shares many of the same properties as Eucalyptus globulus, and the action of both oils is enhanced when blended. Promotes alertness and mental focus; benefits respiratory and urinary system. Not to be used by children under 5. Can be a strong skin irritant. Avoid oil adulterated by turpentine, a low-cost but potentially hazardous filler.

Ravensara (Ravensara aromatica) is referred to by the people of Madagascar as the oil that heals. It has antiseptic properties and is supporting to the nerves and respiratory system.

Rose (Rosa damascena) (Electromagnetic Freq: 320 MHz) has a beautiful fragrance that is intoxicating and aphrodisiac-like. Rose helps bring balance and harmony. In his clinical practice, Dr. Penoel uses this oil for the skin. It is stimulating and elevating to the mind, creating a sense of well-being. It has been called the Queen of oils for women's concerns, establishing harmony throughout the body no matter what life brings. It is also great for circulation and skin care.

Rosemary (Rosmarinus officinalis CT 1,8 cineol) has been researched for its antiseptic properties. It may be beneficial for the skin and for helping overcome mental fatigue. Beneficial for the circulatory, nervous, and muscular system. Has a history of use over the centuries for hair and skin. NOT TO BE used with high blood pressure or epilepsy.

Rosewood (Aniba rosaeodora) is soothing and nourishing to the skin. It has been researched at Weber State University for its inhibition rate against gram positive and gram negative bacterial growth.

Sage (Salvia officinalis) has been used in Europe for numerous skin conditions. It has been recognized for its benefits of strengthening the vital centers and supporting metabolism. It may also help coping with despair and mental fatigue.

Sandalwood (Santalum album) (90% sesquiterpenes) is high in sesquiterpenes and has been researched in Europe for its ability to oxygenate a part of the brain known as the pineal gland, the seat of our emotions. The pineal gland is responsible for releasing melatonin, a powerful hormone that enhances deep sleep. Sandalwood is similar to frankincense oil in its support of nerves and circulation. It was used traditionally for skin revitalization, yoga, and meditation, and has been found to help remove negative programming from the cells (again, another cancer weapon). Also traditionally used for urinary and respiratory systems.

Sea buckthorn is a treatment for a variety of conditions, most of which are now related to skincare. It has been used as a dietary supplement, soap, and even stomach remedy, but it is primarily recognized as a powerful remedy for aged or damaged skin.

Spearmint (Mentha spicata) oil helps support the respiratory and nervous systems. It may help open and release emotional blocks and bring about a feeling of balance.

Spikenard (Nardostachys jatamansi) (93% sesquiterpenes) is highly regarded in India as a perfume, medicinal herb, and skin tonic. Highly prized at the time of Christ, it was used by Mary of Bethany to anoint the feet of Jesus before the Last Supper. This relaxing, soothing oil helps nourish and regenerate the skin.

Spruce (Picea mariana) (38% monoterpenes) oil helps support the respiratory and nervous systems. Its aromatic influences help to open and release emotional blocks, bringing about a feeling of balance.

Tangerine (Citrus nobilis) is a calming essential oil. It helps with anxiety and nervousness.

Tarragon (Artemisia dracunculus) has been used in Europe for its antiseptic functions.

Thyme (Thymus vulgaris) is one of the most antiseptic essential oils and very high in antioxidant rating. It contains thymol, which has been studied for its effect on gingivitis and plaque-causing organisms in the mouth. It may be beneficial in helping to overcome fatigue and exhaustion. Sharp and woody aroma, helps improve circulatory, immune, skeletal, respiratory and nervous systems; anti-microbial use for infections and disinfectant use; dilute with water to clean and disinfect surfaces; especially good to use in a sickroom; makes a good massage oil as it stimulates circulation and can be used to clean burns and wounds; inhaled, it aids in asthma attacks and is a good choice if you are recovering from pneumonia.

Tsuga (Canadensis) (Tsuga canadensis) is distilled from the leaves and twigs of the conifer tree commonly called hemlock. The bark from the hemlock tree was used by American Indians to make poultices for wounds and sores. Tsuga essential oil is used in liniments.

Valerian (Valeriana officinalis) is a root that has been used for thousands of years for its calming, relaxing, grounding, and emotionally balancing influences. During the last three decades, it has been clinically investigated for its tranquilizing properties. Researchers have pinpointed the sesquiterpenes valerenic acid and valerone as the active constituents that exert a calming effect on the central nervous system. German health authorities have pronounced valerian to be an effective treatment for restlessness and for sleep disturbances resulting from nervous conditions.

Vetiver (Vetiveria zanioides) (97% sesquiterpenes) has a heavy, earthy fragrance similar to patchouli with a touch of lemon. Young Living's vetiver oil is hydro-diffused under ultra-low pressure. Vetiver oil is psychologically grounding, calming, and stabilizing. Vetiver may help us cope with stress and recover from emotional traumas and shocks.

Vitex (Vitex negundo) is steam distilled from the inner bark, tiny branches, and leaves of the chaste tree. It has been extensively researched in Europe for its neurological effects. NOTE: Vitex is different from the extract of the chaste berry.

Western Red Cedar Referred to as the "Tree of Life." It has antiseptic properties, is nourishing to the skin, and helps promote a sense of calmness.

White Fir (Albies grandis) is an essential oil with antiseptic properties.

Wintergreen (Gaultheria prcumbens) contains the same active ingredient (methyl salicylate) as birch and is beneficial for massage associated with bone, muscle, and joint discomfort.

Ylang Ylang (Cananga odorata) may be extremely effective in calming, balancing (the nervous system) and bringing about a sense of relaxation. This native flower of Madagascar and the Reunion Islands is symbolic of love, and the fragrant, pale yellow petals are often strewn across the marriage bed. Its soft, floral scent is often used in men's fragrances as an alternative to the sweeter and more feminine rose. Ylang Ylang affects the glandular system, great for hair and skin, stimulates adrenal glands, but at the same time can be used for insomnia and pain. Has been known to have good results for impotence and frigidity. Taken internally, it has been said to lower blood pressure, alleviate problems with PMS, and ease intestinal infections. For depression, rub a drop or two between your palms and inhale the warm aroma.

~°~°~°~°~°~°~°~°~°~°~°~°~°

Superglue:

It can help heal a shallow cut. Align the skin edges together, rub a thin layer of glue over them and hold for 30 seconds.

A tea bag:

For split lips, press a damp black tea bag to the area. Its tannins help halt bleeding in mouth and gum tissue.

~°~°~°~°~°~°~°~°~°~°~°~°

*"What a heavy burden is a name that
has become too famous."*

—Voltaire

~°~°~°~°~°~°~°~°~°~°~°~°

Baby tomatoes:

After planting baby tomatoes, mix wood ashes into the soil around the plant. Remove the top and bottom of a coffee can, place the can over the plant and press into the earth. Remove the can when the plants are a few weeks old and more established.

~°~°~°~°~°~°~°~°~°~°~°~°

Geraniums: like to be fertilized with rinsed coffee grounds once in a while.

~°~°~°~°~°~°~°~°~°~°~°~°

My Special Tips

Chapter Eight

The R's

*"A good laugh and a long sleep
are often the best cures."*

*"A book is a gift you can open
again and again."*

—*Garrison Keillor*

Reduce: Try to fix old things before buying new things. Buy used items whenever possible, at second-hand stores, garage sales, on eBay. See if someone is giving an item you want away.

Reuse: Whenever possible, opt for reusable versions of popular disposable items, including water bottles, coffee cups, diapers, razors. Reuse plastic food containers for storage. Don't just throw away unwanted items. Donate them. Repurpose them. Turn them into craft projects. Be creative.

Recycle: Well all know to do it by now, but a reminder never hurts. It can be so easy to just toss that one tin can into the trash. By being conscientious about everything you throw in the trash, recycling will become second-nature.

Compost: When you say "recycle" most people think of bottles, cans and paper. Composting is nature's original way of recycling—turning "trash" into healthy new soil. You don't need a complicated bin, just set aside a corner of your yard to dump out certain food scraps and yard debris and turn it over every so often. Don't have a yard? Many cities, towns and communities have a public compost pile.

- **Borrow From Friends:** If you only need something temporarily, ask if a friend or neighbour would loan it to you.
- **Share With Friends:** Share things like books, magazines, movies, games, and newspapers between friends and neighbours.
- **Tree-Free Home:** As much as possible, create a tree-free home:

  - replace paper napkins with cloth napkins
  - replace paper towels with a special set of cloth towels/napkins (or cut up old t-shirts for great towels)—store the used ones in a small container in your kitchen and just wash and reuse
  - purchase bleach-free, toilet paper that is made from the highest post-consumer waste content you can find (80% minimum)
  - if you print documents, print on once-used paper and/or bleach-free, recycled paper with the highest post-consumer waste content

available (or <u>hemp</u>/alternative-source paper, if you can afford it)
- reuse envelopes, wrapping paper, the front of gift cards (as postcards) and other paper materials you receive wherever possible
- read books, magazines, and newspapers from your local library
- create and use note pads from once-used paper
- leave messages for family members/roommates on a reusable message board
- make your own cards/letters from once-used products or handmade paper

- **Bulk Purchases:** Avoid products that are packaged for single use (i.e., drinks, school lunches, candy, cat and dog food, salad mixings, etc.). Instead, buy in bulk and transfer the products to your own reusable containers. Many health food stores have bulk bins where they sell everything from grains to cereal to cleaning products.
- **Buy Only What You Need:** Buy only as much as you know you'll use for items such as food, cleaning supplies, and paint.
- **Avoid Creating Trash:** Avoid creating trash wherever possible: when ordering food, avoid receiving any unnecessary plastic utensils, straws, etc. (ask in advance), buy ice cream in a cone instead of a cup, don't accept "free" promotional products, buy products with the least amount of packaging, etc. Every little bit of trash avoided does make a difference!
- **Shopping Bags:** While shopping, if you only buy a few products skip the shopping bag. For larger purchases, bring your own.

- **Junk Mail:** Simplest idea on how to reduce junk mail, just say "NO. thank you!"
- **Toilets:** should not be used as waste-buckets. Every unnecessary flush can use as much as 27 litres of water

~°~°~°~°~°~°~°~°~°~°~°~°~°

Know what you can recycle in your municipality and buy recyclable products more often.

Recycle more than bottles, cans and newspapers. Don't forget to consider the recycling options for other household items including: batteries, refrigerators, computers, electronics, tires, etc.

Remember, recycling is a cyclical process. Support recycling by purchasing recycled products.

~°~°~°~°~°~°~°~°~°~°~°~°~°

A wise shopper knows: No matter how cheap the price. If you don't need it or can't use it. It's no bargain!!

~°~°~°~°~°~°~°~°~°~°~°~°~°

Buy local foods:

Buying food produced locally has several positive effects on the environment and your health.

- **Keeps local farmers working** —Buying from a local farmer cuts out the middle man and keeps local farmers working. Investing in the local economy also helps ensure that future generations have access to local, flavourful, and abundant food.

- **Reduces food transportation**—Food transportation is one of the largest and fastest-growing sources of greenhouse gas emissions on the planet. Some food items, which could be supplied locally, may travel thousands of miles to reach your supermarket.
- **Provides more nutritious foods**—Local food tastes better and is better for you. Produce loses nutrients quickly. Food grown locally was likely picked within the last few days versus the last few weeks or longer. Locally raised meat is typically organic and free from growth hormones and other artificial fillers.

Ways to Reuse Newspaper

Clean windows or glass: Dip crumbled newspaper into water mixed with a splash of white vinegar; clean windows without any streaks or harmful chemicals. *Note ** Wear rubber gloves to keep newsprint ink off hands.*

Burn it up: Instead of a starter log in the fireplace or at a bonfire, use tightly rolled pieces of newspaper instead.

Make a weed barrier: When building a garden bed, lay out pieces of newspaper before you fill it up with dirt. The paper will help keep weeds from invading.

Wrap some gifts: Have fun going through your papers to find unique or colourful pages to use as gift wrap.

Pack it up: Instead of plastic bubble wrap, wrap valuables in newspaper for shipping and pad your box with more crumpled paper. Pay forward and suggest some ideas in the package on how your recipient can reuse all of the paper, also!

As origami paper: Cut your newspaper into squares and get folding! Newsprint is great at holding folds. Just be gentle, since it's a bit more prone to tearing than store bought origami paper.

In the fridge: Keep the bottom of the veggie drawer from getting nasty by lining it with newspaper. It will absorb liquid and odours.

For ripening fruit: If you've picked up some under—ripe peaches, avocados, or other fruit, wrap them in newspaper to ripen them more quickly. Paper bags also work for this.

Shine on: Give the shine back to your stainless steel sink by gently scrubbing it with wadded up, wet newspaper.

Compost it: Newspaper makes great bedding for a worm bin. Tear into strips and let those wigglers turn it into gardening gold.

Papier-mâché: Get crafty with old newsprint. You can make all sorts of fun papier-mâché projects.

Donate them: Your local animal shelter can use newspapers to line their cages. Some even shred them up as kitty litter, when the budget is tight. You can also donate them to thrift stores, where they use them to pack up fragile items that sell.

Line the pet's cage: Pet owners can use old newspapers to line their pet's cage. It makes cleanup much easier.

~°~°~°~°~°~°~°~°~°~°~°~°

Conserve Electricity

Here are so many ways that people can save electricity without necessarily affecting the way that we live.

- Turn off lights, appliances, TV's and computers when you're not using them. According to research one computer monitor that is left on overnight uses enough energy to print more than 5,000 copies.
- Make sure you purchase appliances that have been certified as energy efficient.
- Try to wash clothes inside water that is cold when you can.
- Wrap your water heater and keep the temperature at 130 degrees or lower
- Install a thermostat that can be programmed
- Switch off your AC and open the doors and windows when you can.
- Remove traditional bulbs and get newer bulbs which are longer lasting and energy efficient too.

Save Water. You can help save the global water supply by doing all or any of the following:

- Place a plastic bottle that is full of water inside your toilet water tank. A toilet will use anywhere between 3—5 gallons of water with every single flush. Eliminating some room in the tank may mean that you save up to half a gallon of water each time you flush the tank.

- Fix any leaking pipes or faucets immediately
- Wash your laundry only when you have a complete load.
- Collect and use rainwater in order to water your plants, feed your animals and wash any outdoor furniture and your cars too.

Recycle and Reuse. In a landfill even a biodegradable milk container may take as much as 5 years to decompose.

These recycling tips may help you save the earth:

- Don't buy any disposable utensils such as plates, napkins and cups, try to use washable items and thus save on landfill space and money.
- Fill your community recycling containers. Check in your area to know which type of items can be picked up by recycling carriers.
- Reuse food containers to keep other items such as leftovers and smaller items too.

Go Green. Follow the natural movement by:

- Planting a backyard garden or planting a few trees in your park.
- Switching to cleaning supplies that are made from natural products
- Starting a compost pile in your backyard or together with your neighbours.
- Starting a compost pile in your backyard or with a group of neighbours
- Buy organic foods and other organic products

- Eat only fresh fruits and vegetables. This way you save on packaging waste.

~°~°~°~°~°~°~°~°~°~°~°~°~°

The information below also lists any concerns associated with the safety of the plastics.

Polyethylene terephthalate (PETE) is a clear hard plastic often found in disposable food and drink containers including: water bottles, pop bottles, vegetable oil containers, salad dressing bottles, peanut butter containers and some prepared/frozen food containers. There are many products which can be manufactured in part with recycled PETE such as furniture, carpet, polar fleece and even some containers. There are no health risks connected with this type of plastic.

High density polyethylene (HDPE) is also a hard plastic but is visibly different from PETE as it is not transparent. HDPE is found in household cleaner bottles, shampoo bottles and yogurt containers. Some items it can found in once recycled are pens, recycling containers, laundry detergent bottles, drainage pipe and fencing. There are no known health risks associated with HDPE.

Polyvinyl Chloride (PVC) is less stiff than HDPE but has many of the same uses as HDPE. It can be found as the primary plastic in a variety of bottles including detergent, shampoo, and cooking oil bottles. It is more difficult to recycle than the first two plastics mentioned and is not commonly collected in municipal recycling programs. PVC is known to contain phthalates, a suspected carcinogen.

Low density polyethylene (LDPE) is a soft, flexible plastic. It is typically found in a variety of plastic bags including: bread bags, frozen food bags and plastic shopping bags. Though LDPE can be recycled, traditionally it has not been included in municipal recycling programs. There are no health concerns connected to LDPE.

Polypropylene (PP) is a plastic commonly found in caps, some yogurt containers, medicine bottles and straws. Plastic containers labelled as number 5 plastic are accepted by some, but not all municipal recycling programs. If PP plastics are recycled they are found in items such as brooms, racks, battery casing, and battery cables. There has been no health concerns linked to PP.

Polystyrene (PS) is also known as Styrofoam. It is commonly found in disposable coffee cups and take-out food containers. In the past PS has not typically been accepted by municipal recycling programs. Though this is starting to change, it is still relatively uncommon that it is collected for recycling. If recycled it can be used in insulation. Unfortunately, PS contains styrene which is a known carcinogen.

Number 7 represents miscellaneous plastics but is most often polycarbonate (PC). PC is used in water cooler bottles, other large plastic containers and up until recently baby bottles. Plastics labelled with number 7 are not commonly accepted in municipal recycling programs. PC contains bisphenol-A which is a known hormone disruptor. As a result its use has been banded from some items.

Plastic Bag Facts

Refuse & Reduce

- Take cloth bags when out shopping
- Store reusable bags in vehicle or backpack
- Use sticky note reminders until it becomes a habit

- Hang cloth bags on the door knob to remind you to take them shopping.

Reuse

- Reuse any plastic bag you accumulate
- Next time you shop, use your bag for items from more than one store
- Line your garbage can
- Pick up your pet litter
- As a receptacle for cooled fats, oils and grease from cooking

Recycle

- Recycle clean dry and empty excess bags
- Take back to grocery stores for recycling
- Take shopping bags and your film plastic to a recycling depot

~°~°~°~°~°~°~°~°~°~°~°~°~°

Wash away any food or liquid residue in glass jars, plastic bottles, food cans, beverage bottles and glass bottles

- If it squashes—squash it! Materials such as plastic milk bottles, detergent bottles, shampoo bottles, tetra pak cartons and aluminum cans can all be squashed. This helps you get more into your recycle bin and helps the contractors to recycle more
- Then pop it into your recycle bin for collection at your house or to be brought to your nearest recycling facility

~°~°~°~°~°~°~°~°~°~°~°~°

Put the following packaging in your household recycling bin once it's clean and dry

- Cardboard and paper
- Food tins
- Aluminum drinks cans
- All other aluminum, such as clean tin foil and clean take away food trays
- Plastic for the recycle bin

~°~°~°~°~°~°~°~°~°~°~°~°

Composting tips

- Aerate. Your compost needs oxygen if it is going to break down the materials you add. If it is a tumbler, turn it. If it is static then get a stick/pole/shovel and get in there and move it around.
- Save the worms. If you find a worm while you're gardening carefully relocate it to your compost bin. And it will happily work on breaking down your wastes. The more help you have the better!
- Go Big. Container wise that is. Bigger is better when composting but smaller is better than nothing at all.
- Get cracking! Rinse and break up your egg shells before adding them to your compost pile. This gives them a head start and you will be less likely to find undigested shell later when you go to use your compost.

- Add fluid to your compost. You don't want it too wet but you do not want it too dry either. Water-downed leftover fruit juices are a great treat for your compost instead of pouring them down the drain.

- Sunshine is best! Composters work quicker in sunny locations but if you have to, partial sun will work too (it will just take longer).

- Cover it up. Keep a clear bag of leaves next to the composter so you always have brown material to cover new waste additions. This will also help keep the fly population down in the summer.

- Double duty. If you have the room, two composters are better than one. While you are busy filling one composter the second one can be busy working in the sun. When it's time to empty one they can switch positions and start all over again.

- Cupboard list. Keep a list posted on the inside of one of your cupboard doors so you can see at a glance what can and cannot be composted so there is no confusion.

- Kitchen Aid. You're more likely to compost if you don't have to run out to the composter a few times a day. Keep a lidded container in your kitchen for convenience and empty a few times a week.

Things you can add to compost piles:

Newspaper, cardboard, eggshells, vegetable scraps, lawn clippings, cuttings, hair, manure from herbivores, leaves, sawdust, coffee grounds and filters, tea leaves—basically any plant material that's not too thick.

Things to avoid:

Dog and cat droppings, fish, meat and dairy products, weeds, grease and oil. The reason for avoiding most of these is that there is a disease risk and rodents and other animals may be attracted.

~°~°~°~°~°~°~°~°~°~°~°~°

Take your own shopping bags:

Be sure to take your own shopping bag to the store with you. Both plastic and paper bags have negative effects on the environment.

~°~°~°~°~°~°~°~°~°~°~°~°

Using reusable grocery bags and bins:

Lower the risk of cross-contamination:

- When you are using cloth bags, make sure to wash them frequently, especially after carrying fresh produce, meat, poultry or fish. Some reusable grocery bags may not be machine washable. If you are using this type of grocery bag, you should make sure to frequently wash them inside out by hand with hot soapy water. Plastic bins should be washed using hot soapy water and/or sanitized with a mild bleach solution as described below on a regular basis. It is also important that you dry your grocery bags and bins after washing.

- o Combine 5 mL (1 tsp) of bleach with 750 mL (3 cups) of water in a labelled spray bottle.
- o Spray the bleach solution on the surface of the bin and let stand briefly.
- o Rinse with lots of clean water and air dry (or use clean towels).

- If you notice that juices from your food have leaked into the bag or bin, make sure you wash them thoroughly before using them again.
- You should place fresh or frozen raw meat, poultry and fish in separate bins or bags from fresh produce and other ready to eat foods.
- You can also put your meat, poultry or fish in plastic bags, such as the clear bags you can find in the produce and some meat sections. This will help prevent the juices from leaking out and contaminating your reusable bags and bins and also other foods. Fresh produce should also always be placed in plastic bags to help protect them from contamination.
- If you are using your grocery bags or bins to store or transport non-food items, they should be thoroughly washed before using them for groceries.
- Always follow proper safe food handling and preparation techniques in your kitchen, whether or not you are using reusable grocery bags. The four key steps are: clean, separate, cook and chill.
- After putting your groceries away, clean the areas where you placed your bags or bins while un-bagging your food, especially the kitchen counter and the kitchen table.

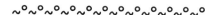

Buy an inexpensive reusable water bottle, and stop buying plastic disposable bottles.

~°~°~°~°~°~°~°~°~°~°~°~°

De-clutter:

Mark four boxes or bags "Keep", "Give Away", "Throw Away", and "Hold for One Year". (The last one's for items you don't need or use but just can't bear to part with yet. If you haven't touched these things in a year, their time has come.)

~°~°~°~°~°~°~°~°~°~°~°~°

60 percent
Amount of Municipal Solid Waste that can be recycled.
13 percent
Amount of Municipal Solid Waste that's actually recycled.
50 percent
Amount of Municipal Solid Waste that can be composted.

~°~°~°~°~°~°~°~°~°~°~°~°

<u>My Special Tips</u>

Chapter Nine

Vehicles

"The winner ain't the one with the fastest car
it's the one who refuses to lose."

—Dale Earnhardt

~°~°~°~°~°~°~°~°~°~°~°~°~°

<u>Winter Survival Kit for Your Car</u>:

Equip your car with these items:

- blankets
- first aid kit
- a can and waterproof matches (to melt snow for water)
- windshield scraper
- booster cables
- road maps
- mobile phone

- compass
- tool kit
- paper towels
- bag of sand or cat litter (to pour on ice or snow for added traction)
- tow rope
- tire chains (in areas with heavy snow)
- collapsible shovel
- container of water and high-calorie canned or dried foods and a can opener
- flashlight and extra batteries
- canned compressed air with sealant (for emergency tire repair)
- brightly coloured cloth

~°~°~°~°~°~°~°~°~°~°~°~°~°

An alternative to a spray wheel cleaner for chrome-plated alloy wheels is a solution of warm water, dishwashing liquid, and a few drops of ammonia wiped on with a soft cloth.

~°~°~°~°~°~°~°~°~°~°~°~°~°

Never work underneath a poorly supported vehicle.

~°~°~°~°~°~°~°~°~°~°~°~°~°

A single misfiring spark plug can decrease your mileage by as much as 10%.

~°~°~°~°~°~°~°~°~°~°~°~°

Underinflated tires can account for a gasoline loss of up to 5%—that's 4 litres every time you fill up.

~°~°~°~°~°~°~°~°~°~°~°~°

Useful Tips for your Holiday Trip:

- *Make copies of your birth certificate, passport, and drivers license and take on the trip with you, but don't keep them in the same place as the originals. If you lose the originals, the copies can help.*
- *Don't use the locks that came in your suitcases, a fingernail file can open them. Buy your own small padlocks and use them instead.*
- *If you normally get an upset stomach while travelling, carry pieces of ginger with you in a plastic baggy. Chew on them and your stomach will soon be better.*
- *Separate your IDs. Only keep one ID with you. That way, if you become the victim of a pickpocket, you'll still have your other IDs to help you out.*

~°~°~°~°~°~°~°~°~°~°~°~°

Mindful tips:

- Clean your windows at least once a week to keep them spotless. Immediately replace cracked glass as they can reflect glare from other vehicle lights.

- Inspect all your vehicle lights (headlights, taillights, signal lights) to make sure that they're clean and in good working condition. Do a general cleaning every week.
- Broken lenses are a big no-no. Always keep your headlights properly adjusted.
- Make sure all headlights are accurately aimed and both headlights point straight ahead and if they hit at the same height.
- Always maintain a longer following distance. Since it's more challenging to see pedestrians and other vehicles on the road, you should keep a longer distance from the vehicle ahead of you. This is all the more true if you're driving a truck as it has a longer stopping distance than a regular vehicle.
- Keep your headlights dim as you drive includes when you are within 250 feet of a vehicle you want to overtake.
- Avoid looking directly at bright lights.
- Watch out for animals on the road. Keep in mind that a lot of creatures are more active at night and are harder to see.
- Avoid smoking while behind the wheel. In fact, avoid multitasking while driving, more so at night. A six-second phone call could cause you a lifetime injury. And that might mean a severe injury at night time.
- Beware of highway hypnosis. You can avoid this night driving hazard by using the radio and taking in cool, fresh air.
- Avoid taking medication before driving as this can cause you to become sleepy or impede your judgment.

- Fatigue, as you know, has caused millions of accidents in the past. When your eyelids are getting heavy or you simply feel fatigue setting in, follow these guidelines:
- Pull over and rest. It's best to take a nap, arrive late in your destination than meet an accident along the way.
- Take frequent breaks. If you're on a long trip, stopping every hour and doing some exercise will help you stay alert.
- Use your visor to cut down on glare from other traffic.

~°~°~°~°~°~°~°~°~°~°~°

"I want to die in my sleep like my grandfather.
Not screaming and yelling like the passengers in his car."

—*Will Shriner*

~°~°~°~°~°~°~°~°~°~°~°

To help keep your windows from fogging up in cold weather, rub lightly with hair shampoo or rubbing alcohol

~°~°~°~°~°~°~°~°~°~°~°

Car lock frozen? Heat the key with a lighter or match and turn in the lock gently

~°~°~°~°~°~°~°~°~°~°~°

To prevent car doors from freezing wipe the rubber gaskets with vegetable oil to seal out winter

~°~°~°~°~°~°~°~°~°~°~°~°~°

Use baking soda on a damp cloth to wipe your car windshield, headlights and chrome

~°~°~°~°~°~°~°~°~°~°~°~°~°

If your chamois has become stiff, soak it in warm water with a spoonful of olive oil.

~°~°~°~°~°~°~°~°~°~°~°~°~°

To help prevent battery corrosion, scrub the terminals with baking soda and water, then smear on petroleum jelly

~°~°~°~°~°~°~°~°~°~°~°~°~°

"The one thing I want to leave my children is an honorable name."

—*Theodore Roosevelt*

~°~°~°~°~°~°~°~°~°~°~°~°~°

Remove bumper stickers soak with nail polish remover before scraping off

~°~°~°~°~°~°~°~°~°~°~°~°~°

Cold steering wheel: Vehicle gets terribly cold in winter and steering wheel doesn't warm up. Use regular foam pipe-wrap, tape the joins then run tape around the entire steering wheel, making wraps about 2 ½ inches apart.

The Basics

Read the owner's manual to become familiar with the various components and systems. Follow the recommended service schedules.

Housekeeping

Wash and wax your vehicle to protect its finish. Inspect lights and bulbs. Replace worn wiper blades; keep plenty of washer fluid on hand; carry emergency gear-a shovel, a blanket, boots, jumper cables, high-energy snacks, and a cell phone.

Battery

The only accurate way to detect a weak battery is with professional equipment. But do-it-yourselves can handle routine care: scrape away corrosion from posts and cable connections, clean all surfaces, and re-tighten connections. (Be sure to wear eye protection and gloves.)

Engine Oil

The oil and filter should be changed as specified in your manual.

Cooling System

Flush and refill as recommended. The level, condition, and concentration of the anti-freeze should be checked periodically. Let the engine cool off before removing the radiator cap. The tightness and conditions of drive belts, clamps, and hoses should be checked by a pro.

Engine Performance

Problems with rough idling, hard starts, stalling, or diminished power should be corrected before cold weather sets in. Describe any changes in performance to a qualified technician.

Heater/Defroster

For comfort and safety, the heater and defroster must be in good working condition.

Tires

Rotate tires about every 5,000 miles. The air pressure should be checked once a month; let the tires "cool down" first. Examine tires for cuts and nicks, uneven wearing and cupping. Check the spare, too. Note that some of today's body styles and tire packages are not compatible with tire chains.

Brakes

Brakes should be inspected as recommended in your manual, or sooner if you notice pulsations, grabbing, noises, or longer stopping distances.

~°~°~°~°~°~°~°~°~°~°~°~°

A broom is the quickest way to clean snow from a car. You can cut the handle down on the broom and store it in the trunk.

In the glove box, keep a few Handy Wipes to remove gas odour from your hands after filling the tank.

Remove auto grease from hands with baking soda and water.

A hubcap can be used as a shovel if your vehicle gets stuck in the snow, mud or mud.

Place a bag of kitty litter in your trunk, in case you get stuck in the snow. Sprinkle some under the tires to get traction.

Make a drip pan to collect oil drips by placing corrugated cardboard in a cookie sheet. Or fill a cookie sheet with kitty litter. Change as needed.

Paint a bright colour strip or use luminous tape on centre of back wall to aim the car down the centre of garage.

If you have poor lighting in garage, place reflector tape on objects that might be hit.

Use carpet strips, foam rubber, or pieces of rubber tire around support studs or framing that car doors open against.

Never warm your car in an attached garage and never with the garage door closed

When tuning up your car, set the gap on the spark plugs using the widest gap that the manufacturer recommends. Your car will run better, idle better and will give you better gas mileage.

Clean hard to reach places such as cup holders with a dampened sponge tipped paintbrush.

Laundry pre-wash liquid removes tar from your vehicle's finish.

Peanut butter has been known to remove tar from vehicle finishes also.

Avoid putting air in tires in extreme cold because the valve stem may freeze and let all the air out. Spray valve stems in the fall with wd40 to help avoid this.

To extend the life of a worn wiper blade rub with sandpaper.

Clean windshield wipers with a good scrubbing of baking soda and water.

A radio antenna will slide up and down easier if a coat of wax is applied occasionally.

Line your car trunk with a plastic rug protector to protect the carpeting. It will make clean up easier if dirty or greasy objects are placed in the trunk.

Prevent rust by keeping the underside of your vehicle clean. Place a lawn sprinkler under the vehicle and let it run full blast. This is a good way to remove salt and road grime.

Leave one window open a crack to prevent frost build-up on the inside of the windows.

If you chip the paint; clean quickly and add a touch of clear nail polish to prevent rusting.

Remove road salt from carpets by using equal parts of vinegar and water.

Make your own washer solvent that won't freeze using 1 quart of rubbing alcohol, 1 cup of water and 2 tablespoons of dish detergent. This mixture will not freeze until -35 below 0

Carry a blackboard eraser if windows tend to steam up easily. Wipe off with eraser.

A dust mop head worn as a mitten is an ideal for washing vehicle

Smushed bugs clean off with baking soda and nylon netting

"Ambition is the path to success.
Persistence is the vehicle you arrive in."

—*Bill Bradley*

~°~°~°~°~°~°~°~°~°~°~°~°~°

~°~°~°~°~°~°~°~°~°~°~°~°~°

"Language is not only the vehicle of thought,
it is a great and efficient instrument in thinking."

—*Humphrey Davy*

~°~°~°~°~°~°~°~°~°~°~°~°~°

Towing Disabled Vehicles:

If your vehicle breaks down, you should get help from a tow truck designed to tow vehicles. If you must use another vehicle to tow, use warning signals or emergency flashers and make sure you attach the vehicles securely. Someone must sit in the disabled vehicle and use the brakes to keep the tow cable tight. If the engine cannot run, don't tow vehicles that have power braking and steering. Without the engine, braking and steering is difficult and towing may lead to a collision.

Trying to start a disabled vehicle by towing is dangerous and could damage both vehicles.

<u>My Special Tips</u>

Chapter Ten

Everything Else

"Remember, your ears aren't made to shut but your mouth is!"

If the cattle are all grazing then the fish are biting.

~°~°~°~°~°~°~°~°~°~°~°~°~°

Cut an empty bleach bottle in half and rinse well. Use the top as a funnel.

~°~°~°~°~°~°~°~°~°~°~°~°~°

To keep nylon cord from fraying, heat the ends with a match or lighter. This will melt the strands together.

~°~°~°~°~°~°~°~°~°~°~°~°~°

If there is thunder in winter it will snow seven days later

~°~°~°~°~°~°~°~°~°~°~°~°~°

When rain is on the way, old sheep turn their backs to the wind, cats sneeze and cows lie down.

~°~°~°~°~°~°~°~°~°~°~°~°~°

Stains on Leather:

Mildew stains. Mix 1 cup (8 fl oz/250 ml) rubbing alcohol with 1 cup (8 fl oz/250 ml) water. Moisten a cloth with the mixture and wipe the affected area. Leave to dry.

Ink stains. Spray the affected area with hairspray, then wipe it off with a clean cloth. Ink can be extremely difficult to remove, so you may need to consult a leather-cleaning professional.

Water stains. Allow a soaked leather garment to dry slowly and naturally. Keep the item away from heat sources, and restore its softness with a leather conditioner after it's dry. For soaked leather shoes, insert shoe trees and let air-dry.

Grease stains. Blot excess grease with a clean cloth. Sprinkle talcum powder or cornstarch on the affected area. Let sit for at least 4 hours, then wipe off the powder.

Protein (Blood, Urine) Stains. Blot excess moisture with a clean, damp cloth. Allow item to dry slowly, away from a heat source.

Gum. Rub with a plastic bag of ice cubes to harden the gum, and then pull off the gum. For any residual gum, heat the area with a hair dryer and rub off the gum with a clean cloth.

Salt Stains. Mix a solution of 3 parts vinegar to 1 part water. Moisten a cloth with the vinegar solution and dab on the affected area.

Discoloration. For leather garments, gloves and bags that are discoloured, use a leather spray designed to restore color. These products are sold at shoe repair shops; choose the color that most closely matches.

~°~°~°~°~°~°~°~°~°~°~°~°~°

When hammering in tight places use needle-nosed pliers to hold the nail instead of bruising your fingers.

~°~°~°~°~°~°~°~°~°~°~°~°~°

Magnet Tip: Instead of groping around your floor for fallen needles and pins, keep a magnet in your sewing kit. Simply sweep it across your rug to pick up these strays.

~°~°~°~°~°~°~°~°~°~°~°~°~°

Crayon on dryer drum: Use "Goof Off," and it worked great! You put a little bit on a rag, wipe off the mess, and you don't have to scrub. After you wipe all the mess away, you go over it with a soapy rag, and let it air out for a day.

~°~°~°~°~°~°~°~°~°~°~°~°~°

Remove dirt stains from the knees of pants: Cut a potato in half, rub it on the stain, and let set for a few hours (or even overnight). Then just launder as usual.

~°~°~°~°~°~°~°~°~°~°~°~°

Cast Iron: If you have cast iron pans, or a wood stove that has collected "gunk" from being used over and over, remove the crusting with a paste made of cream of tartar and vinegar.

~°~°~°~°~°~°~°~°~°~°~°~°

Clean A Vase: To remove those tough stains from the bottom of a glass vase, just fill with water and add two Alka-Seltzer tablets!

~°~°~°~°~°~°~°~°~°~°~°~°

Crayon marks on walls: Spray with WD40 and rub off with a soft cloth

Or

Apply plain white toothpaste to the marks and leave on for a half-hour. Wipe off with a dry cloth.

Or

Just take a blow dryer to it for 5 to 10 seconds. Wipe with a clean, dry towel.

~°~°~°~°~°~°~°~°~°~°~°~°

Cleaning Jewellery: Soak your jewellery in ketchup over night, then rinse in hot water.

~°~°~°~°~°~°~°~°~°~°~°~°

Glass Shower Doors: To keep your shower door clean, shiny, and streak-free rub with a damp sponge soaked in white vinegar.

~°~°~°~°~°~°~°~°~°~°~°~°~°

Loosen Tight Jar Lids: Try using latex dishwashing gloves.

Or

Wrap a rubber band around the lid or top, it will give you enough grip to unscrew it.

~°~°~°~°~°~°~°~°~°~°~°~°~°

Removing Ink & Permanent Marker from Walls: Spray hairspray on the mark then wiping it clean with a dry cloth

~°~°~°~°~°~°~°~°~°~°~°~°~°

Portable Generators: How to use them safely!

Consumers must know that portable generators can be hazardous if used improperly. The hazards are:

1. **Carbon monoxide (CO)** poisoning from the toxic engine exhaust and
2. **Electrocution** from connecting the generator to the home electrical wiring system.

To avoid carbon monoxide (CO) poisoning:

- Never use a generator indoors or in attached garages.

- Only operate the generator outdoors in a well-ventilated, dry area, away from air intakes to the home, and protected from direct exposure to rain and snow, preferably under a canopy, open shed, or carport.

To avoid electrocution:

- Plug individual appliances into the generator using heavy duty, outdoor rated cords with a wire gauge adequate for the appliance load.
- Observe the generator manufacturer's instructions for safe operation.
- Do not plug the generator into a wall outlet.
- If connecting the generator into the house wiring is necessary, have a qualified electrician hook up the standby electrical system, or have the local utility install a linking device if available.

Never store gasoline in the home. Gasoline, kerosene and other flammable liquids should be stored outside of living areas in properly labelled, non-glass safety containers. They should also not be stored in a garage if a fuel-burning appliance is in the garage. The vapour from gasoline can travel invisibly along the ground and be ignited by pilot lights or arcs caused by activating electric switches.

If at all possible, avoid connecting the electrical output of the generator into the house wiring. Instead, connect individual appliances that have their own outdoor rated power cord directly to the receptacle outlet of the generator, or connect these cord-connected appliances to the generator's electrical outlet via a suitable, outdoor-rated extension cord having a sufficient wire gauge to handle the electrical load.

If connecting into the house wiring is necessary on a temporary basis to operate permanently wired equipment, such as a water pump, furnace blower/controls, room lighting, etc., there are important steps that require the utmost care to avoid electrocution. In some locations, the local utility company may offer to install a device at the electric meter socket to permit their customers to connect a portable generator to the household wiring during periods of power outages. If that service is not available or chosen, another method is to have a qualified electrician install a manual transfer switch.

A transfer switch permits transfer of the load from the household power source that is normally supplied by the electric utility over to the portable generator. The transfer switch should be certified by UL, CSA, or other independent test lab for this application, and be mounted within an electrical box. Transfer switches and related accessories designed for connecting a standby system are available from electrical supply stores. The equipment for these accessories includes:

1. cord sets with special locking and recessed connectors
2. electrical boxes with controls for the branch circuits that will receive temporary power from the generator
3. feeder cable to connect the existing electrical panel to the transfer switch

When properly installed, the transfer switch will isolate the circuits supplied by the generator from those normally supplied by the utility. This prevents inadvertently energizing circuits in both systems, and reduces the possibility of electrocution resulting from contact with conductors presumed to be de-energized.

Do not operate more appliances and equipment than the output rating of the generator.

~°~°~°~°~°~°~°~°~°~°~°

Removing Wallpaper: Put boiling hot water in a spray bottle with about one third liquid fabric softener. Spray wallpaper, wait a few minutes and peel off.

~°~°~°~°~°~°~°~°~°~°~°

Sticky labels: Use WD40 to remove sticky labels. Just spray a little WD40 on the label and leave it for a few minutes. The label usually slides right off.

~°~°~°~°~°~°~°~°~°~°~°

Spray Nine: A Product that Does A lot!

CLEANS—Tackles tough soils and stains
DEGREASES—Cuts through heavy grease and grime
DISINFECTS—Kills viruses and bacteria. Controls mould and mildew

Kills viruses and bacteria:

H1N1 Swine Flu, Influenza A2 Virus, Common Flu A2 Virus, Avian Flu H3N2 Virus, Salmonella Choleraesuis, Escherichia coli (E.coli), Hepatitis C Virus, Rhinovirus Type 37, Norwalk Virus, Herpes Simplex I and II, Poliovirus Type I, Rotavirus, MRSA, Streptococcus pyogenes, Shigella dysenteriae.

Use it on:

HOME:

Countertops, stoves, refrigerators, sinks, tubs/showers, toilets, floors, ceramic tile, garbage pails, toys, patio furniture, tools, sporting equipment, BBQ's, fibreglass, vinyl siding and more.

AUTOMOTIVE:

Engines, tires and wheels, bug splatter, consoles, dashboards, door panels, vinyl tops, upholstery, trunks, trailers, RV's and more.

INDUSTRIAL:

Machinery, equipment, tools, motors, conveyors, vents, light fixtures, work benches, floors, walls, cafeterias, showers, change rooms, vinyl, rubber, plastic, metal and more!

~°~°~°~°~°~°~°~°~°~°~°~°~°

This book has also made reference to WD40 and some of its uses:

Here are some of its uses:

1)   Protects silver from tarnishing.
2)   Removes road tar and grime from cars.
3)   Cleans and lubricates guitar strings.

4) Gives floors that 'just-waxed' sheen without making it slippery.
5) Keeps flies off cows.
6) Restores and cleans chalkboards.
7) Removes lipstick stains.
8) Loosens stubborn zippers.
9) Untangles jewellery chains.
10) Removes stains from stainless steel sinks.
11) Removes dirt and grime from the barbecue grill.
12) Keeps ceramic/terra cotta garden pots from oxidizing.
13) Removes tomato stains from clothing.
14) Keeps glass shower doors free of water spots.
15) Camouflages scratches in ceramic and marble floors.
16) Keeps scissors working smoothly.
17) Lubricates noisy door hinges on vehicles and doors in homes
18) It removes black scuff marks from the kitchen floor! Use WD-40 for those nasty tar and scuff marks on flooring. It doesn't seem to harm the finish and you won't have to scrub nearly as hard to get them off.

Just remember to open some windows if you have a lot of marks.

19) Bug guts will eat away the finish on your car if not removed quickly!

Use WD-40!

20) Gives a children's play gym slide a shine for a super fast slide.

21) Lubricates gear shift and mower deck lever for ease of handling on riding mowers.

22) Rids kids rocking chairs and swings of squeaky noises.

23) Lubricates tracks in sticking home windows and makes them easier to open.

24) Spraying an umbrella stem makes it easier to open and close.

25) Restores and cleans padded leather dashboards in vehicles, as well as vinyl bumpers.

26) Restores and cleans roof racks on vehicles.

27) Lubricates and stops squeaks in electric fans.

28) Lubricates wheel sprockets on tricycles, wagons, and bicycles for easy handling.

29) Lubricates fan belts on washers and dryers and keeps them running smoothly.

30) Keeps rust from forming on saws and saw blades, and other tools.

31) Removes splattered grease on stove.

32) Keeps bathroom mirror from fogging.

33) Lubricates prosthetic limbs.

34) Keeps pigeons off the balcony (they hate the smell).

35) Removes all traces of duct tape.

36) Folks even spray it on their arms, hands, and knees to relieve arthritis pain.

37) Florida's favorite use is: "cleans and removes love bugs from grills and bumpers."

38) The favorite use in the state of New York WD-40 protects the Statue of Liberty from the elements.

39) WD-40 attracts fish. Spray a LITTLE on live bait or lures and you will be catching the big one in no time. Also, it's a lot cheaper than the chemical attractants that are made for just that purpose. Keep

in mind though, using some chemical laced baits or lures for fishing are not allowed in some states.

40) Use it for fire ant bites. It takes the sting away immediately and stops the itch.

41) WD-40 is great for removing crayon from walls. Spray on the mark and wipe with a clean rag.

42) Also, if you've discovered that your teenage daughter has washed and dried a tube of lipstick with a load of laundry, saturate the lipstick spots with WD-40 and re-wash. Presto! Lipstick is gone!

43) If you sprayed WD-40 on the distributor cap, it would displace the moisture and allow the car to start.

~°~°~°~°~°~°~°~°~°~°~°~°~°

Ladders Safety: The ladder rule is—the foot of the ladder should be one measure out for every four measures in height. Ladders should be placed on a firm level surface, and the top should be resting on something solid, and not on guttering or a window-sill.

~°~°~°~°~°~°~°~°~°~°~°~°~°

Screws:

- Loosening rusted screws, soak overnight in lemon juice. A tissue wrapped round the area keeps the juice where it can do its work

- The bag of silica gel that you get with your next consumer electronics purchase should not be thrown out. Put it in your tool box and keep them shiny

- Rusty Bolts. Try Coca-Cola, the phosphoric acid in it eats away the rust.

- Rusty Screws. If you are trying to remove a very rusty screw, use the tip of a very hot soldering iron to heat the head of the screw. The heat should expand the screw head and loosen the rust.

- Stuck Screws. If a screw was too tight and the slot gets ruined don't worry, because there is a little trick to rectify this. If the screw head is above the surface use a junior hacksaw blade to cut a new groove.

- Rusty Bolts If you are trying to remove a very rusty bolt, and you don't have wd-40 or anything like that to loosen it, then you can use Tabasco sauce. Just shake a small amount on the bolt and wait for a few minutes then you should have no problem taking it off.

- Glass jars with metal screw tops make excellent storage for screws and other small parts. Drill a hole in the top and screw it to the underside of a shelf, the jar is then screwed up in to the lid,

Nails:

- Try not to run a line of nails along the same wood grain, otherwise the wood could split.

- To help stop a nail from splitting the wood drill a pilot hole or turn the nail over and tap it with a hammer putting a blunt point on it. This helps collapse the wood rather than split it.

Woodworking: Hammering in a nail? Avoid bruised fingers by putting the nail in to a piece of cardboard first.

~°~°~°~°~°~°~°~°~°~°~°~°~°

Drilling Masonry: When drilling masonry always withdraw the tip every 5 seconds or so to stop it overheating. If you don't keep the tip cool it damages the drill bit.

~°~°~°~°~°~°~°~°~°~°~°~°~°

Drilling sheet glass/mirrors: Mark your spot with a felt tip, then make a small well from putty over the marked spot. Fill this well with a touch of light oil. Drill slowly using carbide tipped drill bit. The oil keeps the drill bit cool and makes the job that little bit easier.

~°~°~°~°~°~°~°~°~°~°~°~°~°

If any winged insect, such as a bee or hornet, gets into the house, use hairspray as a repellent. The spray stiffens their wings, so they can't fly anywhere.

~°~°~°~°~°~°~°~°~°~°~°~°~°

Useful Funeral Tips and Facts:

Don't use your will or safety deposit box to hold a description of arrangements you have made for your funeral: Funerals usually take place less than a week after the person dies. Traditionally the Will does not get read until after the funeral has taken place. *A Will, alone will not guarantee that you will have the funeral that you want.*

Final expense insurance: is for burial arrangements but does not protect against inflation. It is just an insurance policy designed to deliver a predetermined lump sum.

Where to start: The family doctor will attend and confirm the fact of death, and will later complete the death certificate and a cremation certificate.

Viewing: Many funeral homes require embalming if the family are planning a viewing or visitation. Embalming generally is not necessary or legally required if the body is buried or cremated shortly after death. Eliminating this service can save you hundreds of dollars.

There are a couple of reasons why funerals are important:

The first is technical—a funeral makes sure that a body is legally buried or cremated.

The second reason is that a funeral helps the family come to terms with the death. *It is very important to remember that a funeral is not for the dead, it is for the living.*

Dispersing the cremated remains after cremation: *Can easily leave family and friends without a place or manner in which to pay tribute.*

One can satisfy both your wishes and those of family and friends through permanent memorialisation. This gives your family and friends a place to visit, which often helps in the recovery process. Always keep in mind that federal, state and local regulations may limit the areas where cremation remains may be scattered.

Children: Should be afforded the opportunity to attend a funeral, especially that of a close relative. They should never be forced to go. Preparing a child is always helpful. Explain what to expect at the funeral before the child is asked to decide if they want to partake in the ceremony. Parents need to make that decision, they are usually aware if a child is likely to be 'too sensitive' to attend or is likely to become hysterical.

Helping: As grieving friend means that you too will share some of the pain. This takes courage and a special kind of friendship. Your friend may want to talk, cry, share, reminisce or even just sit in silence with you. One may ask when is a good time to visit a bereaved friend. Many say *"After the flowers have died"*, that is after about a week or two. Remember it is important to maintain regular contact with your friend six to eight weeks after the death.

Floral tributes: First, check to see if the family want this type of remembrance or a donation to a special interest. Flower tributes can either be sent to the funeral home or the residence. If sent to the residence, usually a planter or a small vase of flowers indicating a person's continued sympathy for the family is suggested. The florist places an identification card on the floral tribute. At the funeral home the cards are removed from the floral tributes and given to the family so they may acknowledge the tributes sent.

Extra funeral services: May include embalming, other preparation of the body, and transfer of the remains from the place of death to the funeral home in town or to or from a location out of town. Facilities and equipment may include use of the funeral home for a viewing or visitation, funeral ceremony, and use of the hearse and flower car, limousine and other automobiles. Merchandise may include the casket, the vault, or the urn.

"Earth shattering events will continue to happen in our lives; we have no control over that . . . . But we do have the ability to control how we respond."

~°~°~°~°~°~°~°~°~°~°~°~°~°~°

Identity Theft Safety Tips:

- Do not carry your extra credit cards, Social Security card, birth certificate, or passport in your wallet or purse except when necessary. This practice minimizes the amount of information a thief can steal. Photocopy everything in your wallet so if it is stolen you know exactly who to call.

- Do not click on links in any emails you receive from financial institutions—even if you're 100% sure they're legitimate. Instead, go to your browser and type in the domain name of the institution (e.g. www.wellsfargo.com or www.paypal.com) and then login to your account. Some emails you receive about your financial accounts are actually fake and are called "phishing" emails.

- Make sure your computer is set to automatically download the latest patches and fixes. Any computer operating systems will have security holes. You will want to install a new fix once they are discovered and patched. Both Microsoft Windows and Mac have an easy method for doing this.

- Install virus and spyware detection software and keep them updated.

- Install a lockable mailbox at your residence to reduce mail theft.

- Take credit card receipts with you. Never toss them in a public trash container.

- Never leave your purse or wallet unattended at work or in church, restaurants, health fitness clubs, parties, or shopping carts. Never leave your purse or wallet in open view in your car, even when your car is locked.

- Destroy all checks immediately after you close a checking account. Destroy or keep in a secure place any courtesy checks that your bank or credit card company sends to you.

- Do not have your bank send your new checks to your home address. Tell the bank that you prefer to pick them up.

- Reconcile your check and credit card statements in a timely fashion, and challenge any purchases you did not make.

- Limit the number of credit cards you have, and cancel any inactive accounts.

- Never give any credit card, bank, or Social Security information to anyone by telephone, even if you made the call, unless you can positively verify that the call is legitimate.

- Minimize exposure of your Social Security and credit card numbers. If the numbers are requested for check-cashing purposes, ask if the business has alternative options such as a check-cashing card.

- Do not allow your financial institution to print your Social Security number on your personal checks.

- Safeguard your credit, debit, and ATM card receipts. <u>Shred them</u> before discarding.

- Scrutinize your utility and subscription bills to make sure the charges are yours.
- Memorize your passwords and personal identification numbers (PINs) so you do not have to write them down. Be aware of your surroundings to make sure no one is watching you input your PIN.
- Keep a list of all your credit accounts and bank accounts in a secure place so you can quickly call the issuers to inform them about missing or stolen cards. Include account numbers, expiration dates, and telephone numbers of customer service and fraud departments.
- Do not toss pre-approved credit offers in your trash or recycling bin without first <u>shredding them</u>. Dumpster divers use these offers to order credit cards in your name and mail them to their address. Always do the same with other sensitive information like credit card receipts, phone bills, and such.
- If you don't receive your billing statement, notify the company immediately.

Making Great Coffee:

The first thing is to buy a good coffee maker. There are a lot of these being sold in appliance stores so the customer should do some research first about the brands to get an idea on the features and benefits of each one.

2. The most important ingredient in making good coffee are the beans. It is recommended that people buy whole beans so this can be grinded prior to use. This may be tedious instead

of just putting in a teaspoon into the cup but there is a big difference that the person will soon appreciate and get to like.

The water that comes out of the faucet or the plastic container has a certain taste. This is influenced by the filtration process to ensure that this is safe for people to drink so customers have to check on it before pouring this into the coffee maker.

Coffee tastes better is by using stainless steel or mesh filters. This is a major improvement from the disposable paper ones that contain bleach, chlorine and dyes that may also affect the flavour. Those who insist on using paper should buy the kind that is unbleached and color brown.

The rule of thumb for brewing is that there should be two tablespoons of coffee for every 6 ounces of water. This must also be spread evenly in the coffee filter before it starts to filter down into the pot.

Coffee can be reheated if it gets cold. The best way to do this is by making sure it reaches 175 degrees. Of course, the other way will be pouring all the contents into a stainless steel Thermos that will keep it warm.

The coffee pot should be cleaned regularly. Using soap and water can do this but if there are still remnants from the old batch, this is the time that vinegar or baking soda have to be used.

It isn't that hard to make a good cup of coffee. It just takes some time to look for a coffee machine and the right beans that will be able to give its rich taste to the user.

Try a cold brew. Some people object to acidity in their cold coffee. Cold brewing greatly reduces the acid content of coffee (with the same coffee it will lower the acidity one full pH point vs hot brew). Put ¾ cup ground coffee in a quart Mason jar, fill with water and stir. Cap it and put in the fridge for 12 hours. The strain the resulting concentrate through a coffee filter to remove he grinds. Add water to taste when you're ready to drink it. You can even heat the reconstituted beverage for a quick, low-acid hot cup.

Make ice cubes from coffee. If you don't like your cold coffee watered down by ice, this is a great way to keep it chilled and avoid dilution.

Don't use "waste" coffee for your iced coffee. Saving some leftover coffee for iced beverage is often fine, but don't be tempted to use the dregs of a burnt pot. If it doesn't taste good hot, it won't taste good cold.

~°~°~°~°~°~°~°~°~°~°~°~°~°

"Enthusiasm is contagious and it increases the likelihood that things will turn out fabulous."

"Say no without guilt—*If you can't get excited about something, don't do it!"*

~°~°~°~°~°~°~°~°~°~°~°~°~°

<u>Beach and Water Safety Tips</u>:

- Learn to swim—it's cheap life insurance.
- Swim in lifeguard patrolled areas.

- Never swim alone—swim with a buddy.
- Supervise children closely even if there is a lifeguard present. They have many people to supervise.
- Inflatable devices are prohibited because they can get caught in a wind, current from tides or even deflate in deep water.
- Alcohol and swimming don't mix.
- Don't dive off piers or swimming rafts. The water has variable depths • Follow the parks by-laws and regulations so everyone can enjoy the facility safely.
- Leave your dog at home or use an off leash area.
- Listen to the lifeguard. They have the expertise to make sure you have a safe time along with others.
- Swim parallel to the shore if you want to swim long distances.
- If you are in trouble call or wave for help if you can.
- Glass containers are not recommended at the beach. Broken glass and bare feet are very dangerous.
- Beach fires can burn feet well after the fire is not lit. The coals can remain hot into the next day if covered with sand.
- BBQ coals should be disposed of in a coal pit. If there is no pit present then douse the coals thoroughly with water before disposing in a garbage can.
- Report any hazardous conditions to lifeguards.
- Stay away from piers and jetties especially during windy conditions.
- Overnight camping and parking on beach areas may be prohibited.
- Kite surfing and kite boarding is not permitted at public beaches. An out of control kite boarder can hurt someone as well as themselves by hitting

another swimmer, or having their nearly transparent lines cut someone severely.

- For any large gathering or special event a permit may be required.
- Use sunscreen on all parts of your exposed body. Watch out for young children getting burnt even in questionable weather. Use a minimum sunscreen of SPF 15 as well as a hat and shirt when you are not swimming.

~°~°~°~°~°~°~°~°~°~°~°~°~°

Looking at want ads, or house's of sale or rent, or cars for sale in your paper, instead of marking the ad, or cutting it out, or copying it, instead take a piece of scotch tape and cover the ad, then just peel it off, the ad sticks to the tape, and that way you can put all the ads on one piece of paper, try it, it works

~°~°~°~°~°~°~°~°~°~°~°~°~°

Cover your snow shovel with spray wax to keep the snow from sticking to it

~°~°~°~°~°~°~°~°~°~°~°~°~°

Winter Water Safety: Ice Safety and Hypothermia:

Falling through ice on frozen bodies of water can cause severe injury or death from drowning or hypothermia. When hunting, fishing, snowmobiling or walking on frozen lakes or rivers, use extreme caution to prevent falling into the very cold water.

Here are steps you can take to prevent drowning:

- Never travel onto frozen bodies of water alone;
- Always wear a personal flotation device (PFD) or a lifejacket;
- Wear a bodysuit that is meant to prevent hypothermia;
- Come well equipped with a rope, small personal safety kit and ice picks;
- Let others know your planned travel route;
- Check the weather and ice conditions before heading out; and
- Avoid traveling on ice at night.

~°~°~°~°~°~°~°~°~°~°~°~°

"Bullying is behaviour that is intentional and repeated over time. Actions are meant to HARM somebody else emotionally, physically, verbally and mentally."

~°~°~°~°~°~°~°~°~°~°~°~°

Chimney:

To keep your chimney clean, throw a handful of salt on the fire.

~°~°~°~°~°~°~°~°~°~°~°~°

Cycle all your plumbing shut off valves (toilet & faucet supply valves) once a year to keep them from seizing up.

To avoid drowning around water:

- Do not drink alcohol when swimming; reaction times are slowed when drinking;
- Take swimming lessons;
- Ensure children wear a PFD or life jacket;
- Build a fence and a gate to keep children away from your pool; and
- Keep the gate on your fence locked at all times when not in use by a responsible person.

~°~°~°~°~°~°~°~°~°~°~°~°~°

CD/DVDs

You can preserve the life of CD/DVD, if you handle and clean it properly, because dirty discs can create errors in reading or writing and soon discs will not work at all. Follow the given steps to care and clean a CD/DVD.

- Avoid to touching the writeable or data side of the CD/DVD.
- Always hold your CD/DVD by its center hole or by the outer edges.
- Keep away your discs from sunlight, heat and anything that may create scratch on the discs.
- Always clean dust with a soft cloth or with a CD/ DVD cleaning kit and avoid to clean with static cloth or harsh detergents.

- Start work to clean from inside to outside in straight lines until the CD/DVD is clean.
- Store your all discs vertically position and in dust free box.

~°~°~°~°~°~°~°~°~°~°~°~°~°

Mold is one of mankind's most silent invaders, spreading in our homes and properties, and worse, profoundly destroying our health.

Mold can affect the systems of the body in the following ways:

Digestive: diarrhoea, vomiting, haemorrhage, liver damage, fibrosis and necrosis

Neurological: tremors, loss of coordination, memory loss, headaches, depression, multiple sclerosis

Reproductive: infertility, changes in reproductive cycles

Immune: Immuno suppression

Respiratory: trouble breathing, bleeding from lungs

Skin: itchy rashes, burning, sloughing, photosensitivity, hair loss

Urinary: kidney toxicity

Vascular: blood vessel fragility, haemorrhage from tissues or lungs

The effects of mold manifest differently in different people in varying degrees, which makes it difficult to diagnose. Some common complaints are associated with mold allergic reactions include: coughing and wheezing, sinus problems, eczema and even muscle and joint pain. Mold can affect any part of the body from head to toe.

Removing Mold:

Seal Off the Room You Are Working In

When removing mold or black mold from a particular room seal it off as best you can from the surrounding areas using plastic sheeting and duct tape.

Dampen the Area You Are Working On

Before you start removing the mold or black mold ensure that you have dampened the area you are working on so as to minimize the release of mold spores.

Mold and Black Mold Removal

The next step in mold and black mold removal is to clean the area as much as possible using soap and water to remove as much of the mold as you can. Then disinfect the area with a bleach and water solution, leave for a few minutes (usually about 15 minutes) and then rinse thoroughly and dry rapidly.

What You Need to Discard

Apart from your clothes there are also a number of other materials within the area that you should discard if they have been exposed to mold or black mold including drywall, paper and carpet padding. Plastic, glass, metal and counter tops can be cleaned effectively but wood must also be sanded down to ensure that all mold has been removed. Place these mold infected items in sealed plastic bags and remove them through the nearest window—do not carry through the whole house.

Before Using the Room after Mold and Black Mold Removal

Before using the room after the mold and black mold removal you should air the room out so as to get rid of any toxins still in the area. After this the room should be safe to use.

Fix the Cause

Once you have removed the mold or black mold it is not enough to simply leave it or the mold will most likely return, you should also have a look for the cause of the problem and work on fixing this as well to prevent future problems. The problem could be related to areas that are regularly flooded, leaking plumbing or leaky roofs. Find out where the problem is in your home and remove this.

Mold and black mold can have serious consequences for your health and so it is important that this is removed. You may either choose to do mold or black mold removal yourself or get in a professional to do this for you. If you are going to do it yourself, you should ensure that you take the necessary precautions and also fix any problems that could have led to the mold.

Mold-proofing your home, room by room:

Basement or crawl space

- Reduce the amount of clothes, paper and furnishings stored in the basement. Discard badly damaged materials. Eliminate clutter to improve air circulation. Only washable items should be stored.
- Dehumidify the basement during the warm months.
- Avoid carpets on slab-on-grade or below grade floors.
- Periodically clean the drain in your basement floor. Use half a cup of bleach, let it stand for a few minutes, then flush with plenty of water. Keep the drain trap filled with water.
- Avoid standing water. Keep sump pits covered (you can use plywood wrapped with plastic).
- Regularly clean and replace furnace filters. Use a pleated one-inch filter, not a coarse filter.
- If you have a heat recovery ventilator (HRV), clean the filter inside the HRV often.
- If you notice molds or signs of dampness, such as water on your windows or wet spots elsewhere, do not humidify. Disconnect furnace humidifiers that are no longer used.
- If you have electric baseboards, vacuum the units, or have a professional clean them for you.

Laundry areas

- Check that your clothes dryer exhausts to the outside.
- Remove lint every time you use the dryer.
- Don't hang-dry laundry indoors.

- Dry your laundry tub and washing machine after you use them.

Bathrooms

- Check the bathroom fan to make sure it exhausts to the outside.
- Turn the bathroom fan on when you shower. Keep it running for a few minutes after you finish your shower.
- Take short showers.
- Keep surfaces that get wet, such as the walls around the bathtub and shower, clean and dry.
- If there is a carpet in your bathroom, remove it.
- Check for water leaks.
- Keep drains in good shape by removing debris from them.

To clean a drain:

- Pour a handful of baking soda into it.
- Add a cup of vinegar.
- Put the plug in the drain.
- Let the vinegar and baking soda work for about 20 minutes.
- Run fresh water into the drain.

If the drain is still clogged, use a small plumbing snake.

Kitchen

- If the fan over your stove exhausts outside, use it when you cook.

- Minimize open boiling.
- Keep your drains in good shape. Follow the steps in the Bathrooms section above.
- There's a drip pan at the back of the refrigerator. Pull the refrigerator out to clean the drip pan. At the same time, vacuum dust from the coils at the back of the refrigerator.
- Check under the kitchen sink to make sure there are no leaks.
- Take out the garbage daily to prevent odours and spoiling.

Closets and bedrooms

- Get rid of clothes and other stored items that you don't use. Keeping your closets and bedrooms tidy makes it easier for air to circulate—and harder for mold to grow.

Other parts of the home

- A dehumidifier helps to reduce moisture in the home during the warmer months. Close the windows when the dehumidifier is running.
- When family and friends come into the home, have them take off their shoes.
- Vacuum often. If you are buying a vacuum cleaner, try to get one with a HEPA filter.
- Clean hard floors with a damp mop.
- Do not bring in furniture, clothing, books etc. that have been stored in a mouldy place into your home.
- Cut down the number of potted plants in the house—soil is a good place for mold.

Exterior

- Regularly check the condition of the roof and exterior finish for any places where water might enter.
- Make sure that eaves troughs and downspouts are connected and working properly and that they are free of debris.
- Install downspout extensions to lead water away from the building.
- Deal promptly with any problems that you find.

~°~°~°~°~°~°~°~°~°~°~°~°

Safety Reminder: Smoke detectors with batteries only can go out while you are on vacation and may not be working when you get back. Remember to test them.

~°~°~°~°~°~°~°~°~°~°~°~°

Trailer Towing Safety Tips:

Start-up Checks

Personally inspect the trailer and hitch safety chains for proper connections. Ensure the electrical hook-ups work for the trailer wiring and brakes. Check tire air, oil, fuel and coolant levels, as always, before taking any trip. Make certain the vehicle and trailer lights operate.

Trailer Loading

Load the trailer heavier toward the front for proper weight distribution. About 60 percent of the cargo weight should be in the trailer's front half. This properly places about 10 percent of the loaded trailer weight on the tow-vehicle hitch.

Practice Driving

If you're not now a trailer-towing veteran, take time to practice before beginning a long haul. When backing up, place one hand on your vehicle's steering wheel at the six o'clock position.

To move the trailer's rear end to the right, turn the steering wheel to the right. In more complex towing situations, such as boat launching, use low-range gears for extra power and control.

Handling Suggestions

Avoid sudden moves that might create side force on the trailer. Allow more room to the inside on right-angle turns since the trailer wheels will be closer to the inside turn path than the vehicle wheels.

Passing; Stopping

When passing a slower motorist or changing lanes, signal well in advance and move gradually into the next lane. After passing, allow the trailer or RV extra room before returning to the driving lane. Avoid passing on steep grades—up or down. Driving while towing a trailer requires a greater distance to stop. A good rule-of-thumb: Allow one vehicle and trailer length between you and the vehicle you're following for each 10 mph of speed. Eliminate panic stops by shifting to a lower gear and pumping brakes lightly to cut vehicle speed.

Parking

When parking your whole kit-and-caboodle, place a foot on the brake and have someone outside your vehicle help you. He/she should place blocks behind the tow vehicle wheels on an upgrade, or in front of the wheels on a downgrade.

Slowly release the brakes until the blocks are holding the vehicle and the trailer is at rest. Fully engage the parking brake and leave the transmission in first or reverse gear if you have a manual shift, or in park for an automatic.

Loading Hints

Keep personal items most-frequently used in the vehicle, not the trailer, for convenience. When packing clothes, use pliable bags and carrying cases that compress when stored, to save space.

Be sure all items stowed in the trailer are tied down. Check RV cupboard latches, closets, bathroom and storage doors to see they are secure before heading down the highway. Distribute passengers equally over the available seating space to promote better vehicle riding and handling characteristics. It's safer not to allow passengers to ride in the RV while it's being towed and it's against the law, too, in some states.

You should make sure both the trailer and your towing vehicle are within load recommendations. Hauling too much can result in handling and trailer-stability problems. Observe all posted speed limits; in bad weather or slippery road conditions, it's always wise to slow down.

Another tip before you get your show on the road: Read the helpful towing information in the owner's manual. Last, but not least, check and make sure anyone else driving your vehicle with a trailer in tow is fully clued in—before the towing begins.

Safety Tips When Driving With A Trailer:

General Handling

- Use the driving gear that the manufacturer recommends for towing.
- Drive at moderate speeds. This will place less strain on your tow vehicle and trailer. Trailer instability (sway) is more likely to occur as speed increases.
- Avoid sudden stops and starts that can cause skidding, sliding, or jackknifing.
- Avoid sudden steering manoeuvres that might create sway or undue side force on the trailer.
- Slow down when traveling over bumpy roads, railroad crossings, and ditches.
- Make wider turns at curves and corners. Because your trailer's wheels are closer to the inside of a turn than the wheels of your tow vehicle, they are more likely to hit or ride up over curbs.
- To control swaying caused by air pressure changes and wind buffeting when larger vehicles pass from either direction, release the accelerator pedal to slow down and keep a firm grip on the steering wheel.

Braking

- Allow considerably more distance for stopping.

- If you have an electric trailer brake controller and excessive sway occurs, activate the trailer brake controller by hand. Do not attempt to control trailer sway by applying the tow vehicle brakes; this will generally make the sway worse.
- Always anticipate the need to slow down. To reduce speed, shift to a lower gear and press the brakes lightly.

Acceleration and Passing

- When passing a slower vehicle or changing lanes, signal well in advance and make sure you allow extra distance to clear the vehicle before you pull back into the lane.
- Pass on level terrain with plenty of clearance. Avoid passing on steep upgrades or downgrades.
- If necessary, downshift for improved acceleration or speed maintenance.
- When passing on narrow roads, be careful not to go onto a soft shoulder. This could cause your trailer to jackknife or go out of control.

Downgrades and Upgrades

- Downshift to assist with braking on downgrades and to add power for climbing hills.
- On long downgrades, apply brakes at intervals to keep speed in check. Never leave brakes on for extended periods of time or they may overheat.
- Some tow vehicles have specifically calibrated transmission tow-modes. Be sure to use the tow-mode recommended by the manufacturer.

Backing Up

- Put your hand at the bottom of the steering wheel. To turn left, move your hand left. To turn right, move your hand right. Back up slowly. Because mirrors cannot provide all of the visibility you may need when backing up, have someone outside at the rear of the trailer to guide you, whenever possible.
- Use slight movements of the steering wheel to adjust direction. Exaggerated movements will cause greater movement of the trailer. If you have difficulty, pull forward and realign the tow vehicle and trailer and start again.

Parking

- Try to avoid parking on grades. If possible, have someone outside to guide you as you park. Once stopped, but before shifting into Park, have someone place blocks on the downhill side of the trailer wheels. Apply the parking brake, shift into Park, and then remove your foot from the brake pedal. Following this parking sequence is important to make sure your vehicle does not become locked in Park because of extra load on the transmission. For manual transmissions, apply the parking brake and then turn the vehicle off in either first or reverse gear.
- When uncoupling a trailer, place blocks at the front and rear of the trailer tires to ensure that the trailer does not roll away when the coupling is released.
- An unbalanced load may cause the tongue to suddenly rotate upward; therefore, before

un-coupling, place jack stands under the rear of the trailer to prevent injury.

Additional Maintenance Suggestions:

Tires

Periodic inspection and maintenance of tow vehicle and trailer tires and wheels are essential to towing safety, including spare tires. Proper tire pressure affects vehicle handling and the safety of your tires. You can find the correct tire pressure for your tow vehicle in the owner's manual or on the tire information placard.

- Under inflation reduces the load-carrying capacity of your tow vehicle or trailer, may cause sway and control problems, and may result in overheating, causing blowouts or other tire failure.
- Over inflation causes premature tire wear and affects the handling characteristics of the tow vehicle or trailer.

Brakes

On a regular basis, have the brakes on both vehicles inspected. Be sure that necessary adjustments are made and any damaged or worn parts are replaced.

Hitch

Check the nuts, bolts, and other fasteners to ensure that the hitch remains secured to the tow vehicle and the coupler remains secured to the trailer. The connection point may require periodic lubrication to permit free movement of the coupler to the hitch ball.

Wiring

Make sure connector-plug prongs and receptacles, light bulb sockets, wire splices, and ground connections are clean and shielded from moisture. Lightly coat all electrical terminal connections with non-conducting (dielectric), light waterproof grease.

Clean the prongs with very fine sandpaper, being careful not to damage the contact area.

Clean the surface deposits in the connector holes. (Make sure the lights are off to prevent blowing a fuse.) Try to clean off only the deposits and lubricate lightly with dielectric, light waterproof grease.

~°~°~°~°~°~°~°~°~°~°~°~°~°

<u>Safest Gun Environment for Your Family:</u>

- Take the ammunition out of the gun.
- Lock the gun and keep it out of reach of kids.
- Lock the ammunition and store it apart from the gun.
- Store the keys for the gun and the ammunition in a different area from where you store household keys. Keep the keys out of reach of children.
- Lock up gun-cleaning supplies, which are often poisonous.

~°~°~°~°~°~°~°~°~°~°~°~°~°

Fireworks Safety Tips:

- Never allow young children to play with or ignite fireworks.
- Avoid buying fireworks that are packaged in brown paper because this is often a sign that the fireworks were made for professional displays and that they could pose a danger to consumers.
- Always have an adult supervise fireworks activities. Parents don't realize that young children suffer injuries from sparklers. Sparklers burn at temperatures of about 2,000 degrees—hot enough to melt some metals.
- Never place any part of your body directly over a fireworks device when lighting the fuse. Back up to a safe distance immediately after lighting fireworks.
- Never try to re-light or pick up fireworks that have not ignited fully.
- Never point or throw fireworks at another person.
- Keep a bucket of water or a garden hose handy in case of fire or other mishap.
- Light fireworks one at a time, then move back quickly.
- Never carry fireworks in a pocket or shoot them off in metal or glass containers.
- After fireworks complete their burning, douse the spent device with plenty of water from a bucket or hose before discarding it to prevent a trash fire.
- Make sure fireworks are legal in your area before buying or using them.

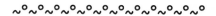

<u>Natural Gas Safety:</u>

1. Make sure that all your gas appliances are in good working order. Follow the manufacturer's maintenance and service schedules.

2. Do not move, install, or remove gas-operated appliances yourself as you could damage the gas distribution lines. Always have a professional install or replace gas appliances.

3. Know how to light the pilot light on any gas appliance that uses one. Never deliberately blow out a pilot light as this allows more gas into the room. Allow any gas build-up to disperse before relighting a pilot light.

4. Never use a gas stove or oven for heat. This not only creates a fire risk, but can cause a deadly carbon monoxide build-up.

5. Know how to shut off the gas to your appliances and your whole house. The gas is on when the handle is parallel to the gas line. To shut off the gas, turn the valve so the handle is 90 degrees from the gas line. You will need a pipe wrench for the outside master shutoff.

6. Install a natural gas detector and a carbon monoxide detector. These will sound an alarm if you have a gas leak or a build-up of carbon monoxide caused by incomplete burning of gas in an appliance.

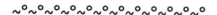

Window Safety:

- Safeguard your children by using window guards or window stops.

  o Install window guards to prevent children from falling out of windows.
  o For windows on the 6th floor and below, install window guards that adults and older children can open easily in case of fire.
  o Install window stops so that windows open no more than 4 inches.

- Never depend on screens to keep children from falling out of windows.
- Whenever possible, open windows from the top—instead of the bottom.
- Keep furniture away from windows to discourage children from climbing near windows.
- Some jurisdictions require landlords to install guards.

~°~°~°~°~°~°~°~°~°~°~°~°

Safe Summer Cycling:

- Protect your head . . . Wear a helmet.
- See and be seen . . . Wear bright fluorescent colors during the day.
- Avoid biking at night . . . If riding at night, equip your bicycle with head and tail lights and wear reflective clothing.
- Stay alert . . . Keep a lookout for obstacles in your path.

- Go with the flow . . . Ride with traffic.
- Check for traffic . . . Be aware of traffic around you.
- Learn the rules of the road . . . Obey traffic laws.
- Assure bicycle readiness . . . Is your bicycle properly adjusted?
- Check brakes before riding.
- Check your wheels . . . "Quick release" wheels should be securely fastened.
- When you get a new bicycle, write your name, address and the bike's serial number on a card. Roll it around a pencil, secure with elastic bands and drop into the frame. (the frame can be reached by removing the seat post) if the ownership of the bicycle is ever in question, you have proof that belongs to you.

~°~°~°~°~°~°~°~°~°~°~°~°~°

Lawn and Garden Equipment Safety:

- Children should never be in the yard while you're mowing, and they should never ride on the mower. More than 800 young children get run over or backed over by riding mowers each year. This happens when children fall while being given rides, or when they approach the operating mower.
- Never assume children will remain where you last saw them. Be alert and turn off the mower if children enter the mowing area. Use extra care when backing up or going around corners, shrubs, trees or other obstacles.
- Many children suffer serious burns to their hands and arms when they touch the hot muffler of

running or recently running engines. Keep children away from power equipment.

- Be sure you know how to operate the equipment. Know where the controls are and what they do. Make sure the equipment is in proper operating condition and guards or other safety devices have not been removed or disabled.

- Dress appropriately for the job. This includes: sturdy shoes with slip-resistant rubber soles, long pants and long-sleeved shirts, close-fitting clothes, eye protection, heavy gloves, hearing protection when needed, and no jewellery, which can get caught in moving parts.

- Before mowing, walk around the area in which you will be working to remove any objects like sticks, glass, metal, wire, stones and string that could cause injury or damage equipment. Nails and wire are the most hazardous objects thrown by mowers, capable of killing bystanders.

- Never work with electric power tools in wet or damp conditions. For protection against electrocution, use a ground fault circuit interrupter (GFCI). GFCIs come in several models, including portable plug-in types and as part of some extension cords.

- Be sure that extension cords are in good condition, are rated for outdoor use, and are the proper gauge for the electrical current capacity of the tool.

- Before making adjustments or clearing jams near moving parts, unplug electric tools and disconnect spark plug wires on gasoline-powered tools.

- Be sure that power tools are turned off and made inoperable if they must be left unattended. This will help prevent use by children.

- Handle gasoline carefully. Remember never to fill gas tanks while machinery is operating or when equipment is still hot. Do not fuel equipment indoors. Wipe up spills. Store gas in an approved container away from the house. Finally, never smoke or use any type of flame around gasoline.

~°~°~°~°~°~°~°~°~°~°~°~°~°

Elderly Safety:

- Install grab bars and slip-resistant surfaces in bathrooms.
- Only use stable step stools with a top handrail. Don't climb alone. Have someone nearby to help you.
- Be sure your telephones and emergency numbers are easily accessible—so you can get help if you fall.
- Always grip the handrails on stairs. Keep stairs well lighted.
- Keep floors clear and slip resistant.

~°~°~°~°~°~°~°~°~°~°~°~°~°

Poison Prevention Safety:

- When hazardous products are in use, never let young children out of your sight, even if you must take them along when answering the phone or doorbell.
- Keep items closed and in their original containers.
- Leave the original labels on all products, and read the label before using.
- Always leave the light on when giving or taking medicine so that you can see what you are taking. Check the dosage every time.

- Avoid taking medicine in front of children. Refer to medicine as "medicine," not "candy."
- Clean out the medicine cabinet periodically and safely dispose of unneeded and outdated medicines.
- Do not put decorative lamps and candles that contain lamp oil where children can reach them. Lamp oil can be very toxic if ingested by young children.

~°~°~°~°~°~°~°~°~°~°~°

Skiers & Snowboarders Safety Tips:

- Select the right equipment, and make sure items such as bindings and boots are adjusted to fit properly.
- Make sure you have the proper training, and don't ski or snowboard beyond your ability.
- Ski and snowboard in control, and follow the rules of the slopes.
- Never ski or snowboard alone. Make sure someone is there to help you if you get hurt.
- Get in shape before you hit the slopes. Making sure you are physically fit before you ski or snowboard can help prevent injuries.
- Wear warm, close-fitting clothing. Loose clothing can become entangled in lifts, tow ropes and ski poles.

~°~°~°~°~°~°~°~°~°~°~°

Public and Home Playgrounds Safety Tips:

- Always supervise children on play equipment to make sure they are safe.

- Purchase playground equipment that meets the latest safety standards.
- Maintain at least 9 inches of protective surfacing, including shredded/recycled rubber, wood chips, wood mulch (non-CCA treated), sand or pea gravel under and around playground equipment to cushion children from falls.
- Check that protective surfacing extends at least 6 feet in all directions from play equipment. For swings, extend protective surfacing in front and back of the swing, twice the height of the suspending bar.
- Repair sharp points or edges on equipment. Replace missing hardware and close "S" hooks that can cause injuries.
- Never attach ropes, jump ropes, clotheslines, pet leashes or cords of any kind to play equipment due to the strangulation hazard.

~°~°~°~°~°~°~°~°~°~°~°~°~°

Prevent Ladder Injuries:

- Make sure the weight your ladder is supporting does not exceed its maximum load rating (user plus materials). There should only be one person on the ladder at one time.
- Use a ladder that is the proper length for the job. Proper length is a minimum of 3 feet extending over the roofline or working surface. The three top rungs of a straight, single or extension ladder should not be stood on.
- Straight, single or extension ladders should be set up at about a 75-degree angle.

- All metal ladders should have slip-resistant feet.
- Metal ladders will conduct electricity. Use a wooden or fibreglass ladder in the vicinity of power lines or electrical equipment. Do not let a ladder made from any material contact live electric wires.
- Be sure all locks on extension ladders are properly engaged.
- The ground under the ladder should be level and firm. Large flat wooden boards braced under the ladder can level a ladder on uneven ground or soft ground. A good practice is to have a helper hold the bottom of the ladder.
- Do not place a ladder in front of a door that is not locked, blocked or guarded.
- Keep your body centered between the rails of the ladder at all times. Do not lean too far to the side while working.
- Do not use a ladder for any purpose other than that for which it was intended.
- Do not step on the top step, bucket shelf or attempt to climb or stand on the rear section of a stepladder.
- Never leave a raised ladder unattended.
- Follow use instruction labels on ladders.

~°~°~°~°~°~°~°~°~°~°~°~°

Uses for Old Pantyhose:

Wash your back. Put a bar of soap in the hose leg, get in the shower, grasp with both hands and rub back and forth across your back

Make a tidy bath sachet. If you like to add things to enhance your bath, like salts or herbs, but them in a section of knotted hose to ensure an easier clean of the tub afterwards.

Conserve old soap. Save small remnants of soap and put them in a section of hose, then tie the ends for a sudsy scrubber.

Secure an ice or heat pack. Put the ice or heat in the leg off a pair of pantyhose, wrap it around the affected area and tie the ends around your body to keep the pack in place.

Pack efficiently. Rolling clothes is a super way to fit a lot in a suitcase without excessive wrinkling. Once you've rolled clothing, encase the roll in a section of pantyhose to keep it secure.

DIY Spandex. Cut the panty part off of support-top hose and wear for support without the hose.

Keep warm. Hose or tights with runs in them can still provide a layer for warmth when worn under pants.

Protect your shoes. Use sections of hose to slip over shoes to prevent them from getting dusty or scuffing while in your closet.

Shine shoes. Pantyhose are slightly abrasive, yet soft enough to not scratch, which makes them perfect for polishing and buffing shoes and boots.

Keep baby socks matched. Baby socks magically become unmatched and orphaned in the laundry. Keep pairs together and place them in the leg of a pair of nylons and tie the ends, then wash and dry as usual

Use instead of twine or bungee cords. Pantyhose legs are perfect for binding anything you would normally use twine or bungee cords for.

Use as a paint strainer. Stretch hose over a can of paint to filter out any lumps of paint to ensure even painting.

Protect paper rolls. Store rolls of wrapping paper in a protective sleeve made of a pantyhose leg.

Secure the trash. Use the elastic waistband from an old hose to secure the top of the trash bag to the bin.

Find lost jewellery. If you've lost something small, place the foot of a pair of pantyhose over the opening of your vacuum and vacuum the area—the item will be sucked against the nylon without being sucked into the vacuum.

Make potpourri. Use sections of hose legs to contain ingredients for potpourri.

Easy dough-rolling. Slip a hose leg over your rolling pin to help keep wet dough from sticking.

Stake plants. Nylon has just the right mix of strength and give to keep plants, like tomatoes, in place without hurting them.

Store plant bulbs, onions, or garlic. Bulbs can get mouldy if too crowded, keep them separated by putting one in a hose leg, tying a knot, putting in another, and so on.

Keep the soil in a potted plant. Fill a hose leg with soil and tie the ends, then line the bottom of a plant pot, blocking the hole, so that loose soil doesn't spill out.

~°~°~°~°~°~°~°~°~°~°~°~°~°

Physical abuse:

- May consist of assault, sexual assault, forcible confinement and / or murder.

Financial abuse:

- Includes theft, theft by person with Power of Attorney, fraud, extortion, forgery and/or stopping mail with intent.

Neglect:

- May involve criminal negligence causing bodily harm or death and/or failing to provide the necessities of life.

Mental cruelty:

- Includes intimidation and/or uttering threats.

Prevention Strategies for Families and Caregivers:

- o Learn how your parent or relative wishes to be cared for in event they become dependent or require medical care.
- o Find out how they want assets spent and/or maintained.
- o Carefully assess your ability to provide care for an increasingly dependent relative.
- o Consult with other members about how care giving arrangements will affect them.
- o Examine the physical layout of potential homes to ensure they are appropriate (i.e.: is a first floor bathroom required?)
- o Learn about all community resources available to help.

Don't:

- o Undertake the care of an older relative on the spur of the moment or out of guilt
- o Assume that a tenuous relationship will miraculously improve when the person comes to live with you.
- o Feel you have failed if you are unable to provide home care at any time and must seek an alternative.

Prevention Suggestions for Older persons:

Do:

- o Plan for your own future when you are well and still independent.
- o Make a will and review it annually.

- o Have your pension and other cheques deposited into your account.
- o Stay active in your community for as long as possible.

Don't:

- o Revise a will without careful thought and before speaking to someone you trust.
- o Leave jewellery, cash or other valuable possessions lying around your home.
- o Rely solely on family members for your social life and care.
- o Allow adult children to return to your home (especially if they have drug, alcohol and /or psychological problems) without carefully considering the situation and consulting others for advice.
- o Be too proud to ask for help when you need it 9 I.E. Public health nurse, church, senior centre, friends).
- o Be intimidated in seeking your rights because of your age.

~°~°~°~°~°~°~°~°~°~°~°~°~°

Stop a scratched CD or DVD from skipping: rub the back of the disk in a circular motion with the inside of the banana peel. Wipe off any residue with a soft cloth, then lightly spray the disk with glass cleaner and buff it until it looks clean. The wax in the peel will fill in scratches without harming the plastic finish.

~°~°~°~°~°~°~°~°~°~°~°~°~°

Common signs of verbal abuse:

- Being called names. Any negative form of name calling is unacceptable. If you feel that it is a put down, then it most likely is. There are names that are obvious and, without question abusive. Verbal abusers love to use constructive criticism to beat a person down. This is the most insidious form of verbal abuse.

- Using words to shame. Critical, sarcastic, mocking words meant to put you down either alone or in front of other people.

- Yelling, swearing and screaming. Living with someone who goes verbally ballistic for very little cause.

- Using threats to intimidate.

- Blaming the victim. The other person blows their top and then blames you for their actions and behaviour. If you were only perfect they wouldn't lose control!

- Your feelings are dismissed. They avoid discussion of any topic where they might have to take responsibility for their actions or words.

- You often wonder why you feel so bad. You bury your feelings, walk on egg shells and work so hard at keeping the peace that every day becomes an emotional chore. You feel depressed and have even wondered if you are crazy.

- Manipulating your actions. The persistent and intense use of threatening words to get you to do something or act in a way you find uncomfortable.

~°~°~°~°~°~°~°~°~°~°~°~°

Commons Signs of Controlling:

- Overt physical violence—they shove, slap or hit you.
- You're afraid you'll trigger a violent rage.
- They make the rules; they control everything—what you do, where you go, who spends the money and what it's spent on.
- You feel emotionally blackmailed, intimidated and drained.
- You're told you're incompetent, helpless and would be alone without them.
- You're told that you're to blame if they hurt you.
- They push boundaries, argue endlessly and withhold approval and love if you don't do exactly what they want.
- Their standards rule—your "no" isn't accepted as "no;" they're always right and you're always wrong.
- They isolate you—they won't allow you to see you friends or your family, go to school or even work.
- They control you with their disapproval, name-calling, putdowns, demeaning, blame and guilt—no matter what you do; you're wrong or not good enough.
- Your concerns generally don't get dealt with.
- They control you with their hyper-sensitive and hurt feelings.

In addition to controlling you by making you afraid, they are the sneaky, manipulative schoolyard bullies who have developed adult ways to dominate, abuse and bully.

~°~°~°~°~°~°~°~°~°~°~°~°~°

Idioms and their meanings:

A Bird In The Hand Is Worth Two In The Bush:
Having something that is certain is much better than taking a risk for more, because chances are you might lose everything.

A Blessing In Disguise:
Something good that isn't recognized at first.

A Chip On Your Shoulder:
Being upset for something that happened in the past.

A Dime A Dozen:
Anything that is common and easy to get.

A Doubting Thomas:
A sceptic who needs physical or personal evidence in order to believe something.

A Drop in the Bucket:
A very small part of something big or whole.

A Fool And His Money Are Easily Parted:
It's easy for a foolish person to lose his/her money.

A House Divided Against Itself Cannot Stand:
Everyone involved must unify and function together or it will not work out.

A Leopard Can't Change His Spots:
You cannot change who you are.

A Penny Saved Is A Penny Earned:
By not spending money, you are saving money (little by little).

A Picture Paints a Thousand Words:
A visual presentation is far more descriptive than words.

A Piece of Cake:
A task that can be accomplished very easily.

A Slap on the Wrist:
A very mild punishment.

A Taste Of Your Own Medicine:
When you are mistreated the same way you mistreat others.

A Toss-Up:
A result that is still unclear and can go either way.

Actions Speak Louder Than Words:
It's better to actually do something than just talk about it.

Add Fuel To The Fire:
Whenever something is done to make a bad situation even worse than it is.

Against The Clock:
Rushed and short on time.

All Bark And No Bite:
When someone is threatening and/or aggressive but not willing to engage in a fight.

All Greek to me:
Meaningless and incomprehensible like someone who cannot read, speak, or understand any of the Greek language would be.

All In The Same Boat:
When everyone is facing the same challenges.

An Arm And A Leg:
Very expensive. A large amount of money.

An Axe To Grind:
To have a dispute with someone.

Apple of My Eye:
Someone who is cherished above all others.

As High As A Kite:
Anything that is high up in the sky.

At The Drop Of A Hat:
Willing to do something immediately.

B

Back Seat Driver:
People who criticize from the sidelines, much like someone giving unwanted advice from the back seat of a vehicle to the driver.

Back To Square One:
Having to start all over again.

Back To The Drawing Board:
When an attempt fails and it's time to start all over.

Baker's Dozen:
Thirteen.

Barking Up The Wrong Tree:
A mistake made in something you are trying to achieve.

Beat A Dead Horse:
To force an issue that has already ended.

Beating Around The Bush:
Avoiding the main topic. Not speaking directly about the issue.

Bend Over Backwards:
Do whatever it takes to help. Willing to do anything.

Between A Rock And A Hard Place:

Stuck between two very bad options.

Bite Off More Than You Can Chew:
To take on a task that is way to big.

Bite Your Tongue:
To avoid talking.

Blood Is Thicker Than Water:
The family bond is closer than anything else.

Blue Moon:
A rare event or occurrence.

Break A Leg:

A superstitious way to say 'good luck' without saying 'good luck', but rather the opposite.

Buy A Lemon:

To purchase a vehicle that constantly gives problems or stops running after you drive it away.

C

Can't Cut The Mustard :

Someone who isn't adequate enough to compete or participate.

Cast Iron Stomach:

Someone who has no problems, complications or ill effects with eating anything or drinking anything.

Charley Horse:

Stiffness in the leg / A leg cramp.

Chew someone out:

Verbally scold someone.

Chip on his Shoulder:

Angry today about something that occured in the past.

Chow Down:

To eat.

Close but no Cigar:

To be very near and almost accomplish a goal, but fall short.

Cock and Bull Story:
An unbelievable tale.

Come Hell Or High Water:
Any difficult situation or obstacle.

Crack Someone Up:
To make someone laugh.

Cross Your Fingers:
To hope that something happens the way you want it to.

Cry Over Spilt Milk:
When you complain about a loss from the past.

Cry Wolf:
Intentionally raise a false alarm.

Cup Of Joe:
A cup of coffee.

Curiosity Killed The Cat:
Being Inquisitive can lead you into a dangerous situation.

Cut to the Chase:
Leave out all the unnecessary details and just get to the point.

D

Dark Horse:
One who was previously unknown and is now prominent.

Dead Ringer:
100% identical. A duplicate.

Devil's Advocate:
Someone who takes a position for the sake of argument without believing in that particular side of the argument. It can also mean one who presents a counter argument for a position they do believe in, to another debater.

Dog Days of Summer:
The hottest days of the summer season.

Don't count your chickens before they hatch:
Don't rely on it until your sure of it.

Don't Look A Gift Horse In The Mouth:
When someone gives you a gift, don't be ungrateful.

Don't Put All Your Eggs In One Basket:
Do not put all your resources in one possibility.

Doozy:
Something outstanding.

Down To The Wire:
Something that ends at the last minute or last few seconds.

Drastic Times Call For Drastic Measures:
When you are extremely desperate you need to take extremely desperate actions.

Drink like a fish:
To drink very heavily.

Drive someone up the wall:
To irritate and/or annoy very much.

Dropping Like Flies:
A large number of people either falling ill or dying.

Dry Run:
Rehearsal.

E

Eighty Six:
A certain item is no longer available. Or this idiom can also mean, to throw away.

Elvis has left the building:
The show has come to an end. It's all over.

Ethnic Cleansing:
Killing of a certain ethnic or religious group on a massive scale.

Every Cloud Has A Silver Lining:
Be optimistic, even difficult times will lead to better days.

Everything But The Kitchen Sink:
Almost everything and anything has been included.

Excuse my French:
Please forgive me for cussing.

Cock and Bull Story:
An unbelievable tale.

Cock and Bull Story:
An unbelievable tale.

F

Feeding Frenzy:
An aggressive attack on someone by a group.

Field Day:
An enjoyable day or circumstance.

Finding Your Feet:
To become more comfortable in whatever you are doing.

Finger lickin' good:
A very tasty food or meal.

Fixed In Your Ways:
Not willing or wanting to change from your normal way of doing something.

Flash In The Pan:
Something that shows potential or looks promising in the beginning but fails to deliver anything in the end.

Flea Market:
A swap meet. A place where people gather to buy and sell inexpensive goods.

Flesh and Blood:
This idiom can mean living material of which people are made of, or it can refer to someone's family.

Flip The Bird:
To raise your middle finger at someone.

Foam at the Mouth:
To be enraged and show it.

Fools' Gold:
Iron pyrites, a worthless rock that resembles real gold.

French Kiss:
An open mouth kiss where tongues touch.

From Rags To Riches:
To go from being very poor to being very wealthy.

Fuddy-duddy:
An old-fashioned and foolish type of person.

Full Monty:
This idiom can mean either, "the whole thing" or "completely nude".

Funny Farm:
A mental institutional facility.

G

Get Down to Brass Tacks:
To become serious about something.

Get Over It:
To move beyond something that is bothering you.

Get Up On The Wrong Side Of The Bed:
Someone who is having a horrible day.

Get Your Walking Papers:
Get fired from a job.

Give Him The Slip:
To get away from. To escape.

Go Down Like A Lead Balloon:
To be received badly by an audience.

Go For Broke:
To gamble everything you have.

Go Out On A Limb:
Put yourself in a tough position in order to support someone/something.

Go The Extra Mile:
Going above and beyond whatever is required for the task at hand.

Good Samaritan:
Someone who helps others when they are in need, with no discussion for compensation, and no thought of a reward.

Graveyard Shift:
Working hours from about 12:00 am to 8:00 am. The time of the day when most other people are sleeping.

Great Minds Think Alike:
Intelligent people think like each other.

Green Room:
The waiting room, especially for those who are about to go on a tv or radio show.

Gut Feeling:
A personal intuition you get, especially when feel something may not be right.

H

Haste Makes Waste:
Quickly doing things results in a poor ending.

Hat Trick:
When one player scores three goals in the same hockey game. This idiom can also mean three scores in any other sport, such as 3 homeruns, 3 touchdowns, 3 soccer goals, etc.

Have an Axe to Grind:
To have a dispute with someone.

He Lost His Head:
Angry and overcome by emotions.

Head Over Heels:
Very excited and/or joyful, especially when in love.

Hell in a Hand basket:
Deteriorating and headed for complete disaster.

High Five:
Slapping palms above each other's heads as celebration gesture.

High on the Hog:
Living in Luxury.

Hit The Books:
To study, especially for a test or exam.

Hit The Hay:
Go to bed or go to sleep.

Hit The Nail on the Head:
Do something exactly right or say something exactly right.

Hit The Sack:
Go to bed or go to sleep.

Hocus Pocus:
In general, a term used in magic or trickery.

Hold Your Horses:
Be patient.

I

Icing On The Cake:
When you already have it good and get something on top of what you already have.

Idle Hands Are The Devil's Tools:
You are more likely to get in trouble if you have nothing to do.

If It's Not One Thing, It's Another:
When one thing goes wrong, then another, and another . . .

In Like Flynn:
To be easily successful, especially when sexual or romantic.

In The Bag:
To have something secured.

In The Buff:
Nude.

In The Heat Of The Moment:
Overwhelmed by what is happening in the moment.

In Your Face:
An aggressive and bold confrontation.

It Takes Two To Tango:
A two person conflict where both people are at fault.

It's A Small World:
You frequently see the same people in different places.

Its Anyone's Call:
A competition where the outcome is difficult to judge or predict.

Ivy League:
Since 1954 the Ivy League has been the following universities: Columbia, Brown, Cornell, Dartmouth, Yale, Pennsylvania, Princeton, and Harvard.

J

Jaywalk:
Crossing the street (from the middle) without using the crosswalk.

Joshing Me:
Tricking me.

K

Keep An Eye On Him:
You should carefully watch him.

Keep body and soul together:
To earn a sufficient amount of money in order to keep yourself alive.

Keep your chin up:
To remain joyful in a tough situation.

Kick The Bucket:
Die.

Kitty-corner:
Diagonally across. Sometimes called Catty-Corner as well.

Knee Jerk Reaction:
A quick and automatic response.

Knock On Wood:
Knuckle tapping on wood in order to avoid some bad luck.

Know the Ropes:
To understand the details.

L

Last but not least:
An introduction phrase to let the audience know that the last person mentioned is no less important than those introduced before him/her.

Lend Me Your Ear:
To politely ask for someone's full attention.

Let Bygones Be Bygones:
To forget about a disagreement or argument.

Let Sleeping Dogs Lie:
To avoid restarting a conflict.

Let The Cat Out Of The Bag:
To share a secret that wasn't supposed to be shared.

Level playing field:
A fair competition where no side has an advantage.

Like a chicken with its head cut off:
To act in a frenzied manner.

liquor someone up:
To get someone drunk.

Long in the Tooth:
Old people (or horses).

Loose Cannon:
Someone who is unpredictable and can cause damage if not kept in check.

M

Make No Bones About:
To state a fact so there are no doubts or objections.

Method To My Madness:
Strange or crazy actions that appear meaningless but in the end are done for a good reason.

Mumbo Jumbo:
Nonsense or meaningless speech.

Mum's the word:
To keep quiet. To say nothing.

N

Nest Egg:
Savings set aside for future use.

Never Bite The Hand That Feeds You:
Don't hurt anyone that helps you.

New kid on the block:
Someone new to the group or area.

New York Minute:
A minute that seems to go by quickly, especially in a fast paced environment.

No Dice:
To not agree. To not accept a proposition.

No Room to Swing a Cat:
An unusually small or confined space.

Not Playing With a Full Deck:
Someone who lacks intelligence.

O

Off On The Wrong Foot:
Getting a bad start on a relationship or task.

Off The Hook:
No longer have to deal with a tough situation.

Off the Record:
Something said in confidence that the one speaking doesn't want attributed to him/her.

On Pins And Needles:
Anxious or nervous, especially in anticipation of something.

On The Fence:
Undecided.

On The Same Page:
When multiple people all agree on the same thing.

Out Of The Blue:
Something that suddenly and unexpectedly occurs.

Out On A Limb:
When someone puts them self in a risky situation.

Out On The Town:
To enjoy yourself by going out.

Over My Dead Body:
When you absolutely will not allow something to happen.

Over the Top:
Very excessive.

P

Pass The Buck:
Avoid responsibility by giving it to someone else.

Pedal to the metal:
To go full speed, especially while driving a vehicle.

Peeping Tom:
Someone who observes people in the nude or sexually active people, mainly for his own gratification.

Pick up your ears:
To listen very carefully.

Pig In A Poke:
A deal that is made without first examining it.

Pig Out :
To eat a lot and eat it quickly.

Pipe Down:
To shut-up or be quiet.

Practice Makes Perfect:
By constantly practicing, you will become better.

Pull the plug:
To stop something. To bring something to an end.

Pulling Your Leg:
Tricking someone as a joke.

Put a sock in it:
To tell noisy person or a group to be quiet.

Q

Queer the pitch:
Destroy or ruin a plan.

R

Rain check:
An offer or deal that is declined right now but willing to accept later.

Raining Cats and Dogs:
A very loud and noisy rain storm.

Ring Fencing:
Separated usual judgement to guarantee protection, especially project funds.

Rise and Shine:
Time to get out of bed and get ready for work/school.

Rome Was Not Built In One Day:
If you want something to be completely properly, then its going to take time.

Rule Of Thumb:
A rough estimate.

Run out of steam:
To be completely out of energy.

S

Saved By The Bell:
Saved at the last possible moment.

Scapegoat:
Someone else who takes the blame.

Scot-free:
To escape and not have to pay.

Sick As A Dog:
To be very sick (with the flu or a cold).

Sitting Shotgun:
Riding in the front passenger seat of a car.

Sixth Sense:
A paranormal sense that allows you to communicate with the dead.

Skid Row:
The rundown area of a city where the homeless and drug users live.

Smell A Rat:
To detect someone in the group is betraying the others.

Smell Something Fishy:
Detecting that something isn't right and there might be a reason for it.

Son of a Gun:
A scamp.

Southpaw:
Someone who is left-handed.

Spitting Image:
The exact likeness or kind.

Start From Scratch:
To do it all over again from the beginning.

T

The Ball Is In Your Court:
It is your decision this time.

The Best Of Both Worlds:
There are two choices and you have them both.

The Bigger They Are The Harder They Fall:
While the bigger and stronger opponent might be alot more difficult to beat, when you do they suffer a much bigger loss.

The Last Straw:
When one small burden after another creates an unbearable situation, the last straw is the last small burden that one can take.

The Whole Nine Yards:
Everything. All of it.

Third times a charm:
After no success the first two times, the third try is a lucky one.

Tie the knot:
To get married.

Til the cows come home:
A long time.

To Make A Long Story Short:
Something someone would say during a long and boring story in order to keep his/her audience from losing attention. Usually the story isn't shortened.

To Steal Someone's Thunder:
To take the credit for something someone else did.

Tongue And Cheek:
humour, not to be taken serious.

Turn A Blind Eye:
Refuse to acknowledge something you know is real or legit.

Twenty three skidoo:
To be turned away.

U

Under the weather:
Feeling ill or sick.

Up a blind alley:
Going down a course of action that leads to a bad outcome.

Use Your Loaf:
Use your head. Think smart.

V

Van Gogh's ear for music:
Tone deaf.

Variety Is The Spice Of Life:
The more experiences you try the more exciting life can be.

W

Wag the Dog:
A diversion away from something of greater importance.

Water Under The Bridge:
Anything from the past that isn't significant or important anymore.

Wear Your Heart On Your Sleeve:
To openly and freely express your emotions.

When It Rains, It Pours:
Since it rarely rains, when it does it will be a huge storm.

When Pigs Fly:
Something that will never ever happen.

Wild and Woolly:
Uncultured and without laws.

Wine and Dine:
When somebody is treated to an expensive meal.

Without A Doubt:
For certain.

X

X marks the spot:
A phrase that is said when someone finds something he/she has been looking for.

Y

You Are What You Eat:
In order to stay healthy you must eat healthy foods.

You Can't Judge A Book By Its Cover:
Decisions shouldn't be made primarily on appearance.

You Can't Take it With You:
Enjoy what you have and not what you don't have, since when you die you cannot take things (such as money) with you.

Your Guess Is As Good As Mine:
I have no idea.

Z

Zero Tolerance:
No crime or law breaking big or small will be overlooked.

~°~°~°~°~°~°~°~°~°~°~°~°~°

Summer Safety Tips:

□ One of the best ways to stay safe this summer is to wear a helmet and other safety gear when biking, skating and skateboarding, and when riding scooters, all-terrain vehicles, and horses. Studies on bicycle helmets have shown they can reduce the risk of head injury by as much as 85 percent.

□ Use layers of protection to prevent a swimming pool tragedy. This includes placing barriers completely around your pool to prevent access, using door and pool alarms, closely supervising your child and being prepared in case of an emergency.

□ Never bring charcoal grills indoors. Burning charcoal produces deadly carbon monoxide.

◻ When cooking outdoors with a <u>gas grill</u>, check the air tubes that lead into the burner for any blockage from insects, spiders, or food grease. Check grill hoses for cracking, brittleness, holes, and leaks. Make sure there are no sharp bends in the hose or tubing. If you ever detect a leak, immediately turn off the gas at the tank and don't attempt to light the grill until the leak is fixed. <u>Newer grills</u> and propane tanks have improved safety devices to prevent gas leaks.

◻ Make sure your <u>home playground</u> is safe. Falls cause 60 percent of playground injuries, so having a safe surface is critical. Concrete, asphalt or packed dirt surfaces are too hard. Use at least 9 inches of wood chips or mulch.

◻ Use softer-than standard baseballs, safety-release bases and batting helmets with face guards to <u>reduce baseball-related injuries</u> to children.

◻ If you are a soccer mom or dad, beware that <u>movable soccer goals</u> can fall over and kill children. Make sure the goal is anchored securely at all times and never allow anyone to climb on the net or goal framework or hang from the cross bar. Remove nets when the goals are not in use.

◻ To prevent serious injuries while using a <u>trampoline</u>, allow only one person on at a time, and do not allow somersaults. Use a shock-absorbing pad that completely covers the springs and place the trampoline away from structures and other play areas. Kids under 6-years-old should not use full-size trampolines.

▢ Don't allow a game of hide-n-seek to become deadly. CPSC has received reports of numerous suffocation deaths involving children who crawled inside <u>old cedar chests</u>, <u>latch-type freezers and refrigerators, iceboxes in campers, clothes dryers and picnic coolers</u>. Childproof old appliances, warn children not to play inside them.

▢ If summer plans include camping and you want heat inside your tent or camper, use one of the <u>new portable heaters</u> that are equipped with an oxygen depletion sensor (ODS). If oxygen levels start to fall inside your tent or camper, the ODS automatically shuts down the heater before it can produce deadly levels of carbon monoxide (CO). Do not attempt to use alternative sources of heat or power to warm a tent or camper. Traditional camping heaters, charcoal grills, camping lanterns, and gas generators also can cause CO poisoning.

▢ Install <u>window guards</u> to prevent children from falling out of open windows. Guards should be installed in children's bedrooms, parents' bedrooms, and other rooms where young children spend time. Or, install window stops that permit windows to open no more than 4 inches. Whenever possible, open windows from the top—not the bottom. Also, keep furniture away from windows to discourage children from climbing near windows.

▢ Summer also means <u>yard work</u>. When mowing, keep small children out of the yard, and turn the mower off if children enter the area. If the lawn slopes, mow across the slope with the walk-behind rotary mower, never up and down. With a <u>riding mower</u>, drive up and down the slope, not across it. Never carry children on a riding mower.

<u>My Special Tips</u>

Food Measuring Equivalents

1 pinch = approx 1/8 teaspoon
½ tablespoon = 1 ½ teaspoons
3 teaspoons = 1 tablespoon
¼ cup = 4 tablespoons
1/3 cup = 5 tablespoons + 1 teaspoon
3/8 cup = 6 tablespoons
½ cup = 8 tablespoons
2/3 cup = 10 tablespoons + 2 teaspoons
¾ cup = 12 tablespoons
1 cup =16 tablespoons
4 cups = 1 quart
8 quarts = 1 peck
4 pecks = 1 bushel

Liquid Measures

1 dash = approx a few drops
1 tablespoon = 3 teaspoons
1 tablespoon = ½ fluid ounce
1 fluid ounce = 2 tablespoons
1 jigger = 3 tablespoons or 1 ½ fluid ounces
¼ cup = 4 tablespoons or 2 fluid ounces
½ cup = 8 tablespoons or 4 fluid ounces
1 cup = 16 tablespoons or 8 fluid ounces
1 pint = 2 cups or 16 fluid ounces
1 quart = 2 pints or 32 fluid ounces
1 gallon = 4 quarts or 64 fluid ounces

Temperature Equivalents

Degrees Fahrenheit = Degrees Celsius
Room Temperature 70 21
Luke warm 90 32
Water's Boiling Point 212 100
Low or Cool Oven 250 120
Slow Oven 300 150
Moderately Slow Oven 325 165
Moderate Oven 350 180
Moderately Hot Oven 375 190
Hot Oven 400 205
Very Hot Oven 450-500 230-260
Broil 550 290

Metric Equivalents

Ounces = Grams

Ounces	Grams
1	28
2	57
3	85
4	113
5	142
6	170
7	198
8	227
9	255
10	284
11	312
12	340
13	368

14	397
15	425
16	454

Grams = Ounces

1	.035
50	1.75
100	3.5
250	8.75
500	17.5
750	26.25
1000 (1 kilogram)	35 (2.21 lbs)

Pounds = Kilograms

1	.45
2	.91
3	1.4
4	1.8
5	2.3
6	2.7
7	3.2
8	3.5
9	4.1
10	4.5
11	

Kilograms = Pounds

1	2.2
2	4.4
3	6.6
4	8.8
5	11

Produce Weights and Measures

Vegetables

Asparagus: 1 pound = 3 cups chopped
Beans (string): 1 pound = 4 cups chopped
Beans, black, kidney or navy: 1 cup dry = ½ pound = 2½ cups cooked
Beets: 1 pound (5 medium) = 2½ cups chopped
Broccoli: ½ pound = 6 cups chopped
Cabbage: 1 pound = 4½ cups shredded
Carrots: 1 pound = 3½ cups sliced or grated
Celery: 1 pound = 4 cups chopped
Cucumbers: 1 pound (2 medium) = 4 cups sliced
Eggplant: 1 pound = 4 cups chopped = 2 cups cooked
Garlic: 1 clove = 1 teaspoon chopped
Leeks: 1 pound = 4 cups chopped = 2 cups cooked
Mushrooms: 1 pound = 5-6 cups sliced = 2 cups cooked
Onions: 1 pound = 4 cups sliced = 2 cups cooked
Parsnips: 1 pound unpeeled = 1½ cups cooked, pureed
Peas: 1 pound whole = 1-1½ cups peeled
Potatoes: 1 pound (3 medium) sliced = 2 cups mashed
Pumpkin: 1 pound = 4 cups chopped = 2 cups cooked, drained
Spinach: 1 pound = ¾-1 cup cooked
Squashes(summer): 1 pound = 4 cups grated = 2 cups sliced, cooked
Squashes (winter): 2 pounds = 2½ cups cooked, pureed
Sweet potatoes: 1 pound = 4 cups grated = 1 cup cooked, pureed

Swiss chard: 1 pound = 5-6 cups packed leaves =1-1½ cups cooked

Tomatoes: 1 pound (3-4 medium) = 1½ cups seeded pulp

Turnips: 1 pound = 4 cups chopped = 2 cups cooked mashed

Zucchini: 1 pound = 3 cups sliced = 2½ cups chopped

Fruit

Apples: 1 pound (3-4 medium) = 3 cups sliced

Bananas: 1 pound (3-4 medium) = 1½ cups mashed

Berries: 1 quart = 3½ cups

Dates: 1 pound = 2½ cups pitted

Lemon: 1 whole = 1-3 tablespoons juice = 1-1½ teaspoons grated rind

Lime: 1 whole = 1½-2 tablespoons juice

Orange: 1 medium = 6-8 tablespoons juice = 2-3 teaspoons grated rind

Peaches: 1 pound (4 medium) = 3 cups sliced

Pears: 1 pound (4 medium) = 2 cups sliced

Rhubarb: 1 pound = 2 cups cooked

Strawberries: 1 quart = 3 cups sliced

"An empty belly is the best cook."

—Estonian Proverb

My Special Tips

EYES CLOSED, TOO HEAR

RJ Woodward

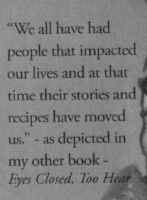

"We all have had people that impacted our lives and at that time their stories and recipes have moved us." - as depicted in my other book - *Eyes Closed, Too Hear*

GENERATIONS
of
FAMILY FAVOURITES

RJ WOODWARD

" We all have had people that impacted our lives and at that time their stories and recipes have moved us" - as depicted in my first book - *Eyes Closed, Too Hear*

GENERATIONS
of
FAMILY FAVOURITES
BOOK TWO

RJ WOODWARD

" We all have had
people that impacted
our lives and at that
time their stories and
recipes have moved
us" - as depicted in
my first book -
Eyes Closed, Too Hear

GENERATIONS
of
FAMILY FAVOURITES
BOOK THREE - SPECIALTY

RJ WOODWARD